HIGH TIMES
CULTIVATION TIPS
TWENTY YEARS AND STILL GROWING
FROM THE EDITORS OF HIGH TIMES

TRANS-HIGH PUBLISHING CORP. NEW YORK

WHY YOU SHOULD GROW YOUR OWN

1. If you're going to use marijuana, growing your own is the best way to avoid contact with any criminal element and insure a safe and uncontaminated supply.

2. Our government's extermination campaign against cannabis is immoral and unjust. By growing your own you stand up for the right of this beneficial plant to exist.

3. Cultivation of any plant draws one closer to nature. Your relationship with cannabis can be extemely rewarding.

4. The financial rewards of home cultivation are mindboggling. The plant is worth its weight in gold and several ounces can be produced every 90 days in a space no bigger than a garbage can. Can anyone tell me a more profitable hobby than this?

—*Steven Hager*

Printed in the China

Editor: Steven Hager
Assistant Editor: Chris Eudaley
Design Concept: Frank Max
Cover Design: Flick Ford
Copy Editor: Steve Wishnia
Cover photograph by Andre Grossmann

ISBN # 0964785846

First edition: September 1995
Second edition: March 1996
Third edition: April 1999

CONTENTS

PART 1
A TALE OF
THE KENTUCKY
HEMP FIELDS
by James Lane Allen

VAN BERG

FIRST PUBLISHED BY THE MACMILLAN COMPANY NEW YORK 1900

The Anglo-Saxon farmers had scarce conquered foothold, stronghold, freehold in the Western wilderness before they became sowers of hemp—with remembrance of Virginia, with remembrance of dear ancestral Britain. Away back in the days when they lived with wife, child, flock in frontier wooden fortresses and hardly ventured forth for water, salt, game, tillage—in the very summer of that wild daylight ride of Tomlinson and Bell, by comparison with which, my children, the midnight ride of Paul Revere was as tame as the pitching of a rocking-horse in a boy's nursery—on that history-making twelfth of August, of the year 1782, when these two backwoods riflemen, during that same Revolution, the Kentuckians then fighting a branch of that same British army, rushed out of Bryan's Station for the rousing of the settlements and the saving of the West—hemp was growing tall and thick near the walls of the fort.

Hemp in Kentucky in 1782—early landmark in the history of the soil, of the people. Cultivated first for the needs of the cabin and clearing solely; for twine and rope, towel and table, sheet and shirt. By and by not for cabin and clearing only; not for tow-homespun, fur-clad Kentucky alone. To the north had begun the building of ships, American ships for American commerce, for American arms, for a nation which Nature had herself created and had distinguished as a seafaring race. To the south had begun the raising of cotton. As the great period of shipbuilding went on—greatest during the 20 years or more ending in 1860; as the great period of cotton-raising and cotton-baling went on—never so great before as in that same year—the two parts of the nation looked equally to the one border plateau lying between them, to several counties of Kentucky, for most of the nation's hemp. It was in those days of the North that the *Constitution* was rigged with Russian hemp on one side, with American hemp on the other, for a patriotic test of the superiority of home-grown, home-prepared fiber; and thanks to the latter, before those days ended with the outbreak of the Civil War, the country had become second to Great Britain alone in her ocean craft, and but little behind that mistress of the seas. So that in response to this double demand for hemp on the American ship and hemp on the Southern plantation, at the close of that period of national history on land and sea, from those few counties of Kentucky, in the year 1859, were taken well-nigh forty thousand tons of the well-cleaned bast.

What history it wrought in those years, directly for the Republic, indirectly for the world! What ineffaceable marks it left on Kentucky itself, land, landowners! To make way for it, a forest the like of which no human eye will ever see again was felled; and with the forest went its pastures, its waters. The roads of Kentucky, those long limestone turnpikes connecting the towns and villages with the farms—they were early made necessary by the hauling of hemp. For the sake of it, slaves were perpetually being trained, hired, bartered; lands perpetually rented and sold; fortunes made or lost. The advancing price of farms, the westward movement of poor families and consequent dispersion of the Kentuckians over cheaper territory, whither they carried the same passion for the cultivation of the same plant—thus

making Missouri the second hemp-producing state in the union—the regulation of the hours in the Kentucky cabin, in the house, at the rope-walk, in the factory, what phase of life went unaffected by the pursuit and fascination of it. Thought, care, hope of the farmer oftentimes throughout the entire year! Upon it depending, it may be, the college of his son, the accomplishments of his daughter, the luxuries of his wife, the house he would build, the stock he could own. His own pleasures also: his deer hunting at home, his fishing on the great lakes, his excursions on the old floating palaces of the Mississippi down to New Orleans—all these depending in large measure upon his hemp, that thickest gold-dust of his golden acres.

With the Civil War began the long decline, lasting still. The record stands that throughout the 125 years elapsing from the entrance of the Anglo-Saxon farmers into the wilderness down to the present time, a few counties of Kentucky have furnished army and navy, the entire country, with all but a small part of the native hemp consumed. Little comparatively is cultivated in Kentucky now. The traveler may still see it here and there, crowning those ever-renewing, self renewing inexhaustible fields. But the time cannot be far distant when the industry there will have become extinct. Its place in the nation's markets will be still further taken by metals, by other fibers, by finer varieties of the same fiber, by the same variety cultivated in soils less valuable. The history of it in Kentucky will be ended, and, being ended, lost.

Some morning when the roar of March winds is no more heard in the tossing woods, but along still brown boughs a faint, veil-like greenness runs; when every spring, welling out of the soaked earth, trickles through banks of sod unbarred by ice; before a bee is abroad under the calling sky; before the red of applebuds becomes a sign in the low orchards, or the high song of the thrush is pouring forth far away at wet pale-green sunsets, the sower, the earliest sower of the hemp, goes forth into the fields.

Warm they must be, soft and warm, those fields, its chosen birthplace. Upturned by the plough, crossed and recrossed by the harrow, clodless, levelled, deep, fine, fertile—some extinct river-bottom, some valley threaded by streams, some tableland of mild rays, moist airs, alluvial or limestone soils—such is the favorite cradle of the hemp in nature. Back and forth with measured tread, with measured distance, broadcast the sower sows, scattering with plenteous hand those small oval-shaped fruits, gray-green, black-striped, heavily packed with living marrow.

Lightly covered over by drag or harrow, under the rolled earth now they lie, those mighty, those inert seeds. Down into the darkness about them the sun rays penetrate day by day, stroking them with the brushes of light, prodding them with spears of flame. Drops of nightly dews, drops from the coursing clouds trickle down to them, moistening the dryness, closing up the little hollows of the ground, drawing the particles of maternal earth more closely. Suddenly—as an insect that has been feigning death cautiously unrolls itself and starts into action—in each seed the great miracle of life begins. Each awakens as from a sleep, as from pretended death. It starts, it moves, it bursts its ashen woody shell, it takes two opposite courses, the white, fibril-tapered root hurrying away from the sun; the tiny stem, bearing its lance-like leaves, ascending graceful, brave like a palm.

Some morning, not many days later, the farmer, walking out into his barn lot and casting a look in the direction of his field, sees—or does he not see?—the surface of it less dark. What is that uncertain flush low on the ground, that irresistible rush of multitudinous green? A fortnight, and the field is brown no longer. Overflowing it, burying it out of sight, is the shallow tidal sea of the hemp, ever rippling. Green are the woods now with their varied greenness. Green are the pastures. Green here and there are the fields: with the bluish green of young oats and wheat; with the gray green of young barley and rye: with orderly dots of dull dark green in vast array——the hills of Indian maize. But as the eye sweeps the whole landscape undulating far and near, from the hues of tree, pasture and corn of every kind, it turns to the color of hemp. With that in view, all other shades in nature seem dead and count for nothing. Far reflected, conspicuous, brilliant, strange; masses of living emerald, saturated with blazing sunlight.

Darker, always darker turns the hemp as it rushes upward: scarce darker as to the stemless stalks, which are hidden now; but darker in the tops. Yet here two shades of greenness: the male plants paler, smaller, maturing earlier, dying first; the females darker, taller, living longer more luxuriant of foliage and flowering heads.

A hundred days from the sowing, and those flowering heads have come forth with their mass of leaves and bloom and earliest fruits, elastic, swaying six, ten, 12 feet from the ground and ripe for cutting. A hundred days reckoning from the last of March or the last of April, so that it is July, it is August. And now, borne far through the steaming air floats an odor, balsamic, startling: the odor of those plumes and stalks and blossoms from which is exuding freely the narcotic resin of the great nettle. The nostril expands quickly, the lungs swell out deeply to draw it in: fragrance once known in childhood, ever in the memory afterward and able to bring back to the wanderer homesick thoughts of midsummer days in the shadowy, many-toned woods, over into which is blown the smell of the hempfields.

Who apparently could number the acres of these in the days gone by? A land of hemp, ready for the cutting! The oats heavy-headed, rustling, have turned to gold and been stacked in the stubble or stored in the lofts of white, bursting barns. The heavy-headed, rustling wheat has turned to gold and been stacked in the stubble or sent through the whirling thresher. The barley and the rye are garnered and gone, the landscape has many bare and open spaces. But separating these everywhere, rise the fields of Indian corn now in blade and tassel; and—more valuable than all else that has been sown and harvested or remains to be—everywhere the impenetrable thickets of the hemp.

Inpenetrable! For close together stand the stalks, making common cause for soil and light, each but one of many, the fiber being better when so grown—as is also the fiber of men. Inpenetrable and therefore weedless; for no plant life can flourish there, nor animal nor bird. Scarce a beetle runs bewilderingly

through those forbidding colossal solitudes. The field-sparrow will flutter away from pollen-bearing to pollen-receiving top, trying to beguile you from its nest hidden near the edge. The crow and the blackbird will seem to love it, having a keen eye for the cutworm, its only enemy. The quail does love it, not for itself, but for the protection, leading her brood into its labyrinths out of the dusty road when danger draws near. Best of all winged creatures it is loved by the iris-eyed, burnish-breasted, murmuring doves, already beginning to gather in the deadened treetops with crops eager for the seed. Well remembered also by the long-flight passenger pigeon, coming into the land for the mast. Best of all wild things whose safety lies not in the wing but in the foot, it is loved by the hare for its young, for refuge. Those lithe, velvety, summer-thin bodies! Observe carefully the tops of the still hemp: are they slightly shaken? Among the bases of those stalks a cotton-tail is threading its way inward beyond the reach of its pursuer. Are they shaken violently, parted clean and wide to right and left? It is the path of the dog following the hot scent—ever baffled.

A hundred days to lift out of those tiny seeds these powerful stalks, hollow, hairy, covered with their tough fiber—that strength of cables when the big ships are tugged at by the joined fury of wind and ocean. And now some morning at the corner of the field stand the black men with hooks and whetstones. The hook, a keen, straight blade, bent at right angles to the handle two feet from the hand. Let these men be the strongest; no weakling can handle the hemp from seed to seed again. A heart, the doors and walls of which are in perfect order, through which flows freely the full stream of a healthy man's red blood; lungs deep, clear, easily filled, easily emptied; a body that can bend and twist and be straightened again in ceaseless rhythmical movement; limbs tireless; the very spirit of primeval man conquering primeval nature—all these go into the cutting of the hemp. The leader strides to the edge, and throwing forward his left arm, along which the muscles play, he grasps as much as it will embrace, bends the stalks over and with his right hand draws the blade through them an inch or more from the ground. When he has gathered his armful, he turns and flings it down behind him, so that it lies spread out, covering when fallen the same space it filled while standing. And so he crosses the broad acres, and so each of the big black followers, stepping one by one to a place behind him, until the long, wavering, whitish green swaths of the prostrate hemp lie shimmering across the fields. Strongest now is the smell of it, impregnating the clothing of the men, spreading far throughout the air.

So it lies a week or more drying, dying, till the sap is out of the stalks, till leaves and blossoms and earliest ripened or unripened fruits wither and drop off, giving back to the soil the nourishment they have drawn from it; the whole top being thus otherwise wasted—that part of the hemp which every year the dreamy millions of the Orient still consume in quantities beyond human computation, and for the love of which the very history of this plant is lost in the antiquity of India and Persia, its home—land of narcotics and desires and dreams.

Then the rakers with enormous wooden rakes; they draw the

stalks into bundles, tying each with the hemp itself. Following the binders, move the wagon-beds or slides, gathering the bundles and carrying them to where, huge, flat, and round, the stacks begin to rise. At last these are well built; the gates of the field are closed or the bars put up; wagons and laborers are gone; the brown fields stand deserted.

One day something is gone from earth and sky: Autumn has come, season of scales and balances, when the Earth, brought to judgement for its fruits, says, "I have done what I could—now let me rest!"

Fall!—and everywhere the sights and sounds of falling. In the woods, through the cool silvery air, the leaves, so indispensible once, so useless now. Bright day after bright day, dripping night after dripping night, the never-ending filtering or gusty fall of leaves. The fall of walnuts, dropping from bare boughs with muffled boom into the deep grass. The fall of the hickory-nut, rattling noisily down through the scaly limbs and scattering its hulls among the stones of the brook below. The fall of buckeyes, rolling like balls of mahogany into the little dust paths made by sheep in the hot months when they had sought those roofs of leaves. The fall of acorns, leaping out of their matted green cups as they strike the rooty earth. The fall of red haw, persimmon and pawpaw, and the odorous wild plum in its valley thickets. The fall of all seeds whatsoever of the forest, now made ripe in their high places and sent back to the ground, there to be folded in against the time when they shall arise again as the living generations; the homing, downward flight of the seeds in the many-colored woods all over the quiet land.

In the fields, too, the sights and sounds of falling, the fall of the standing fatness. The silent fall of the tobacco, to be hung head downward in fragrant sheds and barns. The felling whack of the cornknife and the rustling of the blades, as the workman gathers within his arm the top-heavy stalks and presses them into the bulging shock. The fall of pumpkins into the slow-drawn wagons, the shaded side of them still white with the morning rime. In the orchards, the fall of apples shaken thunderously down and the piling of these in sprawling heaps near the cider mills. In the vineyards the fall of sugaring grapes into the baskets and the bearing of them to the winepress in the cool sunshine, where there is the late droning of bees about the sweet pomace.

But of all that the earth has yielded with or without the farmer's help, of all that he can call his own within the limits of his land, nothing pleases him better than those still, brown fields where the shapely stacks stand amid the deadened trees. Two months have passed, the workmen are at it again. The stacks are torn down, the bundles scattered, the hemp spread out as once before. There to lie till it shall be dew-retted or rotted; there to suffer freeze and thaws, chill rains, locking frosts and loosening snow—all the action of the elements—until the gums holding together the filaments of the fiber rot out and dissolve, until the bast be separated from the woody portion of the stalk, and the stalk itself be decayed and easily broken.

Some day you walk across the spread hemp, your foot goes through at each step, you stoop and taking several stalks, snap them readily in your fingers. The ends stick out clean apart; and lo! hanging between them, there it is at last—a festoon of wet, coarse, dark gray riband, wealth of the hemp, sail of the wild Scythian centuries before Horace ever sang of him, sail of the Roman, dress of the Saxon and Celt, dress of the Kentucky pioneer.

The rakers reappear at intervals of dry weather, and draw the hemp into armfuls and set it up in shocks of convenient size, wide flared at the bottom, well pressed in and bound at the top, so that the slanting sides may catch the drying sun and the sturdy base resist the strong winds. And now the fields are as the dark brown caps of armies—each shock a soldier's tent. Yet not dark always; at times snow-covered; and then the white tents gleam for miles in the winter sunshine—the snow-white tents of the camping hemp.

Throughout the winter and on into early spring, as days may be warm or the hemp dry, the breaking continues. At each nightfall, cleaned and baled, it is hauled on wagon-beds or sleds to the barns or the hemphouses, where it is weighed for the work and wages of the day.

Last of all, the brakes having been taken from the field, some night—dear sport for the lads!—takes place the burning of the "hemphurds," thus returning their elements to the soil. To kindle a handful of tow and fling it as a firebrand into one of those masses of tinder; to see the flames spread and the sparks rush like swarms of red bees skyward through the smoke into the awful abysses of the night; to run from gray heap to gray heap, igniting the long line of signal fires, until the whole earth seems a conflagration and the heavens are as rosy as at morn; to look far away and descry on the horizon an array of answering lights; not in one direction only, but leagues away, to see the fainter ever fainter flow of burning hemphurds—this, too, is one of the experiences, one of the memories.

And now along the turnpikes the great loaded creaking wagons pass slowly to the towns, bearing the hemp to the factories, thence to be scattered over land and sea. Some day, when the winds of March are dying down, the sower enters the field and begins where he began twelve months before.

A round year of the earth's changes enters into the creation of the hemp. The planet has described its vast orbit ere it be grown and finished. All seasons are its servitors; all contradictions and extremes of nature meet in its making. Their vernal patience of the warming soil; the long fierce arrows of the summer heat, the long silvery arrows of the summer rain; autumn's dead skies and sobbing winds; winter's sternest, all-tightening frosts. Of none but strong virtues is it the sum. Sickness or infirmity it knows not. It will have a mother young and vigorous, or none; an old or weak or exhausted soil cannot produce it. It will endure no roof or shade, basking only in the eye of the fatherly sun, and demanding the whole sky for the walls of its nursery.

Ah! type, too, of our life, which also is earth-sown, earth-rooted; which must struggle upward, be cut down, rotted and broken, ere the separation take place between our dross and our worth—poor perishable shard and immortal fiber. Oh, the mystery, the mystery of that growth from the casting of the soul as a seed into the dark earth, until the time when, led through all natural changes and cleansed of weakness, it is borne from the fields of its nativity for the long service.

PART 2
BEGINNER'S GUIDE
TO CANNABIS CULTIVATION

BASIC SKUNK

Just picked.
Mississauga, Ontario, CANADA
#202, June 1992

CANNABIS

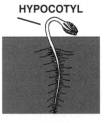

HYPOCOTYL

Cannabis is a tall, erect, annual herb. Provided with an open sunny environment, light well-drained composted soil and ample irrigation, cannabis can grow to a height of six meters in a four-to-six month growing season. Exposed river banks, meadows and agricultural lands are ideal habitats for cannabis since all offer good sunlight. Seeds are planted in the spring and usually germinate in three to seven days. The seedling emerges from the ground by the straightening of the hypocotyl (embryonic stem). The cotyledons (seed leaves) are slightly unequal in size, narrowed to the base and rounded or blunt to the tip. The hypocotyl ranges from one to 10 centimeters in length. About 10 centimeters or less above the cotyledons, the first true leaves arise, a pair of oppositely oriented single leaflets each with a distinct petiole (leaf stem) rotated one-quarter turn from the cotyledons. Subsequent pairs of leaves arise in opposite formation and a variously shaped leaf sequence develops with the second pair of leaves having three leaflets, the third five and so on, up to 11 leaflets.

Marijuana Botany by Robert Connell Clarke.

INTRODUCTION TO CANNABIS

by Mel Frank

Marijuana is a notoriously hardy, fast-growing weed that survives extreme heat, mild frosts, droughts and deluges. Few diseases seriously affect marijuana, and insects and animals generally have little impact on overall growth and yield once the vulnerable seedling stage is past. Mere survival, though, is not the point. Your goal is to raise healthy, potent and fully matured plants.

Every seed contains a certain potential for growth, overall size and potency. Given the seed's potential, the environment then determines the actual size and potency of the plant. In an ideal environment, some marijuana varieties grow from a sprout to 18 feet tall in only six months, and yield up to five pounds of buds. Indoors there is seldom enough space or light to support such robust growth. Consequently, indoor plants are much smaller, sometimes reaching only three or four feet tall, and they yield about half an ounce of buds, although much larger plants easily and more often are grown indoors.

OVERVIEW OF MARIJUANA'S LIFE CYCLE

Marijuana is an annual; a single season completes a generation and all hope for the future is left to the seeds. In nature, seeds germinate when the warmth and rains of spring encourage the start of a new season and life cycle. The first pair of leaves that appear on a sprout are entire (they have smooth edges), and were part of the embryo contained within the seed. The appearance of the second pair begins the seedling stage. The seedling's leaves differ from the embryonic leaves in having serrated margins (toothed edges), and being larger. The first leaves usually have a single, spearhead-shaped blade. With the next pair of leaves, each leaf is larger, and usually has three blades. A basic pattern has been set: Each new pair of leaves is larger and has more blades per leaf, until the leaves reach a maximum size and number of blades per leaf, usually nine or eleven (although 19 blades on an 18-inch-long leaf have been seen). The seedling stage is completed four to six weeks into growth. Next begins vegetative growth (middle stage of life). This is the time of maximum growth, during which branches appear and form the plant into its distinctive shape. After another few weeks, leaf pairs that had been opposite each other (opposite phyllotaxy) begin to form in a staggered position along the top of the stem (alternate phyllotaxy), a sign that the plant is preparing itself for the start of sexual maturation.

Marijuana is *dioecious*, which means that male and female flowers appear on separate plants, and that each plant is then considered either a male or a female plant. During the stage of preflowering, (a two-week period prior to flowering), the plant goes through a quiescent period; rapid growth slows while the plant prepares itself for the growth of flowers.

Males produce pollen-bearing flowers, and females produce seed-bearing flowers. Females are the preferred plant for marijuana because their flower clusters (buds) are more potent and because they yield better marijuana than do male plants. The familiar "buds" of commercial grass are in fact collections of hundreds of individual female flowers that form in masses called "buds" or "colas." (The terminology generally agreed upon is that in marijuana, a bud is a collection of female flowers that form an individual cluster. Colas are collections of buds).

Once the male drops pollen and seeds mature on the female, both plants normally die. This ends a generation, but artificial lighting allows you to alter many aspects of the plant's life by knowledgeable modification of the plant's life processes and manipulation of its normal life cycle. You'll learn these techniques in subsequent chapters. It's actually possible to grow a single plant for several years, or its clones for the rest of your life.

GROWTH AND THE CONCEPT OF LIMITING FACTORS

Marijuana grows best in fertile, well draining soil that gets plenty of water and is exposed to bright light and a warm, airy atmosphere. To reduce the complexities of the environment into factors over which a gardener can maintain some control, think of the environment as consisting of four basic growth factors: light, air, water and soil. Plants live and grow by using:

(1) light energy to make food and biological energy for growth from

(2) carbon dioxide (CO_2) and oxygen from the air,

(3) water from the air and soil and

(4) minerals (nutrients or fertilizers) absorbed from the soil.

Each of these four growth factors is like a link in a chain, and the plant grows no faster than the weakest link will allow. For example, if there is not much light, weak light limits growth no matter how abundant the water is, or how fertile the soil may be. In the same sense, if soil nutrients are scarce, growth is limited by the amount of nutrients, no matter how much light, air or water is given.

Of course, no grower can know exactly if all four growth factors are in perfect balance, but there is no need to know. Only after growers have watered and fertilized the plants to near excess do they need to recognize that low light is the reason their plants are not growing faster. I've seen growers drowning their plants or poisoning them with too much fertilizer when they've had them growing under a 60-watt light bulb and could not understand why they weren't ten feet tall.

A grower does need a sense of balance and a general sensitivity towards what makes plants grow. Hopefully, this book will help you gain this understanding and sensitivity. A brief reading should relieve you of undue worries and misconceptions, and help persuade you to avoid such things as too much watering or fertilizing. A few read-throughs, a little observation and some common sense should be all a sensible grower needs to grow a healthy, potent crop.

One final thought on what constitutes common sense when it comes to plants. Don't overdo it! The demise of many a plant comes from trying to force the issue. If directions prescribe a teaspoon of fertilizer, won't three teaspoons be three times as good? No! Plants do quite well given sensible care, so help them do what comes naturally and never try to force them.

The first crop is always a learning experience and even when the harvest is wonderfully successful, every grower believes that the next will be even better, and generally this is true. Also, each crop gets easier, because questions get answered and doubts gradually disappear, until the process of caring for your crop becomes second nature and more fun than smoking the harvest. Any experienced grower will probably say, "There's no place I'd rather be and nothing I'd rather be doing than sitting among my plants giving them a little TLC (Tender Loving Care)."

SKUNK #1

This fine example of Skunk #1 matured 60 days after first flowers. It was grown indoors under a 250-watt metal-halide lamp (MH), which was switched to a 250-watt high-pressure sodium (HPS) for flowering (with an added 100-watt HPS on the ground). I used high-grade potting soil with vermiculite, perlite and bat guano. Also, CO_2-enrichment was used during flowering to increase size, and a super-high phosphorus (P) fertilizer was added to the water for improved density.

Sticky & Stinky
San Gabriel Valley Posse

#218, October 1993

COMMON PROBLEMS

Wilting: too hot, too dry, too much water.

Plant growing slowly: too much water, too cold, not enough fertilizer.

Brown leaf margins: air too hot and dry, too much water, too much fertilizer.

Spots on leaves: spider mites or other pests, too much fertilizer.

Yellow leaves that fall: not enough humidity, too much water, air too cold, not enough fertilizer.

Yellow leaves stay on: pH problem, water too hard (well water).

Rotting plants: mold or fungus, too much water, too much humidity.

Sudden dropping of leaves or buds: too much water, air too dry, air too cold, transplant shock (not enough water or temperature extremes).

#232, December 1994

SEXING THE PLANTS

BY MEL FRANK

UNDIFFERENTIATED PRIMORDIA

After the plants are at least eight weeks old, look closely (a magnifying glass or photographer's loupe helps) at the junction (node) where the main stem meets with leaf stalks and branches. About two or three nodes below the plant's top, near the base of the main stem's leaf stalks, and just behind the leaf spurs (stipules), you might see a rudimentary flower (preflower). In the best of cases you'll see a single, well-formed female flower with the familiar two white stigmas raised in a "V" sign. If you see a female flower at each internode at two or three successive internodes, this plant is certainly a female. Commonly, you'll see the base of a female flower, a well-formed bract, with no stigmas. If you're

PISTILLATE PRIMORDIA

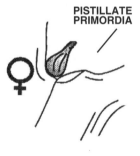

experienced, you'll be able to identify this preflower and the fact that the plant is a female at least 90% of the time.

A male preflower is much harder to identify. A male preflower rarely opens but remains a tightly closed knob or a flat, spade-shaped protrusion raised on a stalk that characteristically identifies the male flower. Often the vegetative overlap of the male preflower superficially looks like a female flower. Once you've learned the difference between male and female preflowers, you'll

STAMINATE PRIMORDIA

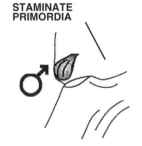

find enough prospective preflowers to remove most males weeks before they actually flower.
#162, February 1989

ILLOS COURTESY SINSEMILLA TIPS

INDOORS OR OUTDOORS: ELECTRIC OR NATURAL LIGHT

The question of where to grow and whether to use natural or electric light depends on your situation: the space you have, the time and funds you have and the quantity of grass you want to harvest. For example, a moderate weekend smoker easily could supply all of the grass he or she might want with a modest indoor setup: a garden under an eight-foot fluorescent fixture, or in a sunny window or back porch. A household that consumes more than an ounce weekly would need a couple of l,OOO-watt HID's (high-intensity discharge lamps, which are halide and sodium-vapor lamps), a greenhouse or a backyard plot.

Sunlight is free; use it whenever possible. The main problem with sunlit gardens is visibility. Window gardens or backyard plots must not be visible to passers-by or to the curious. Greenhouses may innocently attract attention even when using greenhouse plastics that transmit light yet obscure the greenhouses' contents. Furthermore, sunlit gardens usually must be started in the spring and harvested in the fall, following the natural seasonal growth cycle. This restriction can be modified with supplemental lighting and shades. Under exclusively electric lights, growers decide when to start the plants, when the plants will begin to flower and when they'll be ready to harvest. Controlling the basic elements of the environment is then fairly simple and straightforward; indoors there is little concern with wind and rain, cold, poor soil or whether it's springtime or the dead of winter.

SECURITY

Security is the first consideration when setting up any garden. Gardeners should take special care that their gardens and lights aren't visible from outside or accessible to unexpected visitors. Even where marijuana growing is legal, theft is a major concern. Growers must carefully consider the consequences before they tell anyone about their garden and must exercise caution whenever anyone comes to visit. An unfortunate fact of life is that envy, revenge, greed and misplaced morality have made thieves or informers of acquaintances and former friends.

Unlike sunlight, electric lights cost money to buy and operate. First consider the minimal cost for a modest fluorescent garden or the expense of a multi-lamp HID garden. Electric-light gardens require more frequent care than sunlit gardens; on the other hand, they can be cared for at any time since they are inside, and the lights can be on at any time that fits the gardener's schedule. Electric-light gardens are perfect for the working apartment dweller.

You can hide electric-light gardens in closed rooms, basements, attics, closets or garages. Even when hidden, large HID gardens may arouse the suspicions of the utility company. Large metal-halide lamps (MH's), the main light source for many gardeners, draw almost 1,100 watts each. If three or more lamps are used, the utility company may wonder why your electric bill has suddenly gotten so high, and they may make inquiries about your electric usage or investigate a possible short or other problem along your lines. Growers who manage large electric-light gardens sometimes run their lights at night when other tenants are asleep, so that the meter reader doesn't see the electric meter "spinning" when he reads the usage meter. In a home situation, commercial growers limit their electrical consumption so that their usage is less obvious to the electric company. If asked, the best excuse is that you've installed electric heating or central air-conditioning.

Large HID gardens may be too noisy. Ballasts may hum loudly and light balancers (if installed) may cause considerable vibrations. Ballasts manufactured by Jefferson are purportedly the quietest.

Commercial growers who are concerned about the scent of their marijuana may choose to run their lights and ventilation fans at night, when their neighbors are asleep. Consider all possible problems first, before you set up your system, especially if it's a large commercial operation. Small gardens need no special security precautions. But don't tell anyone about the garden and keep the garden hidden from unexpected visitors.

Warning: If your property can be shown to have been purchased with funds from illicit drug sales, it can be confiscated; a vehicle used to transport illegal drugs or to transport materials used in an illegal garden is also subject to confiscation.

Marijuana growing is fun, and more rewarding than you might imagine. In all states except Alaska, growing is illegal, so take some time to consider all of the consequences. The purpose of this book is not to encourage you to grow illegally, but to report how growing is done legally and how it may be done when growing is decriminalized. I hope a thorough reading of this book gives you foresight, a good idea of what to expect and solutions to the problems you might confront.

Starting in 1968, I've experienced more wonderful harvests than I can count, and I've smoked myself into happy oblivion with homegrown more times than I can remember (the excellent quality of the dope definitely affected my memory). Good luck and many happy harvests.

THE SEED

by George Lassen

The proper seed is the single most important thing for the success of your garden.

Pick seed that comes from the best marijuana you can find. If you take seed from average or poor stock, even if it gets the best treatment, grows to be 15 feet tall and weighs five pounds, it will still be poor marijuana.

The real breakthroughs have come from the breeding programs that have recently developed very powerful strains. This breeding is possible because seed is available from all over the world, if you know where to look.

There is no doubt that these botanists have crossbred their way to a product that is excellent. However, it is important to remember that they started with seeds and that there has been legendary marijuana through the ages. Current times include the 1960s with Acapulco Gold (the real thing) that would put four people out on half a joint. And this was heavily seeded pot! We also had heavily seeded Panama Red (again the real thing) from which nobody could finish one joint.

There are many varieties and cross breeds of marijuana. It is up to you to find something that pleases you. The most common types seen today are *indica* and *sativa*. *Indica* produces a very heavy type of high. It has a tendency to push you back into your seat and almost send you into unconsciousness. *Sativa,* on the other hand, is lighter with more of a

SEEDS

BY MEL FRANK
Seeds are all important, since the potency of your crop is hereditary. Potency is genetic: potent "buds" hold seeds that give potent offspring. Also, how early in the season a variety flowers is genetic. The length of daylight ultimately controls this genetic program. When a variety actually flowers depends on the length of day coupled with the variety's predilection to flower at a particular time of the year. The further north your garden is, the later your plants will flower and mature. Some varieties mature as early as mid-August at a mid-line through the country. Other varieties, particularly from a tropical origin, won't mature until late November or December in the same location. Northern gardens should plant Afghani, or another short-season variety so that plants mature before frosts arrive. Many growers prefer to germinate seeds in small pots, transplanting the seedlings to their garden or to larger pots after several weeks of healthy growth. Inexperienced growers find small pots easier to handle, and there is much less chance of over-watering and drowning tender sprouts.
#201, May 1992

SEED ANATOMY

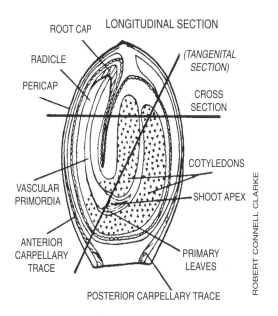

ROOT CAP

LONGITUDINAL SECTION

RADICLE

PERICAP

(TANGENITAL SECTION)

CROSS SECTION

COTYLEDONS

SHOOT APEX

VASCULAR PRIMORDIA

ANTERIOR CARPELLARY TRACE

PRIMARY LEAVES

POSTERIOR CARPELLARY TRACE

ROBERT CONNELL CLARKE

HOW TO YIELD TEN POUNDS FROM A SINGLE PLANT

BY OTIS BIRDSEED

To begin you need to start your seeds indoors during midwinter under lights. Several should be started. The seedlings should grow under 24 hours of light, which keeps the internodes only a couple of inches apart. After three lower branches have formed, the plant may be sexed by taking a cutting off the main stem. Take the cutting, and place it in a glass of water under a regimen of 12 hours light and 12 hours darkness. It will indicate sex in about a week. You want only one female, which will exhibit white hairs or pistils; if you plan on harvesting some seeds, one male should also be kept. Sexing is done in a separate room, so the parent female may continue rapid vegetative growth under 24 hours of light.

TRAINING

When your parent plant has developed new leaves on the three remaining side branches, you are ready to begin pinching. After each branch has three sets of leaves, pinch the tip off each carefully. Each pinched top should form two more leaves, and so on, every seven to 10 days. When three new sets of leaves appear on each branch, pinch again. Keep your light (two fluorescent tubes work fine) just a couple of inches above the plant. Train the branches to grow horizontally by bending, tying or weighting them down. The four branches become eight, then 16, 32, 64, 128...*and so on.*

OUTDOOR TRANSFER

To ready your plant for the outdoors, slowly cut the light cycle down by one hour each week. The idea is to bring the "daylight hours" of the *indoors* in line with the hours of sunshine *outdoors* on the day you move your plant. In May, that's around 15 or 16 hours. Toughen up your plant by taking it outside in the shade only during the daytime, bringing it in at night.

FINISHING TIPS

As your plant grows, keep the branches tied down, or propped up, as needed. Only a few inches of air space are required between the branches and the ground. Most important: If down South, stop pinching your plant during the last week in July; if up North, the last week in June. It will have thousands and thousands of budding sites if you have watered and pinched regularly.

#215, July 1993

sparkle. It gives energy rather than taking it away. A careful crossbreeding program between the two can give the best of both. Be aware that when you cross *indica* and *sativa*, the resulting plant can look like one type and give you the high of the other. You have to go through one generation to harvest before you really know what you have. Trade with your friends and keep complete records of your breeding program. A few years from now you may have the seed that everybody wants.

When choosing seed, consider the area it came from. A plant that comes from the equator is used to almost no change in day length year-round. This means that if you are growing in Northern California, the plants may not mature until the end of November or December. The shortest day of the year is December 21. Having plants which take so long to mature can be disastrous if the rains and frosts come on time, and they usually do. The same problem comes over a month earlier in Northern Idaho. As you get further north, bud rot becomes one of the biggest problems associated with cold, damp weather.

Look for stock that comes from approximately the same latitude that you will grow in. For example, the latitude in Afghanistan is approximately the same as that of the southern half of the United States. This makes Afghani stock a very good choice for gardens at approximately 35 to 45 degrees latitude (or higher, as there is little quality seed stock from higher latitudes at this time).

On the other hand, if you use seed that comes from equatorial areas such as Colombia or Thailand, the plants will mature in cold, wet weather at latitudes above 40 degrees or so.

Some growers, with knowledge, time and patience, have developed and stabilized plants that mature early for high-latitude planting, but this stock is hard to find.

GERMINATION

If you know the history of the seed, or if you have smoked some of the grass and are sure of its potency, you are ready to start. Prior to germination, many growers like to soak the seeds in water overnight. Soaking makes it easier for the seeds to absorb moisture and softens the shell better than just planting and watering. This makes it easier for the tap root to penetrate the hard seed case. The dedicated grower may add a liquid seaweed (like Maxicrop). This increases vigor in the seed because it speeds cell division for faster growth. Germination may be done by taking a few seeds and putting them between two layers of plain white paper towels in a dish. Then add only enough water to saturate the towels, and cover with some plastic wrap. In three to seven days, the seeds will sprout. This procedure is often followed to determine the viability of the seed. Only the seeds that show a tap root are planted.

Seeds should be planted as soon as the root shows. The sprouts are then carefully placed in their individual pots or other containers. This step should be done in subdued light with clean or sterile tools. The roots are delicate, and if they are abused, the growth may be slowed or the plant may die. Seeds are planted with the tip of the root pointing up and covered with about one quarter-inch of fine soil. As the plant develops, the root grows down. It provides the base. At this point the plant is bent in a U-shape. Then the leaf part, still covered by the seed case, unbends, and as it straightens, it pushes its way up through the soil to the light.

Marijuana is sexually flexible (can be male or female), and high stress in the first eight weeks will produce a higher percentage of males.

Because transplanting is stressful, many growers will start seeds in the ground or in a container that will hold the plant until it goes into the ground. Working this way eliminates a lot of handling and a lot of stress. The size of the container will depend on what you want to do or how long you want to keep the plants before transplanting.

For example, starting seeds directly in half- or three-quarter-gallon containers will allow you to go from seed to final home with only one transplant. The older a plant is at transplanting, the more shock it experiences and the longer it takes to recover and get back to growing.

Keeping the above in mind, it may help to note that marijuana is very hardy and will take some abuse. I have seen 60 seedlings in a two-gallon container. These little plants were separated and planted late one spring afternoon with little or no problem. I have also seen two-week-old plants push right up through a very unseasonable April snow. So if you're nice to your plants, you shouldn't have to worry; after all, it is a weed.

Some growers germinate in paper towels, then plant in two-inch pots. A week or two later, they transplant to a four- or six-inch pot and, finally, into the ground. With each transplant they thin out the less desirable plants until only the best are left.

Please Note: You will germinate and start many more seeds than you plan on putting in the ground, and you will put more in the ground than you plan on harvesting. The reason for this is that some will be males. Also, you will lose some along the way, and some will not be vigorous or attractive. These plants offer nothing for genetic improvement and are not useful to your overall purpose. Select only the best plants and cull the rest.

In your starting soil mix do not use soil or dirt that you dig up from your backyard or other outside source. You will not know what is in that dirt, and what you don't know can ruin your entire crop. There are many harmful organisms in what is called native soil. Use only sterile potting soil from your garden supply. That way you are guaranteed a clean start.

Many people have come back to me with sad stories about the things that happened to their plants when they started them using native soil.

POT FOR PENNIES

by Pat and Mike from M.U.D.

This "how-to" guide represents 20 years of personal experience in every phase and involvement with pot imaginable. While we in no way advocate the breaking of any laws, we seek to offer assistance and guidance to those who, for their own reasons, desire to "grow their own."

WINNING YOUR OWN PERSONAL WAR ON DRUGS

The most threatening problem before us is the War on Drugs. The increased penalties, forfeiture of assets, $10,000 fines, harsh prison sentence, and loss of constitutional rights are all attacks on the "drug user" as well as the "drug dealer." The only way to take the heat off the user is to eliminate the true source of conflict: the "drug dealer" and his

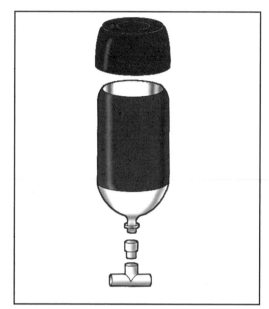

(Top to bottom) Black cap, pot, PVC coupler, PVC "T"-fitting.

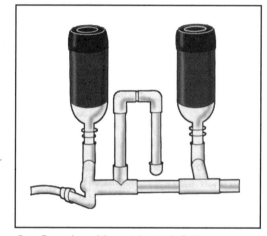

Overflow pipe with vent (center). Later, we realized that not only did this prevent siphoning of the pots, but, through venturi action, actually added air (oxygen) to the water. Inlet and outlet to and from the reservoir (lower left).

The "4x4" or "quad" rack.

BRIAN SPAETH

MARIJUANA STRAINS AND VARIETIES

BY MEL FRANK

Sativas are from eight to 20 feet tall; yields are from 1/3 to five lbs. per plant in sinsemilla buds. *Sativas* may originate from anywhere, but almost all tropical marijuana varieties are *sativas*, and almost invariably all hemps are *sativa*, whether they come from near the Arctic Circle or from equatorial regions. Leaf blades are long and narrow and light green in color. Branching is symmetric to uneven, but usually internodes are long and branches are even and well-spaced. Female stigmas (the two "hairs" of a female flower) are most often pure white. Maturation usually is late in the season from mid-October through December for tropical varieties, but as early as the end of July for temperate hemp strains.

Indicas are shorter, usually between four and eight feet tall, and yield 1/4 to two lbs. of sinsemilla. *Indicas* mostly originate from central Asia, primarily from Afghanistan, Pakistan, Iran and India. Leaves usually are a very dark blue-green, and may develop a purple tinge. Leaf blades are shorter and much wider than *sativas*. Branching is usually symmetric and thick with short internodes. Flower stigmas are usually white, but may be red or purple; buds tend to be fuller and more compact than most *sativas*. Most often *indicas* mature early, from late August through October.

Ruderalises have narrow, *sativa*-like leaf blades; plants are short, from one to five feet tall, and most of them are very sparse with relatively long internodes. (Botanical collections of *ruderalis* from the USSR characterize all *ruderalises* as having narrow blades. Many US marijuana growers describe *ruderalis* as having wide *indica*-like leaf blades, and these might be hybrids.) Often *ruderalis* has only two or three sets of leaves before flowering, and typical yields are only 1/4 to two ounces of sinsemilla. Originally from the USSR, *ruderalis* is very quick to mature and may ripen as early as the middle of July. Generally *ruderalis* begins flowering a few weeks after sprouting, but it won't form decent buds, if ever, until the photoperiod drops to about 18 or 19 hours duration. American hemps are generally six to 12 feet tall with *sativa*-like leaves, coloration and bud characteristics. These weeds are very hardy (in fact authorities have been unable to eradicate this "troublesome" weed), and mature early, from the end of July to early October.

#161, January 1989

enterprise. By drug dealers, we mean those who buy and sell with the sole purpose of making money—not even using the product they push. Drug dealers make obscene profits—amounts so large that corruption cannot be held in check. These "badguys" cause a drain on our economy through money-laundering, evading taxes and by removing large chunks of money from circulation. Later the money circulates back in the form of "big ticket" investments, the financing of revolutions and private armies, real-estate speculation, luxury items, even government bonds, none of which benefits the people who make the whole business possible, the consumer and the farmer.

We believe the ultimate "weapon" in the War on Drugs (which was created and exists because of bad laws) is the *return* of certain inalienable rights. By growing our own we reduce demand, price and profitability and corruption. Great harm is caused by current drug policy; efforts to stop drug use are counterproductive. Enormous benefits, such as tax revenues, import and excise taxes, licensing and the control of drugs through health and safety agencies are lost. If purchasing drugs from drug dealers is equivalent to supporting the murders committed by them, as some would have us believe, then growing our own absolves us. A grow system is the most effective "weapon" in the War on Drugs at our disposal.

We mean that literally. This article presents systems built with disposables—items most people throw away or are willing to give away. These items, we feel, are as good as the best you can buy. We know the people who can least afford to buy an expensive system are the people who most need to grow their own. At today's prices, the financial drain on the average person's income for bud can be considerable (not to mention the bother, anxiety and danger of having to deal with drug dealers). But the rewards of growing your own transcend material comforts. The freedom from dependence on others brings about a wondrous change in the grower.

It used to be hard for the inexperienced grower to produce top-quality bud, especially indoors. But, with advances in grow technology and the exchange of information, this is no longer the case. In fact, if good seed is provided, we can practically guarantee a successful crop on the first try.

YOU DON'T NEED A SEWER PIPE TO GROW GOOD BUD

When we started growing, we faced this problem. Not only did grow systems cost a lot, but the price was more than we could afford to pay. But we had time and ideas: our own and others'. This, along with pocket change, was enough.

The system which we will discuss is similar to the Buddy™ grow system designed by Kyle Roq, a regular contributor to HIGH TIMES. The main part of this system consists of a large diameter (4"-6") PVC sewer pipe, in which the roots of the plants are suspended and fed with aerated nutrient solution by a flood and drain cycle. This seems to be state of the art.

While we in no way copied the Buddy™ system (in fact, it had yet to appear in HIGH TIMES), we took a similar approach. Our system was unique in design, evolutionary in nature and solved problems encountered in earlier systems.

In one system, essentially a large Phototron™, we grew plants in one-gallon containers of perlite, vermiculite and lava rock. The pots sat inside plastic trays, with drain tubes for the runoff from the drip emitters, which supplied nutrient to each of 12 pots. Between plugged emitters and plugged drains, we found the whole affair too time-consuming for our lifestyles. Not that it didn't work; in some ways it was a remarkable system, especially the side-lighting principle. For those who enjoy spending a lot of time with their plants, we can see many reasons for recommending it.

In a still later system, we eliminated the above problem by setting our trusty one-gallon pots on a tray which was flooded and drained twice a day. Our tray was 4' x 12', utilizing two 400-watt metal halides and four 150-watt high-pressure sodium lights. We ran 150 one-gallon pots supplied with starts by air-layering four "mother" plants in another section. Based on the "Sea of Green," it incorporated ideas pioneered by the good folks at Hydro-Farm™. Flooding plastic tubes filled with Geolite™, as opposed to "watering" from above, made it possible to grow three or four *large* plants in an 18" x 24" pot. Later on, Hydro Farm™ developed flooded trays with rockwool slabs and blocks as a grow medium. This, we suspect, was to accommodate the trend towards many small, individual flowering plants.

Being deathly afraid of rockwool for a number of reasons, we looked for a way to flood many small individual containers without expensive and complicated piping. Before we tell you what we found, we'd like to share with you a few of the "most for the least" principles we achieved. Some we figured out through 20 years of fooling around, others we happened upon while reading "Ask Ed," but mostly we just got lucky: (1) for fast growth, feed them often—just like a person who eats constantly and doesn't do any work, they're gonna get fat; (2) just as important as fresh air (CO_2) is to the upper portion of the plant, oxygen (O_2) is to the roots (over 1" a day under a moderate light intensity of about 25 watts/sq.ft.); (3) utilize hydroponics to deliver O_2 and nutrients—it's the most desirable approach for indoor application; (4) make operations low-maintenance and trouble-free so that you don't have to visit the grow area more than once every week or two; and (5) give each plant an individual unit, in order to maximize growing space, light placement, plant size and growth stage—no wasted space.

BUILDING A CHEAP, EFFICIENT, TROUBLE-FREE SYSTEM

We can best act as your guides by telling you our story: what we did, how we did it, and why we did it. Within our story is the seed of an idea. We hope it falls on fertile ground.

Just as I hit on the idea for a cheap, efficient, trouble-free grow system, my partner Mike popped in the door, holding a two-liter Coke bottle upside down, exclaiming, "This is it" over and over. It would be a while before we could say, "It works, we got a system." Once we got started, it didn't take long to become confused about whose idea it was in the first place: Mike ended up damn near perfecting much of the system in ways I was too blind to see.

For example, originally, our method for attaching the bottle to a piece of 3/4" PVC delivery-piping was accomplished by heating the neck of a "T"-fitting and inserting the bottle cap into the opening. This proved impractical for a number of reasons, the main one being that the caps came loose after repeated use. Water consumption and leakage were problems in our system. We solved them by attaching the bottles to a male-threaded coupler which screwed into a "T" with a female-threaded neck. We heated the pipe end of the coupler to make it pliable, dropped in a piece of screen to keep our medium from falling into the

HINDU-KUSH
Pistillate floral clusters.

ROBERT CONNELL CLARKE

ADAM'S GARDEN

Adam said that marijuana changed his life, in that it helped him overcome his cocaine addiction.

"Herb is much more therapeutic for me than any legal prescription drug could be," he added.

The smell of the indoor garden was well-concealed in the downstairs, but when we entered the attic, the aroma of the ripe Purple Kush x (Northern Lights #5 x Hash Plant) blasted the senses.

Some of the buds were profuse with hairy orange "spaghetti" pistils and purple leaves (Kush configuration), some were more leafy (Northern Lights configuration), but all were crusted over with globs of resin. It was time for most of the crop to be harvested.

It was growing in a 7' x 7' area under three high-intensity discharge lamps, two 1,000-watt metal-halide lamps and one 1,000-watt high-pressure sodium. With little more than 4 1/2' vertical space, the lights were kept close to the plants, no more than 8", so adequate air-flow was needed to keep plants from overheating. The soil was organic, the fertilizers completely natural. Adam cautioned that too much bat guano in the mix may have toxified his soil, made it too acidic and thus stunted some plants.

High & Blind
New Hampshire

#223, March 1994

THE GARDEN

BY ANTHONY HADEN-GUEST

There is a smell in the corridors outside Carlton Turner's office and the laboratories of the marijuana project. These, incidentally, are in the pharmaceutical research building, an oblong structure just across the grass and rhododendron from the Ole Miss Alumna House, the Law Building, the Loyalty Foundation and just down the road from a monument to Our Confederate Dead.

Turner got involved on the telephone almost as soon as I arrived at the office. Some stuff about shipments of marijuana seeds from Hawaii and Afghanistan. (They just come by registered mail, in case you're interested, but they have to be specially picked up. And, no, they haven't lost any en route, though one Pakistani supplier was discovered trying to diddle them out of the paid weight.)

The Mississippi project has been budgeted at something between $250,000 and $300,000 a year. The annual harvest has been between three and five tons, and some 500 separate projects in the United States and Europe have submitted form 222C, a white form with elegant brown scrollwork, to the Drug Enforcement Administration, been checked out and duly profited from Turner's carefully standardized crop.

#15, November 1976

piping, coated the bottle threads with PVC cement and shoved it home. The "T"s were joined with short lengths of 3/4" PVC pipe. The configuration we found most suitable for us was what we call the "4 x 4" or "quad"—four rows with four "T"s per row. (We made it 3' x 3' for use under a 400-watt metal halide light.) Later, a 1' x 4' rack with two rows of six staggered bottles proved ideal for starts, utilizing 4' fluorescent side lighting, or a 150-watt overhead.

Meanwhile, I got the pots together by first removing the black bottoms of the bottles (with a hot-water soak they pull off easily). Next, using a razor blade, I cut off the bottoms of the bottles. A hole about 3" in diameter resulted, to serve as the top of the pot. (This opening is necessary to fill it with grow medium. The tops must all be a uniform height as well.) With a one-inch hole in the center, the black bottom became the cap, and gave rigidity to the now-complete "Pot for Pennies."

We put it together for the water test, on a cold night with no heat in our shop. It was just past Christmas, and the leanness of the season was intensified. With absolutely no funds available, Mike and I did what we do best: We used what we had on hand and adjusted our ideas accordingly. The thrill we experienced as we saw an old swamp-cooler pump flood 16 two-liter "grow bulbs" to overflowing is not to be conveyed in mere words. Suffice it to say that our Christmas present that year, though a little late, was one that still hasn't stopped coming.

To finish off the system, we added an overflow pipe which prevented what we had been so happy to see earlier and a fill pipe to make it happen. Our first reservoir was four 3' x 5" x 1/2" pieces of plywood joined at the corners. With the pump and float valve mounted to the cover (another piece of plywood), and heavy-duty plastic draped inside the 3' x 3' frame and tacked on the outside to act like a waterbed liner, our big day was soon upon us.

Naturally, everything still needed to be done, but our starts were ready, even if the grow room wasn't (controls weren't, lights weren't). The day our "medium" arrived, nothing would do but to drop everything. Work would have to wait. For its light weight and porosity, we chose Geolite™ as a medium in our hydroponic system. (Lava rock works about as well at a much lower cost.)

Mike filled the bottles with medium while I busied myself with hanging a light, fan and getting anything else together. Before long, it was time to fill the reservoir with water, add the nutrient and turn on the pump. Mike came into the room with a 5-gallon pail of water and news that it was dark outside already. Somehow we had lost all sense of time. It was an experience that we would have over and over again in the months ahead while refining and fine-tuning our grow system. It was the high that comes with making ideas reality.

We watched the pots flood, from the bottom up, with water/nutrient solution. As the level got to within an inch or so from the tops of the pots, we could see solution flowing through the clear vinyl return hose, back to the reservoir. To our astonishment, as the overflow increased, it began to siphon the pots until they were dry. I looked at Mike, he looked at me. I said, "What the fuck," while he just shook his head. A second later it hit us: We needed a vent to break the vacuum caused by the overflow pipe.

We had to try it. A 1/4" hole drilled in the top of the U-shaped top portion of the pipe broke the siphon effect and allowed the pots to remain flooded while the overflow was then allowed to run at pump capacity.

I could tell you how the next day we placed the peat pellets containing our precious starts into the pots, with the tender shoots and leaves threaded through the 1" hole in the "black cup" which holds it all in place and prevents evaporation through the pot opening; or about the timer Mike made out of a cheap electric clock which feeds our "babies" for five minutes every hour during the light period; or a light mover made out of an old barbecue motor. But that's another story.

What I will say is what can be expected in terms of yield per square foot. Believe it or not, in an area 4' x 4', growing 16 plants, using a 400-watt metal halide light, we harvested 8-12 ounces of trimmed dry bud every 90 days. With two units, we could harvest over five pounds a year. At current prices, if we smoked that much, we would save ourselves $15,000 a year. That's about a half pound per month from an area 4' x 8'.

With nearly a quarter-pound of prime bud apiece every month, our "drug problem" is over.

SEVEN STEPS TO GROWING POT FOR PENNIES

1. Go to the local nursery for peat pellets to start the seeds.
2. Select seeds from your best recent pot purchases. The seed is 90% of a successful crop, so be choosy. Try to select seeds from bud that contains only "a couple of seeds" here and there. Chances are these will be "female seeds."
3. Soak the peat pellets in water to expand them and plant the seeds 1/2" deep, one or two per pellet.
4. During the next several days gather the necessary items with which you will build your "state of the art" grow system:

One "4 x 4"/"Quad" (16 pots)
a. sixteen two-liter soda bottles $0.00
b. sixteen 16-3/4" male NPT X 3/4" PVC couplers ($0.25 ea.) $4.00
c. sixteen 3/4" x 3/4" x 3/4" female NPT T-fittings ($0.40 ea.) $6.50
d. six 3/4" x 3/4" x 3/4" PVC T-fittings ($0.25 ea.) $1.50
e. four 3/4" x 3/4" PVC elbow fittings ($0.25 ea.) $1.00
f. one 22' 3/4" PVC pipe $7.00
   i) eighteen 12" sections
   ii) nine 2" sections
   iii) one 12"-14" section
g. two 3/4" (male) faucet nipples $1.00
h. two hose-to-faucet couplers
i. 6' hose to match (can be two sections of an old water hose
   with female coupler) $5.00
j. six 3' x 5 1/2" x 3/4"(1 x 6 pine #3 or #4, particleboard,
   plywood, etc.) $9.00
k. 4' x 8' heavy plastic $5.00
l. swamp-cooler pump $10.00

TOTAL $50.00

5. Along with a few basic hand tools and some miscellaneous materials, assemble your grow unit by referring to the pictures and the text.
6. Find and read several books on hydroponics and growing pot. Or better yet, order half-a-dozen back issues of HIGH TIMES and tell

LOW-BUDGET GROW ROOMS
BY KEVIN RUDEBOY

I don't have a college degree or a fancy high-paying job. I'm an average Joe. No expensive home in some snobby neighborhood or shiny new car in the garage. My job gets me by and my car gets me home to my little house. I survive.

I had a rec room in my basement, and when I built it I left three feet on all sides to keep it warm, away from the cold brick walls. The room had a door with a padlock and, most importantly, secrecy.

I started with a wooden frame made of el-cheapo two-by-fours. They cost 79 cents each and I didn't care if they were straight or not. I built the frame five feet tall, two feet wide and five feet long. Off-white sheets of posterboard were only 39 cents each, and I used ten of them as ceiling, floor and walls. I then mounted one $7.99 shoplight from the top of my frame by wire so it could be easily moved as the plants grew.

Grow-light bulbs can cost between six and 12 dollars. I couldn't afford all grow lights, so I began with one grow light and one cool white. I built my garden beneath the heat duct to give it warmth in the winter. I plugged my light into a $3.95 K-Mart timer and spent $2.98 for a 30-pound bag of potting soil. Plastic one-gallon milk containers make great starting pots, and since I drink milk anyway, I simply rinsed them out and cut off the tops and punched a few holes in the bottom for drainage.
#168, October 1989

PSYCHOSOMATICS
Infuse flower essences (FE) into the water used to irrigate plants. The theory, practice and availability of FE is available in health food stores. In this way the sublime powers of FE are transmitted directly into the "psychosomatic" genetics of your plants. This ultrawater is used as a magical enrichment, whereas souls partaking of my sacred herb are connected in a very precise way to higher forms of life on this planet.
Bishop Blunt
California

#222, February 1994

KEVIN RUDEBOY

PRUNING FOR GROWTH

BY DR. ZEE

We all know a little about pruning, everyone's battle with hedges and trees, usually to control growth, not enhance it. Pruning, when done properly, will enhance growth as well as yield. Increasing yield gets everyone's attention, from

the closet grower to the outdoor planter. Random pruning can be very harmful, even inducing sex change, something no one wants.

Fig. #1 shows an improperly pruned plant that has resulted in a spindly, weak plant. Cuttings were made indiscriminately, with no knowledge of the correct procedure. Fig. #2 clearly shows a bushy, healthy plant with growth in all directions. A plant like this will easily double the yield of plant #1. Yield is of prime importance to the closet grower, who, because of limited space, wants the maximum results from a few plants.

Fig. #3 shows "double stalking," a process wherein you force the plant to split into two main stalks. Marijuana plants are especially responsive to pruning, and excellent results can be had with a minimal amount of effort. Growth is enhanced with

➔

them to include the Indoor Growers editions. For a *complete* understanding of what you're going to want to know, read *The Marijuana Grower's Guide* by Ed Rosenthal and Mel Frank. The best.

THE MICRO-SECURITY GARDEN

by B.B.

I'll admit it, I'm paranoid about growing marijuana, but I'm even more jittery about buying the stuff. I've grown small crops outdoors and indoors during the last several years. I've gone from 100% organic growing to Geolite based hydroponic units and then to rockwool.

Recently, I've come full circle—back to organics, but supplemented with chemical nutrients. I had gotten so caught up with the procedure that I was in danger of missing my objective—being able to smoke the best bud. Most importantly, we can't smoke it if the garden gets busted. This realization has forced me to come up with an apartment microgarden. It could be used anywhere, but is ideal for apartment or condo dwellers.

The most important considerations in building your own microgarden are listed here in descending order of importance:

• **Security.** Small inconspicuous gardens are the most likely to escape detection for obvious reasons. I've never been busted for growing and I want to keep it that way. I could have been if I had gotten too greedy. Greed is the primary cause of most security screw-ups; it has to be done away with here.

• **Quality.** If you don't start with the best, you can't end up with the best. Small, fast-maturing plants are the goal.

• **Ease of operation.** A little bending, pruning and insect inspection once a week and water every three or four days is about all it takes.

SET UP AND COST

Do not be too cost-conscious in setting up your system. To the extent possible, use the best-quality equipment and materials that you can. It pays off in the long run. A poor man can't afford to buy cheap stuff.

I've watched my cheapskate friends pinch pennies on their gardens and then throw cash away on things like gambling, cocaine and alcohol. They buy cheap, inefficient gear, get mediocre results and then have to turn around and buy decent equipment. It's always best to just skip the first step.

Even at that, a good set-up can be put together for a modest investment. I've listed each piece used in my microgarden and an approximate price. As you can see, the total cost is not that bad—a lot less than a certain toy-like growing chamber that is now on the market.

• **Grow light.** I use a single 150-watt vertical high-pressure sodium light. Vertical? Yes, it fit better into my Bud Box and seemed better built than the mini-horizontal. Cost: $100.

• **Negative-ion generator.** Works like a charm at keeping odors down. I have to stick my head clear into the Bud Box to cop a whiff of the wonderful aroma. Cost: $100.

• **Timer.** Get the digital kind. They cost more but are more reliable. Mine is a lower-capacity model that will only work with a microgarden. Cost: $25.

• **Power strip.** Get one with a built-in breaker. (It should have a red "reset" button on the side.) Cost: $8 on sale and up.

• **Fan.** A tiny 3-inch desk fan with an angle adjustment does the trick for me. It is silent in operation and provides great circulation, although the pink color annoys me a little. Cost: $8.

• **Cardboard box.** Mine is 20 inches square. I tape the sides up and leave one halfway open for access. Cost: $1 or less.

• **Reflective Mylar.** Used to line the Bud Box. Cost: $2.

• **Plastic containers.** Use 1, 2 or 3-gallon tubs or buckets depending on your needs. Cost: $5.

• **Soil.** One large bag of Black Gold. Cost: $9.

• **Thermometer.** Cost: $5.

• **Nutrients.** Cost: $4.

My total cost for gear and nutrients came to $267. My initial seed cost was $150 for two Dutch varieties, but that will of course vary depending on your connections.

The key to my successful operation is the negative-ion generator. Before I bought the generator, the odors were extremely strong. The moment I'd open the front door, bam! There was no mistaking that smell—pot! This was with a well-ventilated bedroom closet with the bedroom door closed. The odors go right through the cracks.

I was always worried about who I brought home, or somebody knocking on the front door and me having to open it. That tiny device has really kept me growing. The peace of mind has been more than worth the modest expense.

I place the ion generator about three feet from the closet on a dresser about level with the tops of the plants. You can't see it work, or tell if anything is happening for a few days, just a small light and a slight hum every 15 seconds. But odor reduction is dramatic, down to nil in about a week. I occasionally shut the generator off for a few days just to smell-sample my crop.

Since the main problem with microgardening—the smell—can be taken care of for about $100, the rest of the site selection and set-up process is just common sense.

In reviewing your own apartment, or especially if you are lucky enough to be shopping for a new one, there are a few things to look for. An upstairs apartment is ideal. Common sense should tell you that foot traffic past your bedroom window can mean trouble. But there is another advantage, often overlooked, to an upstairs garden. If there is no outside access to your bedroom window, it can be left open to provide needed ventilation and fresh air for your plants. An open window at ground level in most areas is an invitation to a bust or rip-off. (For those still stuck on the ground floor or who, due to cool weather, cannot keep a window open, your only option is CO_2 enrichment. I suggest the injection method with compressed CO_2 controlled by a timer.)

Of course, your open window will have to be fitted with blinds or some other covering that will allow air to enter but keep the full glare from your HID lights inside. What you should see from the outside is the dim glow of light through the blinds—nothing unusual. I run my lights to coincide with daylight hours to ensure there are no dark-period light leaks. I don't mean on at dawn and off at dusk. It is necessary to

the addition of more light receptors.

When your seedlings sprout, ignore the first set of leaves as they are merely "pod busters" and will soon be followed by your first set of leaves. When this first set of leaves grows to a minimum of one inch and the second set begins to show, clip one leaf off where the leaf changes into stem. (See illustration.)

When the next set of leaves, sprouts, follow the same procedure but on the opposite side, balancing the plant. Continue this process for four cuttings. Keep your light source as close as possible without causing damage, thus keeping main-stem growth from becoming spindly.

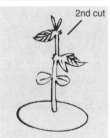

No one wants to waste time growing stalks. After about seven or eight leaf sproutings, you will notice a new shoot growing on the side that you left on the plant when you began pruning.

To "double stalk" your plant, follow the procedure to the fourth cutting, then wait till the sixth sprouting, then take off both sides of the new sprout. The plant will then "double stalk." Practice this procedure on one or two plants until you get the hang of it. See the diagram.

#168, August 1989

FRANK MAX

run the lights for several hours when it is dark outside to maintain the correct photoperiod.

The box itself is just a cardboard box lined with Mylar. Whatever size box you have, your lamp should sit just inside the top to keep the light in the box and not out the window. A box three to four feet high is perfect. The mini-fan is placed at a 8-inch hole cut in the side of the box near the bottom. There is an exhaust hole on the other side near the top of the box. I leave the sliding door open about a foot at the opposite end of the closet. I hang a few coats at the open end of the closet so that everything looks natural.

You can't hear the fan or smell the pot from outside the closet, and in daylight the garden is virtually undetectable. The only clues are the power cord coming out of the closet and the negative ion generator. The cord could be easily concealed. The ion generator? No way. I once spent a whole weekend in bed with a new lady friend not five feet from my growing plants and she never knew they were there.

I've added a lock placed at the bottom of the bedroom door just in case the manager or somebody else were to get into the apartment while I am gone. It's pretty unlikely, I'll admit, but better safe, as they say. If I'm going to be gone for a couple of days, I set the clothes hamper or a couple of towels in front of the lock to keep it looking innocent. If somebody is nosing around, I'd rather have them find a locked door than my box o' buds.

CULTIVATION

Some seeds I start in a clone/seedling chamber that I share with a friend. It's really just a bookshelf with sliding doors that has been fitted with four 18-inch fluorescent tubes. With more expensive or valuable seeds, I plant directly into 1- or 2-gallon containers filled with Black Gold to eliminate transplant shock.

I water with a chemical 20-20-20 nutrient to get the tiny plants off to a good start in phosphorus uptake and to induce dwarfing. I use these nutrients and a 24-hour lights-on cycle for the first two weeks and then switch to a bloom formula for another week, causing the plants to indicate rapidly and to minimize stretching during flowering.

There are some drawbacks to this approach; I seem to get more males (don't ask me why) and a lower total yield, but it also gives me a lot of flexibility. Since I grow from seed, I can keep one or two plants of each strain going, a maximum of eight. I can choose plants to fit the available space in the box—some squat, some a little leaner to fill in gaps.

BREEDING

The basis for all of my hybrids comes from Seed Bank stock. Here are a few I've tried with more or less success:

• **Kush x Kush.** A great simple hybrid. Small solid plants that are great for breeding.

• **Hash Plant.** Beautiful little plants, perfect for small areas and easy to grow. Skimpy yields and a not-so-potent product are minuses.

• **Skunk #1.** When flowered small and under low-watt sodiums, I get only about 33% females, but they are certainly worth it. You can get a mini Skunk with nice buds, but they tend to stretch a bit. I bend them horizontally, making the side buds grow straight up. The quality of the product is superb— my favorite.

• **Northern Lights #5 X Skunk #1.** My second choice. The plants have an enormous amount of resin, even only three weeks into flowering.

• **Haze x Northern Lights #5.** I've done a couple of these, but they are not

SUPER SATIVA

My name is Ace and here's how I grew this fabulous *sativa*. It was my son who suggested we go it as a team and see what we could come up with. I had no idea what was in store for me. After watching my son germinate the seeds in 75 peat pots inside a ten-gallon fish tank in a cold basement, I took charge.

In 30 days I had 18 plants in one-gallon pots. Then I transplanted them into five gallon pots. By this time, I realized I had the right formula because the plants were growing at a rate of 2 inches per day—sometimes more. (Seedlings were started on Upstart B1; after two weeks changed to Peters 20-20-20 for vegetative growth; at 50 days changed to Hydrofarm Blossom 10-30-18.) When the plants reached 50 days old, I went into the flowering cycle: 12 hours on and 12 off. I knew I'd waited too long because some plants were growing into the 1,000-watt HID. I was forced to build a 4-foot-high trellis. I bent the higher limbs of the plants and secured them to the trellis. They responded by turning up toward the light and growing like mad.

Eleven days later, the first male showed his flowers and that was it for him. We ended up with six females, two Thai and four Hawaiian. All were misted daily and I'm sure they liked the attention. Ninety days from planting, one of the Hawaiians was ripe.

#140, April 1987

right for a mini-box. They need at least a 400-watt to get big, tight buds. The product is extremely potent, but there is something in it that turns my stomach just a little. Too sweet or something.

• **Pluton #2.** This one was from SSSC. The picture in the catalog sold me. This pot has no flavor, no aroma and the aphids just love it. Never again.

• **Royal Dutch.** Too leggy for micro systems, but connoisseur-quality if you can get a female. Seemed to be more of an outdoor strain.

• **G-13 x Hash Plant.** I've had trouble germinating these; only three out of 15 and only one of those a lady. The seeds looked weak when I bought them.

I've bred many combinations of my strains. Usually just a very small amount of pollen is used on a number of females. Picking out one father plant and using him on five different females gives me some control. Here are a few of the names/combinations I've come up with: Hash Plant x Kush = Hush; Skunk x Kush = Skush; Skunk x Hash Plant = Skash; Kush x Pluton = Plush; Pluton x Skunk = Plunk, and so on.

I once used three different fathers on six mothers. Each mother had one branch of each father. It got ridiculous—tags everywhere. Although I would pollinate a very small flower for each new seed line, I had seeds up the ying-yang.

Since I only use a 150-watt HPS, I get a lot of non-viable seed. I suspect that one needs at least a 400-watt to get near uniform F-1 hybrid seeds in large numbers. I may get 10 to 15 good seeds out of every 40 or 50, but that's plenty for my needs. I usually start about five seeds from each selected strain to get one or two baby girls.

One of my most promising hybrids arose from a cross between a Northern Lights #5 x Skunk #1 male with a miniature Hash Plant female. The plants come up single-stemmed except for a few bottom branches. The leaves dangle about five inches away from the stem, exposing the node. The buds, although a bit small, are beautiful with lots of curly white hairs from the Skunk #1, pink resin from the Northern Lights #5 and the bud structure of Hash Plant. The smell is unique, a combination of all three with the Northern Lights dominant. The taste is like a pineapple fruit punch. The high is just great.

Dried-bud yields on this unnamed hybrid range between 1/2 and 3/4 ounces. When the buds are ripe, the plant looks like a budded clone. I can easily put four of these in their own 1-gallon container—sort of a micro sea of green. The box has produced 6-1/2 ounces of dried bud from one harvest.

The Skush (Skunk #1 x Kush) is also a fine hybrid. I had a Kush that was in late flowering when it began to produce a few male flowers. So I plucked them and used them on some young females hoping that I had "female pollen" (thanks to Ed Rosenthal for that tip). Sure enough, every seed was a lady Skush. I got one mutant that had beautiful rose-colored calyxes. The plant was only 15 inches high; I'd never seen anything like it. Attempts to breed my purple Skush failed. The high was the same as my regular Skush, but the uniqueness of this baby drew a $500 bid. I should have sold it, but I don't sell for legal reasons.

I've done some breeding with the Haze x Northern Lights #5 with unacceptable results. Crossed with Skunk #1 x Northern Lights #5, it is still tall, leggy and late to flower.

I've had my best results with the Seed Bank's Kush x Kush; it just never fails. Hash Plant is another excellent choice for the micro-box. It responds well to HPS lighting. I think that the *indicas* do better under sodium lamps than the *sativa*-dominant varieties, with Skunk #1 being the exception.

Skunk #1 x Northern Lights #5 buds surprisingly well in my tiny bud box. Some come up single-stemmed and some branch out. The single ones are set in the corners; the branched ones are bent to fit the contours of the box. I have some now that are three weeks into flowering that are already covered

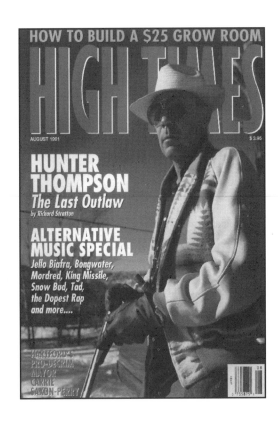

HOW TO BUILD A $25 GROW ROOM

HIGH TIMES

AUGUST 1991 $3.95

HUNTER THOMPSON
The Last Outlaw
by Richard Stratton

ALTERNATIVE MUSIC SPECIAL
Jello Biafra, Bongwater, Mordred, King Missile, Snow Bud, Tad, the Dopest Rap and more....

HALLFORD'S
PRO-DECRIM
MAYOR
CARRIE
SAXON-PERRY

GREEN MERCHANT ALL OVER AGAIN

BY PETER GORMAN AND JOHAN CARLYLE
In the latest development to grow out of Operation Green Merchant, the DEA served dozens of gardening centers throughout the country with administrative subpoenas late this past spring. This action was aimed at securing customer records which might lead them to indoor marijuana cultivators.

The subpoenas, which are not legally binding in any way, were served between May 21 and 24. According to DEA spokesman Maurice Brown, the subpoenas are "a polite way for the DEA to say to an individual: 'Would you, according to the power of the attorney general, please produce any records which we feel is evidence for our investigation?'"

Among those served were not only former HIGH TIMES advertisers—as had been the case in the original Green Merchant operation nearly two years ago—but several stores that never advertised in either HIGH TIMES or *Sinsemilla Tips* (now out of business), as well as the Hydroponic Society of America and the American Orchid Growers' Society. An administrative subpoena is signed by an administrative official (in this case, a DEA official). A warrant is signed by a judge.
#192, August 1991

SELECTING A VARIETY

For outdoor growing I keep about five different varieties to match the surroundings. Pure *indicas* and Afghani are used in evergreen areas because of their dark color and shape. Early-maturing *sativas* are used amongst most deciduous trees, provided they mature before leaves fall. Later-maturing *sativas* are used in swampy areas where natural foliage is lush and tall growth is needed to compete.

If you want to grow indoors but can't afford to stink up your house or don't want the risk of rip-off, then set up a 160-watt fluorescent system, which can easily pump out about 15 cuttings a week. The clones can be traded to other growers who don't want two rooms. A small area and a little time can produce enough cuttings for a bunch of growers. The kickback is enough to keep me satisfied.

Anonymous
Washington

#223, March 1994

THE ELECTRIC GARBAGE CAN

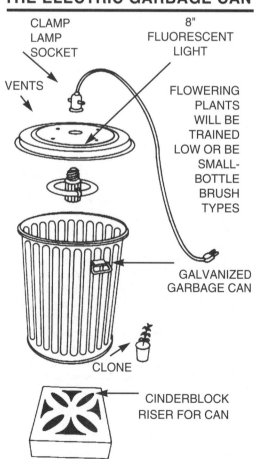

CLAMP LAMP SOCKET

8" FLUORESCENT LIGHT

VENTS

FLOWERING PLANTS WILL BE TRAINED LOW OR BE SMALL-BOTTLE BRUSH TYPES

GALVANIZED GARBAGE CAN

CLONE

CINDERBLOCK RISER FOR CAN

BRIAN SPAETH

---

with resin. These, as with most other varieties, take an extra two weeks to ripen in the bud box, I suspect due to the low light level and the lack of CO_2.

REMEMBER...

Here are a few important points to remember when setting up your own micro security garden:

• The three most important points to keep in mind are location, location and location. Preferably an upstairs unit with a bedroom window facing a "safe" direction for ventilation and, of course, a usable closet of the necessary size and shape. Always think security. With this kind of small set-up, no one should ever know unless you tell them.

• Small, top-quality plants should be your goal. Don't get greedy. Small *indica* strains work best. Don't try *sativas*, except for Skunk. Even at that, be prepared for lower yields. Compact plants ensure a better yield with less maintenance.

• The negative-ion generator is God's gift to apartment growers. I've been told that they can make you feel better by removing pollutants in the air and altering your mood in addition to the peace of mind derived from knowing that your garden's smell won't give you away. I'm going to get another one for my living room. Buy it, you tightwads! It's cheaper than a bust.

• A high-phosphorus formula from the beginning is important to shorten internodal length and keep your low-profile garden low.

• The 150-watt HPS or 175-watt MH is the minimum. Fluorescents can be used successfully. I used to grow minigardens with them 10 years ago, but they are really more expensive in the long run. I notice that they've come out with 25-watt HPS and MH lamps. Looks like a good choice for a microgarden.

• Power consumption is no problem; my 15-watt HPS costs me about $5.25 a month using a 12-hour light cycle. I imagine that a 250-watt light would also be virtually undetectable on your power bill. Higher-wattage systems could be used in a "boxed" system like mine, but with the government monitoring electrical usage, you could be defeating the purpose of the low-profile approach.

Remember, think security, always.

STEALTH METAL: The Electric Garbage Can

by Major Vaportrails

Reality gave me a punch in the jaw last September when I bicycled home from a Cheech & Chong movie party, opened my front door and saw a striking similarity between my home and the house in *Cheech & Chong's Next Movie*. I shook my head to clear the impression and headed to the bathroom to vent my bicycle exhaust. Then I glanced through my bedroom door, and a second dose of reality floored me with laughter.

Thanks to the consumption of two little square party favors before the movie festival, the rapid-pulse electric glare leaking from vents in my trash can looked like a runaway nuclear chain reaction. A rich, warm musk tickled my nostrils as this homemade bomb went off in my brain. "OMIGOD—I'M REALLY GROWING!" I thought.

Like the murky aquarium from which my comic heroes had fished their beers, the electrified garbage can has once again become the icon for a lifestyle. Yes, I built a device that those stoned-out geniuses should have used as a background prop! It consists of an 8" fluorescent circle light, the socket and cord from a clamp-lamp and a galvanized garbage can.

I had long wanted to grow my own, but was always hampered by a tight budget. Then I read an article on "The $50 Grow Room" in HIGH TIMES—but I wanted to cut the cost in half. A fluorescent lamp in a small, reflective-walled enclosure with a fan and vents seemed like the solution. A lack of tools and my uncertainty about building materials delayed the project.

One day, I was walking through my local discount store, past a stack of galvanized garbage cans, when it hit me—I could start my chamber with a mass-produced enclosure! Tilting the stack forward, I saw the silvery interior gleam with promise. My lightweight, fire-proof beauty cost me $9.99. A circle light cost another $7.99, but if I had shopped around, I could have found one for under $5.00. A clamp-lamp I already owned would cost perhaps $7.00.

To mount the light, I perforated the lid just to one side of the handle, with nailholes to make a holey patch about the size of the light's threaded base. I ripped away the metal between these holes with a screwdriver, creating one large hole which the threaded light-base could pass through, though not the socket of the clamp-lamp. I unscrewed the reflector from the lamp, passed the fluorescent's threads through the hole, then screwed the socket onto it from above the lid. The irregularity of the hole and the ripped metal hammered flat on the inside of the lid make the fit less than perfect, but it works. That hole, plus four 1/4" holes in the lid gives top ventilation, while 16 1/4" holes around the bottom of the can let cool air in to replace the lamp-warmed air flowing out the top.

Half of a year has passed since I started the contraption on a 24-hour light regimen for a 3" long clone and a handful of seeds in a pot; I now have 16 plants from seed and five new clones. When I can't get bud, I trim old leaves and growing tips (which induces branching), and I put the fresh, moist material into my copy of Dr. Lunglife's vaporizer for a dirt-cheap stone.

I occasionally take branches for clones (stripping lower leaves for use), and insert the cut ends into the filter-outflow tube in my aquarium, where they root rapidly in the aerated, filtered water. When a cutting has a combined total of six inches of roots, I transfer it to a drinking glass of aquarium water, then press vermiculite gently down into the glass. I change the water a day later to equal parts of aged tap water and aged fertilizer water made with three dropperfuls of Schultz's Liquid per gallon. A week later, I switch to only fertilizer water. When roots encircle the inside of the glass, I transplant to a pot with drainage holes and conventional plant soil. Established plants get only fertilizer water.

I had planned to set up a second can for flowering, but I will probably divide the can I have down the middle with a mylar wall, move the light to one side, mount a new light opposite it and use a timer for half of the can.

I haven't grown buds yet and I need to learn more about fertilizer, but what I have gives me something for nearly nothing.

A HAWAIIAN EXPERIENCE

BY BOB ROBERTS

Three hundred carefully chosen seeds began germinating on Sunday, September 1, 1990. The waning moon wasn't in its proper phase, but we began our project anyway. The time was right: Labor Day weekend gave us enough time off from work to set everything up. We placed the seeds between paper towels in a glass pie dish with a quarter-inch of water (into which we added a drop of multivitamin to catalyze quick germination).

At sunrise, Greg and I checked the sprouts with great anticipation. My eyes lit up and my pulse quickened as I saw the first white embryos peeking through the narrowly split seed castings. Approximately 30% of the seeds had sprouted overnight. Relieved and satisfied, we replenished the water and retired to the beach for the rest of the day. For the ride down the mountain I rolled a fatty so we would be baked before we reached the sand and surf.

Finding a safe place to grow marijuana is a major problem in Hawaii. The site must be either dangerously remote or insanely obvious (and thus overlooked by snoops). After much searching, Greg and I chose a remote area up the mountain, yet relatively close to our place so the drive would not be too long. Although we were able to leave our vehicle at a secure house, the hike through the lava flows, scrub brush and ohia trees was a job in itself.

#196, December 1991

MOJAVE GREEN
BY KOMMANDER KOLA

Call me Kommander Kola. I got that nickname when I used to grow outdoors in 15-gallon buckets. But I don't grow outdoors anymore. Even with drip irrigation and polymers, it seemed a full-time job to keep the females from drying up in the hot California sun.

That was then, this is now....

Instead of growing with multiple lights and hundreds of plants all year long, I grow in a 5' X 5' area with just one 400-watt high-pressure sodium (HPS) bulb with metal halide (MH) conversion. I switch to the MH bulb for flowering, when the plants are placed under 12-hours-of-light, 12-hours-of-darkness flowering cycle. With only one bulb, the plants just need to be moved around more often. This time I let a few males from the batch pollinate freely. Shit...with Dutch seeds so hard to find in the USA, it was about time for these strains to repopulate.

Most of these skunky plants are a mixture of Fallbrook and Mendocino varieties. The seeds were getting old, so I had to sprout 'em soon. For added therapeutic value and mind-high intensity, I also bred a few super-sweet *sativas* into the crop.

I go only organic. Kelp meal and green sand mixed with soil is essential. During the vegetative-growth phase, I water with nitrogen A-35 and bat guano (powdered or ground) in a tea. For flowering, it's high-P bat guano and A-35 with either sugar or berry or apple juice mixed in. The pH of both of those potions is almost 8, so I use about a 1/2- to 1-gallon of tea per 5-gallon container. The plants also get an alternating fusion feeding of liquid kelp (to pep up from the nitrogen) and Spray'N'Grow. Never have I had any micro- or macro-deficiencies.

I'd like to see more people grow more seeds! Who cares if a pal or fellow smoker gets a little less smokeable material from you? This is a God-given plant that belongs to everyone. It should be more wild and free...more feral. Just for fun, sometimes I wait 'til about July 4 and plant a few where excess water from sprinklers runs through fields. When I come back in August, I find many of them flowering and producing big, healthy seeds. What if all herbalists did this with their stash seeds?

Since I grow Mojave Green only for personal stash, the more than 2-1/2 pounds harvested every 3-4 month cycle is well enough to last me all year. I think it's the best pot around.

Why do you think they call me Kommander Kola?

#208, December 1992

THE 10 MOST-ASKED GROW QUESTIONS
by mary jane green

There are, of course, many excellent, in-depth publications on the cultivation of cannabis which should be required reading for the serious grower. They include *Indoor Marijuana Horticulture* by Jorge Cervantes, *Marijuana: The Cultivator's Handbook* by Bill Drake, and *The Marijuana Grower's Guide* by Ed Rosenthal and Mel Frank. Or you could go through every HIGH TIMES issue and piece together all the tips from "Ask Ed." But for the novice grower, here's a quick review of the basics:

1. FOR THE AVERAGE SMOKER, IS IT WORTH GROWING YOUR OWN RATHER THAN PAYING CURRENT STREET PRICES?

The average indoor garden, perfected over several harvests, produces quality smoke for a fraction of the street price. Price, however, is the least of the would-be grower's concerns. Cultivation carries penalties ranging from a mandatory year behind bars to life imprisonment. Persons convicted in state courts often find themselves facing additional federal charges and time. Many accused gardeners face forfeiture of their home and assets—whether they are convicted or not.

Simple possession carries far more lenient penalties in most states, ranging from small fines and probation to short jail terms. Grow-store mailing lists, license-plate checks in grow-store parking lots, high electric bills, informants and heat-sensing devices have all been used to nab growers. Besides the legal risks, would-be growers must also consider their own temperament and abilities. It often takes several seasons to produce the first harvest of smokable buds, and growing any plant requires time, dedication and patience.

2. HOW DO YOU DETERMINE THE SEX OF CANNABIS SEEDLINGS?

Any seedling, regardless of size, can be induced to flower and show sex by providing it with 12 hours of total darkness a day for two weeks. Female plants will produce teardrop-shaped balls (calyxes) at the nodes between leaf and stem, each sprouting two white hairs (pistils). Males will produce clusters of balls (pollen sacs) at the branch internodes. Once the sex is determined, the plants can be returned to the vegetative cycle. The males should be separated to prevent seeds from forming.

Cervantes recommends taking cuttings from each plant and rooting them under a 12-hour light cycle to determine sex, so as not to stress the original plants.

3. HOW DO YOU TELL WHEN THE BUDS ARE READY FOR HARVEST, AND HOW DO YOU CURE THE FINAL PRODUCT?

Plants require about eight to 12 weeks of flowering to produce ripe buds. Look at the clear crystals encrusting the flowers with a magnifying glass. These crystals (trichomes and gland heads) contain the THC resin that gives the flower its flavor and potency. When they change from clear to amber, the buds are ready for harvest.

Harvest when humidity is low. Use a sharp, clean knife and firmly sever the plant below the lower leaves. Trim as much leaf and stem from the buds as possible. Dry them in a dark area with good ventilation, low humidity and a steady (68-75°F) temperature. To reduce molding, hang the buds from a rack or lay them on a screen, turning often.

Drying generally takes seven to 14 days. When the buds feel firm and crisp, seal them in an airtight, light-proof container and store in a cool place (preferably the freezer). If mold develops, separate the moldy buds and expose them to direct sunlight for up to 24 hours.

If some of the buds aren't ripe, you can harvest the topmost and let the lower buds mature. (Do not remove the leaves.) If you wish to rejuvenate a plant for a second harvest or to take clones, cut off only the buds, leaving as many leaves as possible, and return the pruned plant to the vegetative light cycle. In an emergency, buds can be "finished" in the microwave (medium heat for 15-second intervals) or in a convection oven (below 150°F) with no loss in potency, though the taste and aroma will diminish.

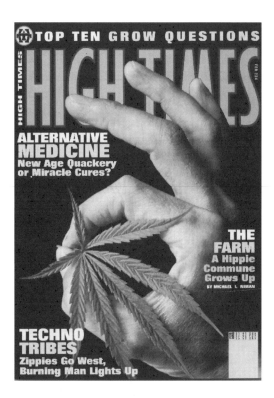

4. HOW MUCH LIGHT IS NEEDED IN AN INDOOR GARDEN, AND HOW LONG SHOULD THE LIGHTS BE ON EACH DAY?

Generally, a garden requires around 2,000 lumens of light per square foot. If a high-intensity-discharge (HID) light is used (metal-halide or high-pressure sodium), roughly 12-20 watts will be needed per square foot. Fluorescent lights are easier to obtain but less efficient, so use 20-30 watts per square foot.

Plants in the flowering stage require 12 hours of uninterrupted darkness each day. Giving them less than 12 hours will slow flower production and reduce yield. Plants in the vegetative-growth cycle should have 18-20 hours of light for optimum growth.

5. WHAT KINDS OF FERTILIZERS SHOULD BE USED AND HOW OFTEN SHOULD THEY BE APPLIED?

Fertilizers supplement the nutrients found in the soil, which are used up as the plant ages. Use a commercial potting soil or mix your own. One simple recipe is to blend equal parts worm castings, dehydrated cow manure and perlite.

Fertilizers are rated with three numbers showing their ratio of nitrogen, potassium and phosphorus. During vegetative growth, use a fertilizer high in all three elements. Moderate (biweekly) use of a well-balanced (20-20-20) fertilizer with micronutrients will prevent or eliminate most deficiencies. Flowering plants will require a fertilizer with higher levels of potassium (15-30-15).

How do you know if you're using too much? The ends of the leaves will curl and turn black. If this occurs, leach the plants by rinsing the soil with lukewarm water (two gallons of water per gallon of soil).

THE FARM

BY MICHAEL I. NIMAN

Resident Farm historian Michael Traugot describes the early Farm as a "grass church." Farm folks "depended upon marijuana for insight, for ceremonial value and to enhance lovemaking." They shunned, however, commerce in pot. Traugot explains that since pot was a "sacrament and an aid to consciousness, one absorbed some of the karma of those who produced and distributed." "The cleanest form of pot, most suitable for the kind of loving consciousness and clear mind" that Farm folks were seeking, he adds, "was pot lovingly grown, over which no money changed hands." With their reverence for pot and their aversion to buying, growing seemed to be the only choice. They were not, however, subtle. "Not only did they plant it," said Gaskin, "but they sat nude and played flute to it, and got caught by people doing that, until they just aroused the curiosity of the neighbors." The bust was cordial. In fact, Gaskin and the sheriff later went on to become close friends. The congeniality of the police, however, didn't alter the fact that they were enforcing what The Farm saw as an unjust law. Rather than proclaim ignorance of the pot, Gaskin took full responsibility. With The Farm's legal defense crew, he spent three years fighting the case in court, claiming that marijuana prohibition violated their religious-freedom rights. The case was brought to the Supreme Court, which refused to hear it. Gaskin spent a year in jail.
#234, February 1995

HOW TO RECOGNISE COMMERCIAL AND NON COMMERCIAL MARIJUANA GROWING OPERATIONS

BY WES JULIANA

You're probably asking yourself: Why would anyone want to recognize a noncommercial growing operation?

The reason is the law in California (and some other states) "recognizes" a big difference between a commercial operation and a noncommercial operation. If you ever have the misfortune of being busted, it could play an important role in your defense. Right now in California, cultivating marijuana is a felony with a maximum penalty of three years in state prison and/or a $10,000 fine. Along with the cultivation charge, you will probably get charged with possession of marijuana for sale, a second felony charge that carries the same maximum penalty as the cultivation charge. Other states have similar and sometimes much harsher penalties. (Check with your attorney or your local law library to find out what the maximum penalties are in your state.)

COMMERCIAL OPERATIONS

1) A greenhouse to start the plants in, with starter trays and plant pots that are filled with potting mix
2) Large gardens that are away from the residence
3) Tight fences around the gardens; elaborate plant supports and animal deterrents
4) Plants in large holes and/or containers filled with powerful fertilizers
5) A sophisticated watering system that includes pumps, holding tanks, timers, chemical feeders and drip-irrigation systems
6) Drying sheds and processing areas with heating and dehumidification systems, manicuring scissors, scales and packaging materials
7) Other support equipment such as all-terrain vehicles, scanners, citizen-band radios, alarm systems and camouflaging materials
8) An excess of materials which usually includes extra fencing, water pipes, fertilizer, plant pots and miscellaneous hardware
9) An unusually large number of gardening tools
10) Business records which list transactions, expenses and work assignments
11) Large amounts of cash
12) Processed marijuana of exact weights in uniform packagings ⟶

Buildup occurs more quickly in small containers, so use the largest pots possible. One sure way to avoid fertilizer burn is foliar feeding—biweekly applications of diluted fertilizer, sprayed directly on the leaves in a fine mist and followed by a plain-water mist two days later.

6. SHOULD PESTICIDES BE USED, AND HOW OFTEN SHOULD THEY BE APPLIED?

Most pest problems can be avoided by keeping the garden area clean, clearing dead leaves and debris from the soil pots, not reusing soil and not carrying pests into the garden on clothes, shoes or tools. Healthy plants grown with good ventilation and low humidity (around 50 percent) will resist most insect attacks.

Frequent inspection is the best way to avoid pest infestation. Yellow sticky-strips (pesticide-free) can be used to detect white flies. Also check the underside of the leaves on each plant regularly for spider mites. Small infestations can be stopped by spraying the plants with nontoxic Safer's Soap. If the pests persist, a natural pyrethrum-based fogger can be used, but not in the last week before harvest (you don't want to end up smoking it). Always follow applications of pest controls with generous plain-water misting. Chemical pesticides and pest strips are toxic and should be avoided.

7. WHAT IS THE OPTIMUM INDOOR ENVIRONMENT FOR GROWING?

A plant requires certain things for healthy growth: light, nutrients, ventilation, CO_2 (for photosynthesis), heat and humidity. Too much or too little of any of these can affect the plant's health and the resulting harvest.

Cannabis thrives at 70-80°F. Growth stops below 50°F or above 95°F. Pots should be kept up off cold floors: to warm the roots, use heating mats, available at most garden-supply stores.

The humidity level should be kept around 50 percent for plants and 70-80 percent for clones and seedlings. Misting increases humidity and ventilation decreases it. A hygrometer (available at garden-supply stores) can be used to monitor the air moisture.

Make sure the garden area has adequate ventilation (a vent fan or open door) and air circulation (a fan inside the room, not blowing directly on the plants). Fans should completely replace the air in the room every 10-15 minutes. Check the fan rating, which is measured in cubic feet per minute (cfm). An 8' x 8' x 10' room, for example, would need a fan rated at 42-64 cfm. Fresh air circulation provides CO_2 for photosynthesis. Increasing the CO_2 content of the grow-room air will increase growth, but it is not necessary for a healthy garden.

Plants should be spaced to allow for adequate side growth, generally one to two square feet per plant. They can be pruned and tied to optimize light exposure and minimize side growth.

To control the odor of the ripening harvest, an ionizer may be purchased from any department store. Ionizers (a type of air cleaner) cause positively-charged odor particles to be neutralized so that they settle on room surfaces. Some growers maintain that using an ionizer inside the grow room will neutralize the aromatic qualities of the buds. They suggest placing it just outside the door.

8. IS CLONING BETTER THAN STARTING FROM SEED, AND WHAT'S THE BEST WAY TO TAKE CUTTINGS?

Once plants are established and sexed, a garden can be pepetuated by taking cuttings before the plants flower. These clones retain all the characteristics of the original plant, including age and sex, but can flower as soon as they reach 12". Thus, cloning can shorten total growing time, normally six to eight months from seed to harvest, to as little as three months. Cuttings can also be taken from clones with no deterioration of potency or vigor.

New stock grown from seed should be introduced periodically for breeding purposes and to further the quest for the ultimate strain. Cuttings are usually taken from the side shoots, which appear between the leaf and stem. Slice the cutting off with a new razor blade, being sure to make a clean, diagonal slice. Dip the cutting in a commercial rooting product, such as Root-Tone, and then place it in a prepared seedling flat or small pot, and water it with Upstart or a similar transplanting solution which has added hormones.

Clones shold be kept warm (74-80°F) and covered with clear plastic (baggies or fitted plastic tops for seed flats work well), and should receive 18-24 hours of light a day. Check them often to make sure they remain moist (water only) during the critical rooting period. Generally, 50-60 percent of cuttings will produce healthy plants. Transplant after roots have formed—usually in two to four weeks. Once the clones reach 12", they are essentially mature plants ready for blooming. Harden them for outdoor growing by placing them outside for several hours each day for a couple weeks before transplanting.

9. IS OUTDOOR CULTIVATION BETTER THAN INDOOR GARDENING?

It is always easier to grow plants in their natural setting than it is to recreate Mother Nature indoors. Indoor gardening has the advantage of being viable year-round, while outdoor harvests are usually limited to one per year. Outdoor plants can also take longer to ripen, depending on the climate in your area. More importantly, outdoor gardens risk detection by the cops—not to mention other four-footed and two-footed predators.

Indoor detection is more difficult, generally requiring the use of informants or observation of suspicious activity. You can play it safe by watching for license-plate traces at grow stores and never ordering supplies by mail. In terms of harvest quality, both methods appear to produce extremely fine smoke, with growers being divided about which is best.

10. IS HYDROPONIC GROWING BETTER THAN TRADITIONAL SOIL-POT METHODS?

Hydroponics is a soilless method of growing in which a plant's roots are suspended in an inert medium and fed with a time-release nutrient solution. Purchasing a hydroponic system and the nutrient mixes to

Some other factors to consider are the grower's source of income and if there is a large accumulation of unaccountable wealth. A commercial operation is a business, and it looks like a business.

NONCOMMERCIAL OPERATIONS

1) No fence, or a fence that is not well made or adequate for the job
2) Small gardens near the residence
3) Plants in small holes and/or containers with a small amount of fertilizer
4) The watering system usually primitive, often done by hand
5) No separate drying shed or processing area
6) Random sizes of stash and personal-use paraphernalia usually present
7) Little or no garden security and camouflaging
8) A lack of the items listed under commercial operations
#157, September 1988

COLORADO LADIES

This is living proof that Colorado is beautiful. I planted these ladies in the first part of April. By the first part of August, I harvested the first one. I picked the last one in November. We can't forget to mention how beautiful Colorado sunsets are.

R.N.
Grand Junction, Colorado
#109, September 1984

operate one can be very risky in this age of parking-lot surveillance and mail-order probes. Many books, such as *Hydroponic Gardening* by Raymond Bridwell, contain easy-to-follow plans for building your own hydroponic system using common materials found at any hardware store.

One advantage of hydroponic growing is that it allows you to better control the plants' nutrient intake, eliminating fetrtilizer burn and nutrient deficiencies. Hydroponic systems also require less floor space than soil pots, and you don't have to go through the hassle of buying and handling bulky soil mixtures. The added cost of nutrient mixes generally balances out against the cost of soil and fertilizers for conventional gardening.

Hydroponic systems do require diligent care, as the failure of a feed pump can cause root systems to dry out, quickly killing the plants. But when properly run, a hydroponic system will consistently produce more vigorous plants and higher yields than soil-pot methods.

....

BEACH GROWER

BY WILEY E. COYOTE

I have been a grower for five years and every year is better. I live in an old beach house in Southern California. I converted one of the rooms into a beautiful garden. I ran all new electrical wires and circuit breakers because this old house would have burned with the old system. I use two 1,000-watt MH and one 1,000-watt HPS for a room that is approximately 12' x 7' x 8' high. This is the first year I have used clones and it's great. This crop yielded six pounds of the stickiest skunk buds we have ever seen.

I start my clones in small pots, then switch to 5-gallon pots. I use 23-19-17 for vegetative growth and 12-55-6 for flowering.

The outside of my room is covered by giant boysenberry bushes and some of the vines have grown in through the baseboard. I think these bushes have affected my plants. Some of the buds have such a sweet berry aroma, you almost want to eat them.

I love growing. This is the best hobby in the world.

#159, November 1988

28

PART 3
INDOOR CULTIVATION

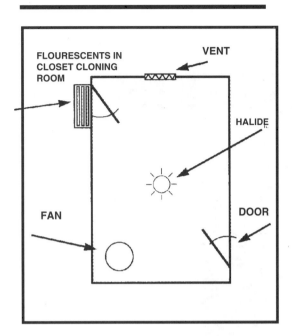

FLOURESCENTS IN CLOSET CLONING ROOM

VENT

HALIDE

FAN

DOOR

TEN STEPS TO SETTING UP A GROW ROOM

by Jorge Cervantes

When the indoor revolution took off in the late '70s, Jorge Cervantes's Indoor Marijuana Horticulture became the user-friendly choice for a new generation of ganja farmers. Now updated and revised for 1993, Horticulture has become even more essential to any serious indoor grower's library. The following is Jorge's step-by-step on how to build a successful indoor garden.

Before any plants are introduced, the grow room should be set up. Construction requires space and planning. There are just a few things that need to be accomplished before the room is ready for plants.

STEP ONE:
Choose an out-of-the-way space with little or no traffic. A dark corner in the basement would be perfect. Make sure the room is the right size. A 1,000-watt HID, properly set up, will efficiently illuminate up to a 10' x 10' room if a light balancer is used. The ceiling should be at least 5' high. Remember, plants are set up about one foot off the ground in containers and the lamp needs about a foot of space to hang from the ceiling. This leaves only three feet of vertical space for plants to grow. However, if forced to grow in an attic or basement with a low 4' ceiling, much can be done to compensate for the loss of height, including cloning, bending and pruning.

STEP TWO:
Enclose the room, if not already enclosed. Remove everything not having to do with the garden. Furniture and especially drapes or curtains may harbor fungi. A totally enclosed room will permit easy, precise control of everything and everyone that enters, exits and who and what goes on inside. For most growers, enclosing the grow room is simply a matter of tacking up some sheetrock in the basement or attic and painting it flat white. Make sure no light is visible from outside. At night, bright light leaking from a crack in an uncovered window is like a beacon to curious neighbors or bandits.

STEP THREE:
Cover walls, ceiling, floor, everything with a highly reflective material like flat white paint or whitewash. The more reflection, the more light energy is available to plants. Good reflective light will allow effective coverage of a 1,000-watt HID lamp to increase from 36 square feet with no reflective material to a maximum of 100 square feet just by putting $10-$20 worth of paint on the walls.

STEP FOUR:
Constant circulation and a supply of fresh air are essential. There should be at least one fresh air vent in a 10' x 10' room, preferably two. Vents may be an open door, window or heat vent. Most growers have found that a small

exhaust fan, vented outdoors, pulling new fresh air through an open door, will create an ideal air flow. A small oscillating fan works well for circulation. When installing such a fan, make sure it is not set in a fixed position and blowing too hard on tender plants. It could cause wind burn, or in the case of young seedlings and clones, dry them out. If the room contains a heat vent, it may be opened to supply extra heat or air circulation.

STEP FIVE:

The larger your garden gets, the more water it will need. A 10' x 10' garden may need as many as 30 gallons a week. You may carry water in, one container at a time (one gallon of water weighs eight pounds). It is much easier to run in a hose with an on/off valve or install a hose bib in the room. A 3'-4' watering wand may be attached to the hose on/off valve. When watering in dense foliage, the wand will save many broken branches. It is best to hook the hose up to a hot-and-cold-water source so the water temperature may be easily regulated.

STEP SIX:

Ideally the floor should be concrete or a smooth surface that can be swept and/or washed down. A floor drain is very handy. In grow rooms with carpet or wood floors, a large white painter's drop cloth or thick white visqueen plastic will save floors from moisture. Trays may also be placed beneath each container for added protection and convenience.

STEP SEVEN:

Mount a hook strong enough to support 30 pounds in the center of the growing area to be serviced by the lamp. Attach an adjustable chain or cord and pulley between the ceiling hook and the lamp fixture. This will make it easy to keep the lamp at the proper distance from the growing plants and up out of the way when maintaining them.

STEP EIGHT:

There are some tools an indoor gardener must have and a few extra tools that make indoor horticulture much more precise and cost-effective. Besides helping the horticulturist play Mother Nature, the extra tools make the garden so efficient, they pay for themselves within a few weeks. It is best to purchase or find around the house all tools needed before the plants are brought into the room. If the tools are here when needed, chances are they will be put to use. A good example is a hygrometer. If plants show signs of slow, sickly growth, due to high humidity, most growers will not notice the exact cause right away. They will wait and guess, wait and guess, and maybe figure it out before a fungus attacks and the plant dies. When a hygrometer is installed before plants are in the grow room, the horticulturist will know, from the start, when the humidity is too high and causing sickly growth.

STEP NINE:

Read "Electric Light For Plant Growth" (Page 46). Set up your light.

STEP TEN:

Move the seedlings or rooted clones into room. Huddle them closely together under the lamp. Make sure the HID is not so close to small plants that it burns their leaves. Usually seedlings require the lamp to be at least 24 inches away.

FIRST TIME INDOORS

This was my first time growing indoors. I was surprised at what I could do with some reading skills and a few great books. Total harvest was 4-1/4 oz out of three plants.

The plants were sown November 1st, and the buds were harvested January 6th. I used worm castings, bat guano and potting soil. The lamp was a 300-watt HPS. The plant was a Hawaiian cross.

Feelin' Irie
San Gabriel Valley, CA

#211, March 1993

WORLD'S SMALLEST GROW ROOM

It measures 12" wide and 21" high. For light I use three 18" (15-watt) fluorescent lights in the corners and one 15-watt soft-white bulb. I also have a 6" fan taped into one side which exhausts the hot air while drawing in cool air. The box maintains an average temperature of 79 and 81 degrees. All sides are covered with mylar or foil, and the eight young plants sit on a tray of moist pebbles. I will thin the plants to a total of between one and four for flowering depending on their configuration.

Cannknowlabis
New York City

#145, September 1987

NECESSARY TOOLS

- Spray bottle
- pH & soil test kit
- Liquid biodegradable soap concentrate
- Hygrometer
- Pruner or scissors
- Wire (bread-sack) ties
- Hammer and nails
- Measuring cup
- Pencil or pen
- Measuring spoons
- Notebook
- Moisture meter
- Yardstick (to measure growth)
- Vent fan
- Light baffle
- CO_2 tank
- Visqueen plastic

INDOOR FLOW-SYSTEM

Here are some pictures of the constant-flow system that I constructed using gutter pipe. The room is lined with metallic reflective material. I use 1,000-watt high-pressure sodium (HPS) lamps.

It works like this: I place 4" squares of rockwool in the gutters. A simple plumbing faucet regulates the flow rate for each gutter. The water flows the length of the pipe and drains into a pan holding a sump pump. The pump pushes the water to a reservoir above the garden. The water then flows from the reservoir back to the gutters.

I also grow a few plants in 5-gallon buckets. I water these by hand.

Chris
Pennsylvania

#200, April 1992

INDOOR GROWING FOR BEGINNERS

PART ONE

Beginning indoor growers always have more enthusiasm than ability. The temptation to run out and buy some hi-tech equipment, hoping the advertised promises will replace inexperience, leads to all sorts of expensive disappointments, including a mediocre crop.

Clearly, beginners give far too little consideration to the basic requirements of setting up a grow room. And when faced with the three basic growing medium options, can't tell in advance which is likely to be the easiest to learn while doing.

While setting up a grow room for a friend new to the business, I made careful note of the various steps my experience dictated, and relate them below.

Picking the right site is essential. Security requires a door you can lock, walls thick enough to block noise, and it needs to be lightproof. The plants require temperature and humidity regulation independent of the rest of the dwelling, a way to introduce fresh air and a way to exhaust spent air while minimizing unintentional air exchanges to trap CO_2 gas you introduce. Keep in mind that water, dirt and plant matter will wind up on the floor.

An area in the basement is the very best choice. An upstairs bedroom is a poor second and a spare room in an apartment isn't worth the trouble. Whatever you choose, your first job is to clean it 'til it's spotless, including the ceiling, which should be at least seven feet tall.

After a thorough cleaning, buy a small container of general purpose fungicide (Captan or Maneb), a quart spray bottle and some liquid bleach. Mix separate quart solutions, 1/4 cup bleach and one quart of water, and one tablespoon fungicide and one quart water. Spray the entire area down with one, then the other, and leave for 12 hours. This kills the bugs and spores likely to attack the plants as seedlings.

Next, you need to maximize light reflection. Mylar is a bit expensive. Painting the walls flat white is fairly easy, but to enclose an area in the basement, the best choice is four-by-eight sheets of Styrofoam, one inch thick. It's flat white, has insulating properties to aid in temperature control and is easily cut to shape with an electric knife. You can frame in the area with two-inch square strips of furring wood.

Note that the black plastic was put over every basement window to prevent sightseeing, and a black plastic sheet was hung to block light on the exposed side. Joints in the Styrofoam were sealed with three-inch clear tape.

The size of the room is dependent on the number of plants you want to grow. If you grow from seed, as most first-timers do, figure that 50 percent will be male and all but one or two (saved for breeding) will be culled. So your space requirements are likely to change during the growing cycle.

The first time, I think, coping with 10 to 15 females grown four to five months from seeds will be plenty to deal with. This means you start with 20 to 30 plants. This will fit in a 10- by 12-foot area using one phosphor-coated 1,000-watt metal-halide HID. During flowering you add a second high-pressure sodium 1,000-watt bulb, which requires its own firing system (ballast, socket, etc.). A rough measure is seven flowering plants, four or five feet tall, from soil line per bulb and that's the max.

If you're already thinking ahead to yield, throw out your fantasy. A good first crop would produce one to two ounces of manicured bud per plant on average if you use an *indica*-dominant strain. Through breeding and experienced gardening technique, four to six ounces per plant can be achieved sometimes. While this is not a seed-selection article, I strongly urge you to use *indica* strains if you can.

Sativa needs more light, more root space, is too sensitive to high root moisture and atmospheric humidity and has a narrower range of fertilizer tolerance than a beginner can handle.

An exhaust fan sucks out humid, spent air, drawing in fresh air. The fan you buy will come with a cfm (cubic feet per minute) rating. Buy one that is rated at one-fifth the volume of your grow room. A 10-by 12-foot room seven feet high is 840 cubic feet. It needs a cfm rating of approximately 175 cfm. This allows the fan to run about five minutes for one complete air exchange, all you need each exhaust cycle.

Mount the fan close to the ceiling, no more than two feet down, maximum. The exhausted air has to go someplace. Likely, you'll have bought a "squirrel cage" or "ram's horn" style fan and the outlet is easily mated to a four-inch diameter clothes-dryer exhaust-hose kit. If you go out a nearby window, camouflage the exit port, but be conscious of close neighbors who may hear noise or smell flowering cannabis. A better choice is the ash door at the base of the furnace chimney. Be sure to tap in below the furnace smoke exhaust tap or the grow room will fill with smoke.

To hang the HID bulb fixture, use pulleys and parachute cord. You'll raise and lower it a lot. A reflector is necessary in my opinion—four feet wide, a shallow cone. In the basement a 30-amp, 220-volt dryer outlet may be available. If it's not, strongly consider paying an electrician $100 to install one before starting on the project. Keeping

THE BUDS FROM BRAZIL
BY DR. INDOORS

The secret to a successful garden is cloning. Cloning insures females for harvest and allows the grower to take full advantage of his or her gene stock. Just like Dr. Mengele, who clones Hitler with the future in mind, you can clone cannabis with your future gardens in mind. The immediate harvest is a bonus. What you're looking for is to establish a baseline on continual, identical gardens.

Let's assume you have a closet that can be turned into a minigarden. The closet is 3' x 4' with a ceiling (see diagram). The top two-thirds of this space will be the main grow area and the bottom third will contain your clone room.

ASSEMBLING THE ROOM

Place the table in the closet, flush against the back wall. Put the 5-gallon bucket underneath to one side. Tape black plastic underneath the table. The plastic tray fits on top of the table. First, however, drill two 1/2" holes on one side of the plastic tray as close to the bottom as possible. (Drilling these holes in the side will allow you to drain the tray without cutting a hole in the table.) Put a bead of silicon onto the threads of the nipple fittings and screw them into the holes.

#158, October 1988

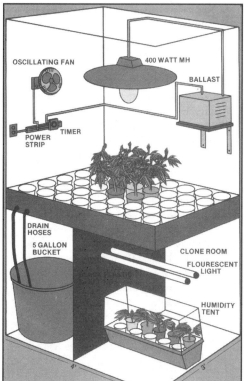

BRIAN SPAETH

THE BUDDY SYSTEM

BY KYLE ROQ

"It's simple. I maintain the mothers, clones, and vegetate. I turn clones over to my buddy, who flowers them. This limits the amount of plants in our apartments—as well as the space and electricity needed. We split the proceeds fifty-fifty.

"I vegetate. He flowers. It's perfect. Different plants are maturing and being replaced constantly. Something like Higher Yield's system, where the plants are individually contained in plastic drinking glasses, makes the transfer a snap. A lot of grass passes through, but it's gone as soon as it's harvested. At any one time, I doubt if we have more than a few ounces on hand—with constant turn-over and up-to-date techniques, almost one-half pound a month is realistic—with one 400 HPS and one 400 MH. Not bad, huh?

"And here's the best part." His grin took up the whole room as he held up a baggie marked THAI. "Best there is. The buds run forever, but with one chamber just to flower, it doesn't hold anything up. It can flower as long as it wants!

"And this Thai is not for sale," he said before taking a draw, smiling, as he slipped into his new stereo headphones.

#141, May 1987

HID ballast amp demand within circuit load capacity is crucial. On a 30-amp, 220-volt dryer, circuit the ballast draws 4.5 amps. There's room to spare using three 1,000-watt HIDs wired for 220 volts. On a 110-volt circuit, the ballast draws nine amps and the majority of household circuits for 110 volts are 15 to 20 amp capacity, which means one HID per circuit. The ballast needs 50 percent above its base operating amp draw for start-up. HID ballasts are wired for 220 or 110. Buy the right one.

The HID is regulated by a timer. Get one equal to the amp rating of your circuit. I recommend the 18-hour vegetative cycle run from 3 PM to 8 AM when you are likely to be home. Wire everything up working backwards from socket to plug; wipe the bulb with alcohol after screwing it in, then fire it up.

As the bulb fires up, get your air-circulation fan, bought beforehand. It should be eight inches or larger in diameter and have a sweep of 90 degrees or better. Set it on something or aim it upward so it's moving air in the three to five foot layer. Turn it on and then bring in a note pad, a mercury thermometer with at least a six-inch reading tube and a hygrometer (it measures humidity), also purchased beforehand. Put both instruments about four or five inches off the floor and take readings every four to six hours for a full 18-hour light-cycle. This phase is crucial! The temperature range during light-cycle must be between 66 and 80 degrees and the humidity can go no higher than 60 percent.

If the temperature is over 80 degrees, move the ballast out of the grow room; if not, leave it in; the dry heat lowers humidity. If the temperature approaches 80 degrees only at the tail end of the 18-hour light cycle, it's okay. If it's over 80 degrees earlier in the light-cycle, run the exhaust fan for one five-minute cycle, then see how far the temperature drops and for how long.

Basically, you're identifying specific times to run the exhaust fan to keep temperature within tolerable ranges. Record the necessary exhaust - cycle intervals. Humidity in basements could be a problem. If it is over 60 percent with no plants in the grow room, it will certainly go higher with them in, and mold and fungus can become a problem. The answer is a dehumidifier or a vigilant eye for mold.

After the light-cycle ends, the temperature will drop. Down to 56 degrees is OK. Humidity will rise. After the plants are in, adding exhaust cycles to lower humidity during the dark period will work as the basement will be relatively drier outside the grow area.

If the humidity and temperature ranges are OK then the timer you buy to control the exhaust fan only needs to cycle it two times per day, 12 hours apart, to introduce enough fresh air for steady growth. After you are an experienced grower, a thermostat/humidistat can be used to control the exhaust fan. But in my own grow house, I've found that coordinating them with CO_2 injection is a real handful. Also, in my experience, the best pot I've grown has been in conditions of a low "night" temperature of around 60 degrees with a day maximum temperature of 80 degrees and humidity about 40 percent. The buds seem to have a higher resin content.

The subject of CO_2 injection can be confusing. I'm going to skip a lot of detail and give you a quick formula. First, the air-circulation fan stays on 24 hours per day. Rent a five-pound CO_2 tank; aluminum ones are much easier to lift if you have a choice. You'll also need a pressure regulator to step the tank pressure down to safe levels for the flow meter and a short-interval electric timer, one that has on/off settings in one-minute intervals, plus a solenoid regulator for the timer to activate on the tank. Regardless of what regulator/flow meter you buy, make absolutely sure you know how it works and can regulate the final discharge flow to 20 cubic feet per hour. This isn't what you inject! Read on.

Calculate the cubic-foot volume of your room. The one I set up was 840 cubic feet. Multiply your volume in cubic feet by .0014.

The result here, 1.176, is the cubic feet of CO_2 you release per injection. If your flow meter is set at 20 cubic feet per hour, that's .333 cubic feet per minute. Divide your CO_2 cubic feet objective, here 1.176, by .333. The result here is 3.52 or the equivalent of four minutes. So every injection cycle, regulated by the short-term timer, should be four minutes. Then set the timer to inject four minutes of CO_2 every 2-1/2 hours after the beginning of the light cycle, to the end. Don't add CO_2 during the dark cycle, there is no need for it. Make sure each CO_2 timer cycle happens just after any exhaust cycle and synchronize timers or you'll waste CO_2. Run the CO_2 outlet tube to the center of the ceiling to allow the gas to drift down over the plants and get mixed by the air-circulating fan, which runs 24 hours a day.

All of this may sound complicated, and frankly, a good grow room is harder to do than most think. But if you do it right the first time it is like riding a bike, you never forget, and the plants will thrive.

The lure of high-tech hydroponic units and its promise of a bigger, better crop is hard to resist. But you're a beginner, resist it. The truth is that some of the simplest approaches work as well as any and are much easier to learn while doing.

Hydro set-ups are tricky to regulate. The nutrient solution has a critical pH range to maintain at all times. Full-recovery systems require close nutrient-combinations monitoring. And trace-mineral problems—too much or too little—can give even the pros fits. All in all, they are not that bad once you've had some experience, but not the first time out.

Organic soil mixes in containers are expensive. Correct supplement-fertilization ratios require continual adjustment as plants exhaust the container's original contents, and trace-mineral problems are difficult to deal with. They are also less forgiving of overwatering or overfertilizing.

Of all the approaches, a soilless mix is best. It is porous enough to drain easily (beginners tend to overwater), can be leached of excess fertilizers with a heavy clean-water rinse (beginners tend to overfertilize) and is lightweight. Rather than grow bags, I recommend the five-gallon plastic buckets used to ship food products. You need a five-gallon size for a four-to five-month old flowered plant to avoid root constriction and stunting. Plants in too small a container tend to flower prematurely.

Drill six 1/4-inch holes in the bottom for drainage. A five-gallon bucket is close to one cubic foot. A good mix is 50 percent perlite, 25 percent vermiculite, 12.5 percent peat moss (no more) and 12.5 percent clean, coarse sand. Add one cup of finely ground dolomite lime to each bucket's mix. Buy the amount you need of each for the number of buckets you have and mix the ingredients thoroughly. This is an awful job: Wear a mask and be glad you do it once a crop. Fill the buckets to the rim and put them in the grow room.

The next concern is water and fertilizer application. Hand-watering is best for the first few weeks of seedling life, when plant needs vary a

THE NORTHWEST POT PASSAGE

BY NATE EATON

In the Northwest it was discovered that early-maturing *indicas* could achieve four grow seasons per year under lights. By the late '70s, when the halide shops first opened, growers had got hold of the same basic varieties grown by breeders in California and worked with them. In 13 years they were able to cover an astounding 50 years of breeding.

Because of this rapid evolution, the Northwest would quickly advance their strains in stellar ways. With indoor pot, a grower must consider time. How much time does an indoor grower have? Most people would rather spend less time producing more.

Legendary strains known to have been developed in the Northwest include Big Bud, Hash Plant, and Northern Lights #1, #2 and #5. These strains were developed specifically for growing indoors.

As superkind strains became easier to find, growers were able to concentrate on the quality of the indoor environment. In the '60s and most of the '70s, Seattle and Portland growers were using fluorescents. While an excellent crop can be raised with fluorescents, they lack intensity and must be kept two inches away from the plants. It was a very labor-intensive task that made large setups especially difficult to manage. People started looking for other light sources.

#216, August 1993

CURING, DRYING & STORING

BY PROFESSOR AFGHANI

Freshly harvested sinsemilla is usually dried in branch and cola form on clotheslines and placed loosely across screen racks. Drying should be done in the dark. Ideal atmospheric conditions for this four-to-seven day process seem to be 70 to 80°F with a relative humidity of about 75% tapering down to 40% toward the end.

Circulation fans are deployed in the drying area to create a gentle, non-direct breeze which, along with adequate ventilation, slowly extracts moisture from the buds. Once the buds are dry enough to burn, the curing process begins.

Years of trial and examination shows that this process continues for at least a month. The buds seem to improve with each day when they are cured correctly. The high becomes more complex in character; the potency of the herb increases by more than 20%. After drying, the buds are loosely placed in Rubbermaid™ or similar-type boxes for curing. These bins are commonly found in department stores, ranging in size from shoebox to footlocker. At least once a day the herbs are carefully tossed. The lid is manipulated, from sealed to ajar to off, to regulate the speed of moisture loss and escape of gases.

#224, April 1994

lot and they are most sensitive to more or less than optimum levels. After that, you knock the plants around too much making a path. By the time the plants are three months old, there won't be room to move around in the grow room much anyway.

Regular delivery of water and fertilizer is best done through a drip system. Correctly set up, a drip system is similar to a nonrecovery hydroponic unit and you get many of the same benefits. A good drip system allows irrigation at a slow, steady rate, avoiding soil compaction or unintentional leaching. You've got the adjustment just right when only a small trickle, 1/2 cup or less, emerges from the drain holes after a water cycle. As the plants grow, you will have to add more watering cycles as the plants consume more. It is preferable to add short watering cycles rather than having a longer one. A wand-style water meter is inexpensive and by probing the mix at varying levels in a few spots you can tell if the plants are getting enough water. Test three pots for every 10 in the room to get a representative sample. The meter reads higher or lower relative to root moisture. I've never seen one that came with guidelines for correct cannabis root moisture, but after using a few, the high one to low two reading level seems the objective to maintain.

A mixer-proportioner (MP) can inject a dilute fertilizer into the drip system each time you water. The emphasis is on dilute. I think Peter's brand products are the best to learn with, are easily available and dissolve completely even in the highly concentrated solution you load the MP with. Somewhere between 1/3 and 2/3 of the recommended outdoor application levels is right. Read the instructions that come with the MP and the Peter's to figure out how to load the MP correctly. It is always better to slightly underfertilize than risk burning the plants' roots. They do not recover from the latter very well.

Peter's sells a number of mixes but the following applies to nearly all commercially available mixes. In the first few weeks of seedling life, hand-water with a root-stimulating substance like Ortho Upstart. At three weeks, switch to a balanced NPK combination like Peter's 20-20-20. This is a transition fertilizer. At six weeks switch to Peter's Pete Lite 20-10-20. The higher relative N level promotes leaf/branch growth. The lower P level slows root growth and prevents premature flowering. At three to four months when you flower, switch to Peter's Blossom Booster 10-30-10 to aid floral (bud) formation.

As a convenience I like a self-contained programmable timer controlling the watering cycles. The Rainmatic models advertised in *Tips* are reliable and easy to program. You can get by without them but they never forget or have to go out of town for a few days. And when correctly adjusted, do it exactly right every time.

Linking the drip system, MP and water timer together requires a bit of experimentation. Remember two things: A little trickle out the bottom of the bucket is your objective, and the faucet pressure is the real key. When puzzled about how to regulate the system, think faucet pressure—more, faster drip rate; less, slower drip rate.

You've gotten this far and I still haven't even mentioned germinating a seed. When you see how much work is involved in set-up you might wonder why the hell homegrown appealed to you in the first place. But take heart, the hard part is over. The rest, the actual growing, is easy if your grow room is set up right in the beginning.

First printed in *Sinsemilla Tips*, Vol. 6, No. 2

PART TWO

Each time you grow a crop, you'll go through some close variation of the techniques described here. Follow them rather closely your first time so you can develop basic plant skills needed to improve quality and quantity in subsequent harvests.

The critical plant skill is the ability to tell at a glance whether a plant is healthy and growing at close to the optimum rate, and if not, what's likely to be wrong with it. This skill is learned through careful, regular observation of the plants and the intentional variation of fertilizer and water-quantity application to a few test buckets—more on this below.

When growing from seed, as you probably will the first time, the emphasis will be on yield per plant. But as you grow your first crop, you'll learn to clone, and with clones the emphasis shifts to yield per growing area. This is the production basis for commercial growing operations.

Unless you intentionally grow a variety of strains, your crop plants will be of relatively similar size and appearance up to the point you induce flowering.

Start with a larger number of seeds than your mature plant objective—about 100 seeds for 25 adults. Both are reliable and provide the strains as advertised. Soak the seed in room-temperature water for one hour to soften the hull and begin germination.

Peat root cubes are the preferred germination environment. Purchased compressed and dry, they swell to full size when soaked in water for a half hour. After soaking, slit the covering mesh to ease later removal and place one seed in each cube 1/8 to 1/4 inch below the cube surface.

Note the texture and color of the moist cubes. It's essential to maintain this until the cubes are planted in the larger grow buckets. Initially, place all the seeded cubes in a waterproof lined box 2-1/2 feet below the bottom edge of the HID (1,000-watt, clear or phosphor-coated). Begin the 18-hour timer-controlled light-cycles that characterize the vegetative cycle now. If you can control grow-room temperature, push it up to 80 to 85 degrees and keep it at that level for the first seven days. If the room is cooler, raise the cube container a foot or two off the floor (adjust the HID above that) where it will be warmer.

Start a grow-room diary the day you seed the cubes. Record regularly key measures, such as air temperature, humidity, root moisture, growth rate and general comments about your activities and observations in the grow room. A good diary will be more useful than you can imagine.

Ordinarily, I'm strongly opposed to any fungicide/pesticide application on the plants. The one exception I make regards damp off prevention. The micro-organisms that cause this are everywhere in the environment, plague even the cleanest grow rooms and can quickly kill young seedlings. Apply a dilute Captan (or Maneb) fungicide spray after you seed the cubes, again in three days, and again three days later. A light mist is better than a heavy drench. Rinse the plants with a room-temperature plain-water spray one day after each application.

At 80 to 85 degrees, seeds sprout in two or three days. First to emerge will be opposing, single, paddle-shaped leaves called cotyledon leaves. Keep track of the first to sprout. Colored toothpicks in the cube margin help.

After sprouts show give them a dilute (33 percent of the recommended strength) Ortho Upstart root-stimulator solution each

PLANTING TIPS

Mix soil or soilless medium in trash bags by holding bag closed and rolling it around. Add water to the bag after mixing but before pouring out to eliminate dust. Cut out one corner of the bag and let the mix pour into containers. This cuts dust and is fast and clean.

Have you ever watered your plants only to find exposed roots after the water is absorbed? As easy cure for this is to cut a piece of one-inch thick, open-celled foam rubber to the size of the top of your container. Cut a slot in this piece to fit around the plant's base. It can be put on or removed easily.

All this could easily be avoided by using open-celled rubber as a medium. Using seven-foot rain gutters, I cut the foam rubber to fit. I seal one end of the gutter off and raise that end an inch or two. The water flows to the open end and into a drip tray. Plants are started in pellets and are set in precut holes in the foam.

This medium is cheap and clean, and plants respond to feeding and leaching overnight. If black trash bags are cut and taped to the sides with a slit provided for each plant, it may be folded over the foam to help retain moisture and keep algae from growing on the foam.

Galloping Growroom Gourmet
Gulfport, Mississippi

#148, December 1987

INDOOR DUTCH SKUNK

The plants are Dutch Skunk. They were started in a small grow chamber and placed under a 250-watt HPS. The plants were trained to grow horizontally because of the limited height of my closet. The tops were filled with buds.

Sully
North London
ENGLAND

#218, October 1993

MONDO HYDRO

BY SHADY GROVE

Upon coming out of my winter hibernation in the Great Northwest last Spring, I wandered upon a hydroponic conference happening in Portland, OR. Always a fan of the many great microbreweries of that great city, a high-tech gardening conference was all the excuse I needed to grab my camera and check things out.

Attending this event was a curious cross-section of people whose only common interest was hydroponics, the science of growing plants without soil. The exhibitors included a local community college, companies that sold greenhouses by the acre and purveyors of many

small systems designed or adapted for the hobby gardener.

The most unique system at the show, the Pearlflow System, was designed in Scotland and is sold by Cropking Inc. in the USA. Pictured here are the passive wick-style single units (the larger ebb-and-flow systems support up to 10 trays).

A medialess system, the aquaduct combines NFT, ebb-and-flow and aeroponics principles. Plants are started in small rockwool cubes and

transferred to the rigid V-channel units, available up to 20' long. Not pictured here is the new 400-watt halide

lamp from Hydrofarm, which features a built-in cooling fan, safety shield and reflector (sized for the 400-watt bulb). This might be the culmination of all new trends in lighting.

Suncor showed a new passive system, pictured

here, that is most useful for cloning and salad greens. Their truly excellent "White Lightning," which uses NFT technique, comes up to 8' long and is capable of some truly awesome results. It was not displayed at the conference.

#226, June 1994

watering. To water, pour some of this mix in the cube container, let them soak it up and remove the excess in a few minutes. Don't let them stand in water, they'll die.

You'll want to select the most vigorous starts to transplant into the grow buckets. Keep in mind that the most robust seedlings make the most vigorous plants. Desirable sprouts are those that emerge first, have the thickest stems and have their first true leaves emerge one to two inches above the cube surface. This last point assumes a 1,000-watt HID 2-1/2 feet above the cubes. If your seedlings' first true leaves (true leaves have serrated edges and look like a cannabis leaf) emerge above three inches, the light intensity is too low or the grow room humidity is very high. Leggy seedlings do not make very good plants.

You may be surprised at the variation in seedling appearance in a sample as small as 100 seeds, but the more vigorous starts are usually easy to spot. Good experience can be gained by germinating seeds from commercial junk pot and noting the changes they go through in a week.

Transplant selected starts into the grow buckets three days after they emerge. Any longer often results in roots penetrating the cube's containing mesh. These roots will be broken off when removing the net as you transplant and this will shock and slow down the plants.

Just before transplanting, soak the soilless mix in the grow buckets. I try to bring it up to No. 7 on a Sudbury moisture meter. Scoop out two holes near the container center, carefully remove the mesh keeping the exposed cube intact and place it in a hole with the cube top even with the soilless level. Fill in around them and pat down to insure contact. Place the drip system emitter between them. Repeat this process until all 25 buckets have two starts in them.

Leftover, lower-quality starts should go into several extra buckets; "more fertilizer," "less fertilizer," "more water" and "less water." The relative level of water and fertilizer applied to these buckets will teach you a lot about plant tolerances. Only the crop plants are on the drip system. You must hand-apply variables to the test buckets. Carefully watch and record the effects. Test plants are more or less damaged by the extremes. Plant tolerances are, by the way, relatively narrow. I give "more" buckets twice as much and "less" buckets half as much as the crop plants. Any more variation than that would not provide useful information.

Huddle the grow buckets under the HID. A five-gallon bucket is one foot across, and 30 fill a five-by-six-foot area. Keep the HID 2-1/2 feet above the seedlings. The seedlings on the outside suffer a bit from lower light intensity. Compensate by using four by eight sheets of Styrofoam to create temporary walls around the grow buckets' perimeter.

As soon as plants sprout they begin making chlorophyll (the green in the leaves) and can benefit from the CO_2 supplementation schedule described in the preceding article "Indoor Growing, Part One". The exhaust-fan timer should also be activated at this time.

For the first seven days most growth is below the soil line. The root structure rapidly expands (it will nearly fill a five-gallon bucket in four weeks) to support later vegetative growth. At 10 days, survey the buckets and remove the second-best start in each by clipping at the soil line. Do not pull it up as you'll damage the remaining plant's root structure.

You now have 25 buckets with one plant each as your main crop plants and four test buckets with two or three plants in them. Test buckets do not need to be thinned to one plant. Two or three are OK.

During the first two to three weeks, aim for a water-meter-indicated root moisture of 2 to 2-1/2. To achieve this, apply 15 to 25 ounces of water/fertilizer Monday, Wednesday and Friday, one hour after lights-on. This is applied to the crop buckets using the timer-controlled drip system with an in-line fertilizer mixer/proportioner. On Sundays, override the timer control and add an additional amount of water depending on the root moisture reading, growth rate and plant appearance. The test buckets receive their water and fertilizer by hand.

You read a lot about pH and plant health. Soilless mixes have a buffering effect, moderating water which is too alkaline or acid closer to the desirable range of 6.6 to 7.1. In rare cases the tap water feeding your drip system can be so acid or base it results in a pH measure in the buckets above or below this range. If that happens, pH-up or pH-down concentrates can be bought from sources that supply the hydroponic gardener, who's much more concerned about pH regulation. These pH adjusters are added to the mixer/proportioner along with the fertilizer concentrate until the drip solution has an acceptable pH.

As the plants grow, you must adjust the drip-control timer. Aim to maintain a slightly lower root-moisture-meter reading of one to two. Obviously the meter readings will fluctuate. Just after the drip cycle it will be higher and on the off days, drier. A good general perspective on watering is to note that in nature, plants start in the wetter months of spring and grow and mature under the drier environmental conditions of summer.

Fertilizer application takes place with each watering using the drip system described. The first five days, apply a dilute (33 percent) Ortho Upstart Solution. Then switch to Peter's 20-20-20 applied at the rate of 1/2 teaspoon per gallon for two weeks. After that, switch to Peter's Pete Lite 20-10-20 for the balance of the vegetative cycle.

The most reliable measure of water/fertilizer application effectiveness is growth rate. At four weeks from start date, expect plants to average nine inches tall, and all to be over six inches. *Indica* plants may be a bit shorter but they will be very wide. *Sativa* will be taller and narrower. Around the fourth week the plants will take off and average 1/2 to 1 inch minimum growth per day. Measure them every four days and chart all plants. Growth should be steady throughout the vegetative period. A sudden spurt or lag can foreshadow a problem. Refer to diary notes taken three to five days before to see if anything changed. Changes in fertilizer and water application do not show immediate effects, although continually underwatered plants often shoot up overnight after a good soak.

An even, green color should predominate. The plants in the "more" fertilizer buckets may be a very dark green and show leaf burn at the edges. The plants in the "less" fertilizer bucket will grow slowly before they yellow, but you can slowly back off on fertilizer and watch the effect to gain experience. "Less" water plants usually look OK, but are smaller. Interestingly, "more" water, if it's severe enough, will drown the roots, and the growing tips of the plant will yellow, mimicking a nutrient deficiency. A classic beginner disaster is to overwater until the plants yellow, mistake it for a nutrient deficiency and apply a big shot of fertilizer and burn the daylights out of the plants. Lest you think anybody is a born expert, note that I speak from experience on this last point.

Light intensity is increased by getting the HID bulb closer to the

HYDROSPEAK

HYDROPONICS—Growing plants in a soilless medium (natural media include lava rock, and pea gravel; rockwool is spun from fiberglass). All systems include some sort of reservoir, a tank to hold the water and nutrient mix. In a passive system, the nutrients are usually brought to the plants by a wick, like the ones in an oil lamp. All other systems use a pump of some kind.

EBB-AND-FLOW SYSTEM—Uses a pump to flood roots with nutrient solution for a few minutes. Then the pump shuts off and the liquid runs back to the reservoir.

AEROPONICS—Roots hang in a closet and are constantly bathed in a fine mist of nutrients and air. (The mist nozzles can be tricky, though.)

TOP-FEED SYSTEM—Drips the nutrients down the top of the media out an always open drain in the bottom. May pump continuously, as does the NFT, or intermittently, similar to the ebb-and-flow.

NUTRIENT-FILM TECHNIQUE (NFT)—Plant roots are placed in a high channel or slightly tilted trench that contains a shallow flow of nutrient solution mixed with abundant air. The nutrient solution is constantly pumped up and down the channel, which gives the roots the thin film of nutrients for which the system is named.

#226, June 1994

SPRAY-N-GROW

I experimented with a product called Spray-N-Grow. It is all natural and can be sprayed on the plant up to the day of harvest. It claims to dramatically increase the weight and yield of tomatoes and other vegetables. Bottom line: It works on cannabis, too.

The plants I treated with Spray-N-Grow produced huge, dense, heavy buds. The dried buds are rock-hard and have a pleasant, fruity flavor.

D.K.B.
Sheridan, Oregon

#228, August 1994

INDOOR HYDRO

This bud is 115 days old from a 6'4" tall *indica/sativa* cross. Its weight was 21.5 grams dried and manicured. My garden system is hydroponics using growing nutrient and switching to 10-30-18 flowering nutrient. I use a MS 1,000-watt halide, negative-ion generator, CO2 system and a high-velocity air circulator (low setting) to strengthen the limbs. This strain has by far a superior yield to any I've grown before.

The Professor
Long Beach, CA

#125, January 1986

HEAD START FOR CLONES

One way to give clones a head start is to oxygenate the water. I do this by filling a container halfway with water, then sealing it. I shake it vigorously for a few moments. As you remove the lid you will notice that there is a partial vacuum—some of the air dissolved in the water.

The Slasher
Ann Arbor, Michigan

#162, February 1989

---

plants. Leave it at 2-1/2 feet above the soilless mix surface for the first four weeks, letting plants grow toward it. At four weeks, lower it to 12 inches from the closest plant. A week later, adjust it to six inches above the closest plant. After this you'll be raising the light as the plants grow to keep it six inches above the plants.

Spread the plants out as they grow to avoid extreme plant-leaf overlap. At four to six weeks the buckets will spread over about one-half a 10- by 12-foot grow room. At eight to 10 weeks, they'll fill it.

The vegetative period lasts, most economically and practically, until plants average 30 to 36 inches tall from the soil line. A room with higher (80 to 85 degrees) light-cycle temperatures, CO_2 supplementation and plants carefully tended with correct fertilizer/water application will be ready in eight weeks. Cooler rooms, with no CO_2 and erratic plant-care procedures, could require four to six weeks more. The next installment will cover exactly what happens when you shift from the end of the vegetative to the flowering cycle.

Cloning is the key to increasing yields without increasing electrical consumption. It allows you to raise only female plants if you choose—and the best ones at that.

Cloning is somewhat mystified in the literature. It's actually fairly simple. Here is a "foolproof" method. Plants should be two months old and two feet tall. Pour a gallon of plain water through the bucket once a day for three to four days. Wait two days and do not apply any water or fertilizer during this time. Select lower, if not the lowest, branches. They should be at least as big as a farmer's match in diameter. Cut off a length approximately six inches from the tip and midway between sets of leaves.

Snip off one set of leaves above the cut line, leaving two 1/8-inch nubs. Dip the stem in a root stimulator like Rootone to a point 1/4 inch above the nubs, and stick it in a quart container of soilless mix. The soilless mix should be presoaked. Make a guide hole with a tool larger than the stem so you don't scrape off rooting powder during insertion. Insert the stem to a point equal with the rooting powder level and tamp the soilless mix into contact with it.

Keep the soilless mix evenly moist, watering with a 50% Upstart solution as needed. Cover the clones under a clear plastic sheet with an open air passage, to raise humidity while allowing air exchange. Put the clones in boxes two feet off the floor, where the temperature is likely to be higher. For the first week, keep them in a corner away from the HID, until the clone root structure starts up and can supply the plant nutrients and moisture more intense light will require. Mist the clones lightly each day. At the end of one week move them closer to the HID and remove the tent. They may wilt a bit along the way, but they will perk up seven days after cutting if they are going to make it.

The clones will outgrow the quart container in two to three weeks. Transplant them into larger containers before they get root-bound. A plant grown from seed needs a container equal to one gallon per month of plant life. A five-gallon bucket sustains a plant for five months before it becomes root-bound and sickens. I put clones in three-gallon containers, anticipating 30 days of vegetative growth after placement in the bucket and then a maximum eight-week flowering cycle. (More on this in Part Three.)

When you clone, carefully record the parent plant for each. To establish a perpetual clone crop with these starts you'll need a second, smaller grow room. Follow carefully, the clones can stay in the main grow room while the 18-hour light-cycle is maintained. But soon after cloning you drop to 12 hours for flowering. To avoid flowering the clones, they go into the second grow room which stays on an 18-hour light cycle. As the crop plants flower, the males will be easy to identify. If you kept track of the clone's source, toss the clones taken from them leaving only females. To insure a full grow room with your clone crop, take two cuttings from each parent plant. (More on this in Part Three.)

Bringing your first crop to this point will be an enormous education. If you've read Jorge Cervantes's *Indoor Marijuana Horticulture*, a true classic, take the next step and read Robert Connell Clarke's *Marijuana Botany*. These books are the best I've read and are written by experienced growers, not inexperienced, but widely read students of the subject.

One last point. Cannabis thrives in the correct mental as well as physical climate. Relax around the plants. Beginners are forever meddling with their plants. Don't. They often do a little better with less attention than too much. And Sister Marijuana knows if you have a positive mental attitude. Growers driven by greed and other shallow irresponsible motives don't do very well, and they shouldn't.

First printed in *Sinsemilla Tips*, Vol. 6, No. 3

PART THREE

Even though I've watched over many a crop, I still find flowering and harvest utterly fascinating. In just a few short weeks, the appearance and character of the plants changes dramatically. Experiencing it gives truth to all the hype you read and hear about the psychological rewards of home growing.

Causing the plants to flower is essentially a matter of reducing the timer-controlled light-cycle from 18 to 12 hours by taking six hours off the front or back end of the original schedule. The new 12-hour cycle is maintained until the plants are harvested. When you flower is your choice, but certain practical considerations will generally determine the timing.

Plants from seed should not be flowered before they are four to six weeks old. Prior to that, the ratio between bud and shake will be low and sex-reversal problems can crop up. Further, the younger a seed-grown plant, the longer it takes for it to react to photoperiod reduction and begin vigorous floral formation. The best rule of thumb is to flower seed-started plants when they are three feet tall from soil line to growing tip or three months old, whichever comes first. If you do everything right with light, water and fertilizer, plus add CO_2, they will be ready in eight to nine weeks. Before or after this time, the yield ratio of bud to plant size is less favorable for most strains.

When you set back the light-cycle you must make other modifications:
● Reduce the CO_2 injection period by six hours because of the reduced light-cycle. Plants do not require significant amounts during the "night" period.
● Carefully monitor the hygrometer's humidity reading at "lights on" the first 10 days and add exhaust cycles during the "night" to keep it below 60 percent as necessary. The longer dark period results in a lower bottom temperature, which will raise humidity. To prevent this from sponsoring a mold attack on the buds, add exhaust cycles.
● Check for any light leaks, particularly at the top and bottom of the grow-room door. The grow room must be absolutely dark during the "night" period. No "midnight" inspections with flashlight in hand,

THAI PLANT

This top kola is from a clone of a Thai plant. It was grown in potting soil, with one month of continuous light and 4-1/2 months of flowering cycle (12 on/12 off).
Total time 5-1/2 months.

Big "A"
Atlanta, Georgia

#174, February 1990

INDOOR WEEKLY CHECKLIST

Air ventilation
Air circulation
Humidity (40-50%)
Temperature: day (70-75°F); night (50-60°F)
Soil moisture
Cultivate soil surface
Check pH
Rotate plants
Check for spider mites (underside of leaves)
Check for fungi or algae
Check for nutrient deficiencies
Move lamp (12" from plants)
Cleanup!
#136, December 1986

THE ART OF CLONING

BY PROFESSOR AFGHANI

My method incorporates 1 5/8" 1 5/8" wrapped Grodan rockwool cubes and 10" x 20" clear-domed, black propagation trays. These domes have dime-sized holes cut from the top corners. I soak the cubes in Olivia's Cloning Solution diluted to 200 parts per million. I set the pH at 4.5, then maintain it at 5.5 or 5.6.

At least one node must be available to clip clean and bury in the rockwool. The final base cut of the stem is made at a 45-degree angle, never dissecting a node.

An air bubble that can suffocate a new clone may develop in the stem's central hole if the stem is not immediately submerged in liquid. The fresh-cut clones should immediately be placed in a vessel (I use a shot glass) filled with enough liquid to cover the stem and clipped nodes. If you prefer powered rooting compounds, such as Hormex #8 or Rootone F, simple water or Olivia's will do. If you use a liquid rooting compound, such as Dip'n Grow, then dip the stems in that. I tend to make just four cuttings at a time, filling the shot glass and then planting them by poking individual holes in the rockwool with a thin, wood shish-kabob skewer. Exercise special care not to squeeze or kink the cutting while planting.

#239, July 1995

either.

● Change the fertilizer from the growth formula (20-10-20) to a bloom booster with a higher proportion of phosphorus (10-30-10). After the first three to four weeks of flowering, discontinue fertilizing and use plain water. Do not alter the fertilizer-application concentration or frequency, just the NPK mix.

Also, do not withhold water to promote resin formation. Instead, you will reduce harvest. A number of growers I know use a home brew the last couple of weeks before harvest. Usually it's a dilute fruit-juice mixture like orange juice, apple or pineapple. They feel it sweetens the bud. I think it gunks up the drip system and acidifies the soil. I've not been able to taste the difference myself, but plants harvested with no let-up in fertilizer application do taste a bit bitter.

● Lastly, no sprays of any kind can be used in the grow room from now on. They can cause bud mold, and smoking the plant transfers all spray residues to your lungs. Never, ever use any type of poison on a crop you smoke or sell.

Adding a second light now will increase light intensity and, consequently, bud formation. The preferred choice is a 1,000-watt high-pressure sodium (HPS) bulb. The yellow/orange cast of the light discharged indicates the particular segment of the light spectrum emphasized. The combination of HPS and MH light approximates the harvest-sun spectral mix that occurs in nature during the fall months and encourages floral growth. The bulbs and reflectors should be offset, equidistant from the ceiling center to insure even light distribution. A circular light balancer is beneficial but not necessary. Rail-type light balancers, in my opinion, travel the circuit too slowly. I do not recommend them.

Plan to check your garden every day for at least a half hour the first two weeks of flowering, unless you want an early male to spread pollen and fertilize every female in the room. After your first crop, you'll probably be able to distinguish males from females when they are only four to six weeks old.

Specifically, you look for the single immature sex organs (flowers) they display at the branch crotches on the upper third of the plant. A 10-power magnifier helps to spot them. Male plants produce pollen sacs that look like tiny cantaloupes when closed and umbrellas with dangling bags of pollen when about to release. One flower, even though it's the size of a pencil eraser, can pollinate an unbelievable number of female calyxes, ruining your sinsemilla crop. Female flowers look like two hairs emerging from a small pod. The hairs are anywhere from 1/8 to 1/2-inch long and can be white (most common), green, reddish-purple to a beautiful lavender, in certain strains of *indica* from Afghanistan.

Watch your plants' development closely. As they mature and males are identified, remove them before their flowers open. If you started with 30 plants, expect about 12 to 15 to be male (there are slightly more females in any seed sample). Most growers immediately harvest all identified males except for one or two saved for breeding. The saved males go into a different room with a sunny window. Except during the summer months, the males will mature enough flowers to be a pollen source for breeding.

If your plant strain is relatively potent, the males will be smokable/saleable, although harsher and not nearly as potent as the females.

While total yield from the grow room is a combination of good gardening and genetic potential, the potency is solely determined by the genetic makeup of the plants and a sufficient flower period to mature the bud. How long it takes your particular plants to mature will vary. Rather than tell you to wait four, six or eight weeks, then cut and dry, it's better to learn to recognize a mature bud. The following is open to debate but here's what I teach others and use myself.

In the first 10 to 14 days, the plants will elongate the upper one-third of each branch anywhere from eight to 14 inches. After that nearly all vegetative growth will stop; no more multibladed leaves will form. Lower fan leaves will begin to yellow partially due to the lower nitrogen level in the fertilizer. The plants also find it convenient to cannibalize lower fan leaves for assimilated nutrients, thus conserving energy to reproduce.

The plants, if healthy, will rapidly form calyxes one atop another into bud formations of varying length, with the biggest forming on the main stem. During the first 10 days, use your 10-power magnifier to watch the resin glands pop out on the buds. There are a few types of glands, but check for those which look like a mushroom, a small clear globule on a clear stalk. The first few weeks of flowering, the buds will usually smell faintly sweet, the hairs protruding from the calyxes will retain their original color and the resin glands will be clear.

After that point, the odor will become coarser. Some strains are quite acrid smelling, like gasoline, skunks or anything else that comes to mind. Odor and resin-gland formation are linked and a sign of increasing potency. The calyx hairs will begin to wither and turn brown toward the base of the bud and this will progress toward the top. If a male flower releases pollen and fertilizes the calyx the hairs will turn brown immediately. Grossly pollinated plants will immediately slow new calyx production and begin to emphasize seed production. Lightly pollinated plants will keep going.

The key indicator of maturity is the resin heads. As the majority on the central bud cloud to a milk white or turn a reddish color, that bud is ripe and the rest of the plant is close behind. If you've regularly observed the plants with your 10-power magnifier you won't miss this.

Generally, all females from the same strain will mature at the same time. You'll have to watch yours to know, but when a few are ready, most will be.

The fan leaves will yellow and drop rapidly as the plants ready for harvest. Some of them, as well as small leaves subtending the bud, may turn shades of purple or rust. This isn't a sign of higher relative potency as many believe. It's genetically linked, but essentially expresses declining vigor, much as trees outdoors turn assorted colors and lose their leaves in autumn.

In the final days before harvest, the plant may produce tiny unserrated leaves near the bud tips. These leaves will look like the first cotyledon leaves that emerged on the seedling. When all of these circumstances have occurred, you have reached peak floral development and harvest is called for.

Most growers attempt improvements in their particular strains by selectively breeding for certain traits. The subject of selective breeding is beyond the scope of this article, but the practical techniques are not.

Once you've isolated one or two selected male plants as pollen

CHEAP CO₂

Mixing vinegar (dilute acetic acid) with a slurry of baking soda (sodium bicarbonate) is a fantastic low-technology way to produce CO_2 on demand. There are several advantages to this technique.

1) Waste products are simply disposed of down the toilet without hurting the environment.

2) There is no burning of hydrocarbons such as gas or oil, which produce pollution.

3) No heat is produced, so less has to be removed from the grow room.

4) This technique is more convenient than lugging big, heavy CO_2 cylinders.

5) Purchasing baking soda and vinegar at your local supermarket and transporting these items in grocery bags garners a lot less attention than the tanks.

6) You don't have to purchase an expensive gas regulator-metering device.

Producing CO_2 by fermenting sugar is interesting, but a molecule of CO_2 from fermentation costs more than the vinegar/baking soda method and fermentation requires more maintenance.

My grow closet is 2' x 3' x 3'. I use a 150-watt HPS for all stages of growth. I feel it is necessary to supplement the closed environment with CO_2 to enhance the growth rate. The space has virtually no ventilation.

I put 1/3 cup of baking soda in a 2.25 quart pitcher, cover with a minimum amount of water to make a slurry of baking soda. I built a little platform on the pitcher mouth which holds an 8-ounce cup of vinegar. The cup has a strip of tissue placed in the inside bottom which extends over the top and below the bottom, so that is acts as a siphon. It takes several hours to drain the cup, one drop every 15-30 seconds, into a pitcher. I add more vinegar to the cup as needed. When the pitcher is nearly full, I simply pour the contents down the toilet and refill the cup and pitcher.

The High Chemical Engineer
Houston, Texas

#161, January 1989

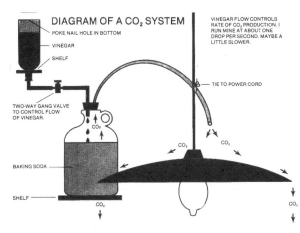

DIAGRAM OF A CO₂ SYSTEM

POKE NAIL HOLE IN BOTTOM
VINEGAR
SHELF
VINEGAR FLOW CONTROLS RATE OF CO₂ PRODUCTION. I RUN MINE AT ABOUT ONE DROP PER SECOND. MAYBE A LITTLE SLOWER.
TWO-WAY GANG VALVE TO CONTROL FLOW OF VINEGAR.
TIE TO POWER CORD
CO₂
BAKING SODA
SHELF
CO₂
CO₂
CO₂
CO₂

BRIAN SPAETH

PRACTICAL GAS: CO₂

BY JOHN BUSHWELL

Due to concern about the effects of the rising CO_2 level in the general atmosphere (the "greenhouse effect"), a great deal of research demonstrating the effects of CO_2 on plants has recently come to light. In an assemblage of 430 prior observations, B.A. Kimball's paper on the effects of carbon dioxide on agricultural yields notes four areas of marked improvement:

1) CO_2 enrichment at ideal levels (above 1,000 ppm) produces an improved yield of all crops tested averaging 68 percent.

2) CO_2 improves the speed of flowering.

3) CO_2 lowers water consumption and improves water utilization efficiency.

4) CO_2 increases leaf area, branch numbers, fruit size, germination and the rooting of cuttings.

Any plant has an ideal temperature for growth, the point at which photosynthesis is the farthest ahead of respiration. By adding CO_2 enrichment, this ideal temperature can be raised for many crops by 10 or 15 degrees.

My basic rule of thumb is this: Close off the grow room as if you were going to use CO_2. Turn the lighting on and leave it on for a full day cycle. If the temperature goes over 100°F for more than two or three hours, then using CO_2 enrichment is probably out of the question, at least until cooler weather sets in. If the temperature stabilizes to between 80 and 90 degrees, then CO_2 can be used with confidence.

#113, January 1985

donors, place them in a sunny room before their flowers mature and release pollen. A pollen trap can be made from a small brown-paper bag. Cut a three-inch square hole in one side and tape down Saran Wrap to cover it. The bag will breathe enough to avoid harming the plant. Slip it over the top stalk of the plant and secure at the base with a garbage bag twist-tie. Keep the bag closed but don't pinch off the flow in the plant stalk. In about 10 days, you'll see a number of male flowers open up and shed pollen.

To capture the pollen, give the bag a healthy shake to part pollen from plant. Cut the stalk off a couple inches below the bag neck. Invert the bag, loosen the seal and carefully draw out the top of the stalk while gently shaking to toss pollen off into the bag. Next, lay a 12-inch square sheet of wax paper, creased in the middle, on a flat surface in a draft-free room. Turn the paper bag upside down a few inches above it, and pollen and flowers will cascade onto the wax paper. Then collect the pollen in the crease by holding the wax paper "taco-style" and chase it with a brush into a dry 35mm film canister. Label the canister with the source. Wash the brush between collections from different donors and use fresh sheets of wax paper each time to avoid unintended mixing.

There are two common ways to pollinate females you select. A small amount of pollen can be put in a baggie, which is then placed over a lower branch bud on a plant with fresh, ripe pistils (calyx hairs). Use a twist-tie to seal the baggie neck and shake the branch to insure pistil/pollen contact. Leave it on a day or two; any longer and the inside of the bag will be soaked. Putting the bag on and taking it off risks spreading pollen to other plants.

Consequently, I prefer to apply pollen directly from the 35mm container using a small paint brush. Lightly touch the end of the brush in the pollen and then touch it directly to the fresh pistils. You can easily create 20 or 30 viable seeds this way in just a minute. I find it much easier to control the pollen this way. Turn off the grow-room fan when you're doing this.

If a shitload of seeds from a great male and female is your goal, there is only one way to go. Wait until the female is heavily flowered but the pistils are still fresh. Then place her right next to the male in the sunny room for a couple of days. Periodically shake the male to liberally distribute pollen over the female. Then return the female to the grow room, but first take a small fan or blower and "dust" the female of loose pollen or it'll blow around in the main grow room, pollinating the rest of the plants.

Seed must fully mature to be viable. Pollinated lower branches need to be left unharvested and attached to the lower third of the plant stalk. As the seeds develop they'll split the containing calyx and turn dark brown. Spread newspapers under the plant to catch seeds which fall early. Seeds must be dark brown and "rattle in the pod" or drop easily to be reliably ripe. It takes three to six weeks from fertilization for seeds to form and ripen. When harvesting a plant with some lower branches intentionally seeded, cut off all the rest of the bud and branch ends, leaving one-third of the main stalk with seeded branches attached. The plant will still be able to ripen the seeds. If there are only a few seeded plants, concentrate them under the HID and turn off the HPS lamp after the main harvest. The seeds will turn out fine.

Always change clothes and wash your hands between visits to the male room and the female room or you'll carry in unwanted pollen.

After each intentional pollination, record the info in your grow-room diary and tag the seeded branches with relevant information so you won't lose track of what you've done. Again, let the seeded plants/branches go on under the HID as long as necessary after the bud harvest. The seeds cannot be planted right away. You should store them after they are completely dry in a film canister with a dash of Captan fungicide to prevent mold. They'll need three to four months in storage in a cool place to stabilize before they will germinate vigorously and produce healthy plants.

The harvest process needs the same patient attention you gave to growing. It's best to cut one branch at a time and do a wet manicure. Remove the fan leaves for "Grade B" shake. They dry fine in a paper bag. Toss the bag contents occasionally to prevent compression rot. Then trim back the small leaves in the buds, leaving a small amount protruding, 1/4 to 1/2 inch. I think it's best to suspend the buds upside down during drying. The trimmed small leaf is separated into "Grade A" shake. The stubs left will curl down over the bud and dry to a shield protecting the resin-covered calyxes. The smallest buds can dry on screens, but all bigger ones benefit from a rack. A fan in the drying room helps air circulation and discourages mold. A room temperature of 72 degrees is a good minimum.

Take it easy when manicuring and drying. Rough handling will cause the resin glands to break off the bud, carrying away THC. Afghani pure strains bred for hashish manufacture need very tender care.

The buds are dry when the central stems snap when bent and the calyx/leaf portion feels slightly flexible and moist. The buds should then be packaged for market. Zip-lock bags are the "plain brown wrapper" of the industry and do not adequately protect the harvest. If you're serious about your business, buy a Seal-a-Meal plastic bag closer. These bags are airtight, so the buds better be dry or they will mold on the way to market.

It will take you about 10 to 12 hours to manicure a pound of bud. Allow one or two weeks to slow-dry the crop unless you use a hurry-up method, like a room dehumidifier or forced, heated air circulation. Unless you wear rubber gloves, your hands will be coated with resin. Periodically rub your hands together and save the little resin balls. Dip the scissors in alcohol to wash off accumulating resins and keep them sharp. The phrase "snip 'til you flip" is accurate. If you have surplus pollen, take a dab of alcohol and mix it with the collected resins, then dry. This delicate and rare smoke is quite satisfying.

Going back a couple of stages, if you cloned per the guidelines in Part Two, this is the basis for your second crop. If you did two for every plant and carefully recorded the mother source, you'll know which are males to toss and females to keep.

The clones must be moved to a second grow room with a 1,000-watt HID when you flower the main grow room. After harvest and seed collection are finished, clean the main room thoroughly and move in the clones. I recommend that you grow two or three clone crops this way before going on to another technique.

Eventually I'd recommend you evolve to what is commonly called the "Sea of Green" method if you want to maximize your production capacity and make it your main income source. It is not a complicated technique and reduces your dependence on yield per plant to yield per area by raising a very large number of short clones. The main skill is to be able to start a lot of clones simultaneously, keep them all healthy and put them into the flower phase just as they root. The result is a grow room that looks like the floor is carpeted with green spikes 12 to

SKUNKY PETE

A friend turned me on to this strain from seeds he had acquired in Amsterdam. When he purchased them, he had asked for the skunkiest stuff. Not knowing what they were going to produce, I named them Skunky Pete, in my friend's honor.

I set up my grow room in September in an uninsulated barn loft. The plants were put in a 5' x 5' frame built out of 1 x 4's and lined with polyethylene plastic, Styrofoam and another layer of polyethylene. The inside was then lined with removable panels covered with Mylar, held in place using Velcro.

A small ceramic heater aimed away from the plants was used to keep temperature in the mid-60s to high-80s. The temperature did get a little high, despite the exhaust fan and circulating fan.

Seeds were started October 1st under a 400-watt metal halide. I chose the three best plants of the 20 Beatrix Choice specimens at six weeks and induced flowering to prevent them from getting too leggy. At the same time, I turned on an additional light: a 400-watt HPS lamp. Within a week, sex expression indicated. The male SPs were removed for pollen collection, and the bottom branches of the SP females were pollinated. I left the Beatrix alone, as past cross-pollination with a Skunk #1 x NL #5 proved disappointing.

The two SPs were ripe in six weeks and yielded 4-5 ounces each. The odor is very pungent, but not particularly skunky. The high is pure *sativa*. The BCs were ready in 10 weeks and yielded 3-1/2 ounces each. It has a minty-pine taste and smell and a good high, but it's a poor second to the SPs.

T.H. Seed Co.
Brookline, MA

#203, July 1992

IONIZERS

I have started using ionizers in my grow room and I have noticed the following benefits: White fly infestation reduced by 90-100%; Yield increased by 10-20%; Flowering time reduced by approximately 7 days.

Stoned-Way Up North
Westminster BC

#163, March 1989

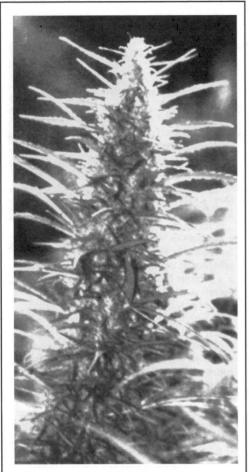

INDOOR LIGHTING

This baby grew under a 1,000-watt MH with CO₂ and all the fixings. Things have gotten better every harvest.

Brother Bilbo
San Bernadino, CA

#181, September 1990

SON-AGRO BULB

A fairly recent development the Bush Doctor neglected to mention in "A Heavy Essay on Lights," (Dec. '93 HT) is the Son-Agro 430-watt bulb manufactured by Phillips, which fits in a standard 400-watt system. The Son-Agro has 30% more blue light and emits 6% more lumens overall than a standard 400-watt HPS bulb. I currently use this bulb and highly recommend it.

Mezz Mezzrow
Boston

#224, April 1994

18 inches tall in one-gallon pots.

If you've come this far you've learned a lot. But there is more to know. Selective breeding can do much to custom produce your own super plant, producing a yield, appearance and high closely matching your own tastes. Robert Connell Clarke's *Marijuana Botany* stands far above any other book on breeding and along with Jorge's bible, *Indoor Marijuana Horticulture*, is a must-read.

First printed in *Sinsemilla Tips*, Vol. 6, No. 4

ELECTRIC LIGHTS FOR PLANT GROWTH

by Mel Frank

The light system is the heart of any electric-light garden. The amount of light and space your plants have determines how fast, large and robust the plants will grow. In a well-maintained garden, it's relatively simple to supply indoor plants with all the water, air and nutrients they need, so that light becomes the only limiting factor which might restrict growth. The amount of light also determines the garden's dimensions, the overall size of the plants and even what varieties of marijuana a grower chooses to cultivate. Most other aspects of gardening can be considered when you come to them, but the kind of lights and the amount of light that illuminates a garden must be decided before any seed is sown.

PRIMARY LIGHT SOURCES: TYPES OF LAMPS FLUORESCENTS (MODEST INDOOR GARDENS)

Fluorescents are common, inexpensive, cheap to run and effective in illuminating modest indoor marijuana gardens. Fluorescent fixtures contain a ballast and two end sockets in which the tube (bulb or lamp) is held. If possible, purchase fixtures with built-in reflectors. There are innumerable types of fluorescent tubes and many lengths and wattages available to the homegrower. Only those sizes and types that are the most effective as growing lamps are described here.

Fluorescents have gotten a bad rap from many growers who were disappointed with the results. Good results require almost daily care while the plants are flowering. Fluorescents generate weaker light than other recommended lamps. While flowering, plants must be carefully tended to keep the tops of all plants at the same height and as close to the fluorescents as possible; otherwise the final crop will amount to no more than some skimpy buds and a lot of leaf. Many fine crops are raised under fluorescents by conscientious growers who spend the necessary time and who are sensitive to the plants' needs. Fluorescents are an inexpensive alternative to other lamps for the moderate smoker who can't invest much money or devote much space to a larger light system. The type of light makes little difference to the potency.

Fluorescent fixtures may be found or scavenged, tubes are cheap, and the garden contributes little to the electric bills. On the other hand, if cost and space are no object, high-intensity discharge (HID) lamps support larger and more robust plants, and require less careful attention and less frequent care.

Fluorescents are cheaper and better than HIDs for rooting clones, raising males for pollen, and starting seedlings up to about eight weeks of growth before they are transferred to an HID system; on all of these, the high energy output and expense of HIDs are wasted. Commercial growers use fluorescents to start plants when they rotate crops to successively larger light systems, particularly when using high-pressure sodium (HPS) lamps.

Ironically, some of the largest commercial indoor gardens use the lowly fluorescent exclusively. These "growing factories" use growing shelves and clones for rotating fast-turnover gardens. For the homegrower growing for personal use, a shelf garden under fluorescents might be your best option in terms of your initial cost, electrical consumption and subterfuge.

STANDARD FLUORESCENT FIXTURES

Standard fluorescents (the long tubes you see in industrial and some home lighting) come in lengths from six inches to 12 feet, and all of them use about 10 watts per linear foot. This means that a standard four-foot fixture with its tube uses about 40 watts per tube and an eight-footer uses about 80 watts. These two sizes, four-foot and eight-foot lengths, are the most common sizes available and the most popular with marijuana growers. You can find tubes of five, six and seven-foot lengths, and you should use them if they will fit your space.

Any tube less than four feet long emits too little light to grow a vigorous crop of marijuana. Tubes longer than eight feet are hard to find and somewhat unwieldy to raise and lower, but they work very well if you have the space.

Fluorescents are also manufactured in efficient-use tubes. GE sells their Watt-Miser line and Sylvania has their SuperSaver line. Europeans look for TL tubes, and most manufacturers sell a line of watt-saving standard fluorescents which emit more light per watts consumed than standard tubes. Typically, "watt-saving" tubes consume about 20% less electricity and emit 10% less light than standard tubes. Look for these watt-saving lines when setting up a large shelf garden where you're concerned about electrical consumption. Many fluorescents are manufactured as "power twists" or "power grooves." These tubes have indentations or are twisted, which gives the bulb more surface area, and they emit about 10 to 15% more light per watt consumed. Most manufacturers offer tubes in "efficient use," "power groove" and "higher output versions."

HIGHER-OUTPUT FLUORESCENTS

Fluorescents also come in higher-wattage sizes, the most common being Very High Output (VHO), at 215 watts per eight-foot tube, and High Output (HO), at 110 watts per eight-foot tube. VHOs emit about 2.25 times as much light and consume almost three times as much power as standard fluorescents of the same length. They also require a special VHO fixture (a VHO ballast and end sockets). HO tubes also require an HO ballast and different end sockets than standard bulbs use. HOs use about 45 to 50% more electricity and emit about 45% more light than standard fluorescents of the same length. VHO and

ESSAY ON LIGHTS

BY THE BUSH DOCTOR

What you need to understand are four basic parameters: how much, what color, photoperiod and efficiency—plus a smattering of other considerations like safety and hardware costs. The amount of light required can be measured in two ways—quantity and energy. Light quantity is measured by the brightness cast by a candle onto a square foot of surface one foot away (one foot-candle or one lumen). This is what the "exposure meter" in your camera measures. In the metric world, candle light upon a square meter one meter away equals one lux. One lumen equals 10.76 lux. Ordinary indoor light averages 150 lux, too dim for cannabis, a plant that requires lots of light.

Researchers have grown cannabis plants under as little as 600 lux (Aringer & Nagy, 1971). Paris et al. (1975) used fluorescent and incandescent lamps emitting 14,000-18,000 lux. Sunlight approaches 100,000 lux atop Mauna Loa. Color is a function of wavelength, measured in nanometers (nm). Plants, like people, prefer certain colors. Plants reject (reflect) green-yellow light (500-600 nm). Photosynthesis works best at red and blue wavelengths. Incandescent bulbs burn toward the yellow/orange side of the rainbow—they lack blue. On the other hand, MH bulbs emit mostly blue and lack yellows. Fluorescent bulbs are white, producing a balanced light. Enhance the fluorescent spectrum by combining warm whites (more red) with cool whites (more blue). HPS bulbs emit a brittle pink-orange light; Frank (1988) says HPS bulbs serve mature plants (flowering requires more red light), but seedlings, needing more blue, do poorly. Low-pressure sodium (LPS) bulbs produce pure, monochromatic yellow light that is no good for plants.
#220, December 1993

LIGHT BALANCERS

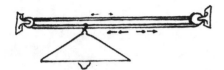

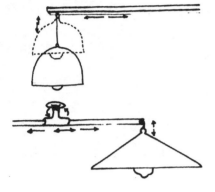

LOW-COST LIGHT MOVER

I use a 175-watt vertical MH in a small garden in my closet. The garden had "hot" and "cold" spots. I needed a light mover, but being budget-conscious, I discovered a way to do it for pennies. Swing it.

I set up the mover using a few fish-eye screws and 40-lb test fishing line. I tied the line to the fan guard on one side and to the light's chain, about 2" below the hook holding the light on the other side. I adjusted the line so that it gives a gentle tug on the chain. Too much resistance will eventually wear out the oscillating gear of the fan. On most fans one side of the arc is stronger than the other, so that should be considered. With a little bit of experimenting you should be able to get your light to swing gently back and forth or even in a circular pattern. My lamp has been moving for over a 5" diameter for over a month now.

David
Shawnee Mission, Kansas

#163, March 1989

HO tubes in four-foot lengths are rated at about half the wattage of the eight-foot tubes. HO tubes in five, six and seven-foot lengths with correspondingly higher wattages are hard to find, but they can be ordered. VHO tubes also come in five-foot and six-foot lengths. For better results, always use the longest tube you can fit in your prospective garden.

Generally, VHO and HO "watt-saving" tubes consume less watts with a correspondingly lower output in overall light. In other words, they aren't necessarily more efficient, they just put out proportionally less light, while they consume correspondingly fewer watts. A "watt-saving" eight-foot VHO consumes about 185 watts, and a "watt-saving" eight-foot HO uses about 95 watts.

Although all higher-output fluorescents work well for growing marijuana, VHOs are not better than HID lamps; they cost about the same, and the light system is more unwieldy and less efficient in terms of light delivered per watt consumed. Set-up and care is easier with HID lamps; when the plants get larger, growth is more robust under the higher intensity of HID lamps. However, HO tubes draw less current, are cheaper and work very well with moderate electric costs after the initial investment in the HO fixture.

One advantage of fluorescent tubes is that they may conform to an odd space with limited headroom, such as a shelf, overhead closet, attic, crawl-space, half-basement, nook or space beneath a loft bed; they come in many lengths and take up less vertical space for gardening than HIDs.

METAL-HALIDES AND SODIUM-VAPOR LAMPS

Metal-halide (MH) lamps and high-pressure sodium vapor (HPS) lamps are the most effective and efficient electric light sources available to the indoor gardener. These bulbs are a point source of light, rather than a linear source like fluorescents. Because the light radiates from a point, it's more intense and can penetrate leaves and illuminate a deeper cubic area than fluorescents. *A 1,000-watt HID will grow larger plants with a deeper layer of worthwhile buds than five VHO fluorescents using 1,075 watts.*

Both MH and HPS bulbs come in many sizes: The halides range from 175 to 1,500 watts; the sodium-vapor bulbs from 35 to 1,500 watts. For most situations I recommend only two sizes, 400 and 1,000 watts, and only a few basic bulb types which are listed later. A 1,500-watt bulb lasts only 25% as long as the smaller sizes do, including the 1,000-watt bulb, so 1,500-watt bulbs are not recommended because of excessive bulb costs. Most bulbs of less than 400 watts are not as effective for plant growth, and it's considerably more expensive for growers to set up several smaller units than to use either of the two larger, recommended sizes. The GE Watt-Miser, or similarly efficient bulbs of 325 watts, and the Duro-test Optimarc of 250 watts are the only smaller bulbs recommended for typical gardens. With special circumstances—for instance, if the only place you can grow is in a small closet, consider buying a smaller, horizontally mounted MH or HPS. These minihorizontals range from a 150-watt HPS or 175-watt MH to 250-watt sizes. The horizontal fixture delivers from 20 to 45% more light to the plants than conventional, vertically hung bulbs. *The most productive, modest setup you can buy is a 400-watt HPS with a horizontal reflector.* It doesn't add much to your electric bill, and the bulb lasts for about three years. For about the same costs, one 400-watt ballast runs any 400-watt MH and a 1,000-watt ballast runs any 1,000-

watt MH. HPS bulbs require their own particular ballast, which should be purchased along with the HPS bulb.

LIGHT BALANCERS (MOVERS)

Light balancers (also called movers) are mechanical arms from which hang MH or HPS bulbs; their small motors move the lights slowly across a garden. Light balancers come in two basic configurations, linear or circular. Linear balancers move the lights back and forth along a linear track, and are best employed in a rectangular garden. Circular balancers either rotate the lights continuously in a circle, or move 180 degrees and back to repeat a cycle. After the initial cost, light balancers save considerable electrical costs, considering the extended area that they illuminate versus their running costs, which are negligible (only 14 to 24 watts). Light balancers increase the effective size of any garden significantly without additional bulbs or any appreciable increase in electrical costs.

SUPPLEMENTAL LIGHTS: TYPES OF LAMPS
MERCURY-VAPOR

Mercury-vapor lamps can be screwed into a standard incandescent light socket, yet they produce a lot of light. Mercury lamps are relatively inefficient in terms of usable light versus electrical consumption. Use mercury-vapor bulbs only to add light to a natural-light garden. Mercury vapor bulbs do produce a very high-intensity light compared to most bulbs that work in a standard light socket. The best bulb in terms of light-spectrum is the *Duro-test Fluomeric Safe-T-Vapor* lamp, because, as the name implies, the bulb is safe to use in home situations and the light spectrum is excellent for growing plants, whereas the light spectrum of other mercury-vapor lamps is quite poor. Wattages range from 160 watts up to 1,250 watts (although bulbs with wattages higher than 250 watts from Duro-test or Duro-lite may not be available by the time you read this). Buy mercury-vapor lamps with built-in reflective coatings, and mount them as you would a spotlight. The Fluomeric is an excellent bulb to supplement natural light, but any HID is more economical and a better light to use as a sole source of light. A 400-watt MH or HPS covers more area with considerably cheaper bulb-replacement costs.

For supplementing natural light, mercury-vapor lamps add much useful light, and when extending the photoperiod there is no shading from a bulky fixture. Installing the lamp is as simple as screwing it into a standard light socket. The disadvantages with mercury-vapor lamps are that they burn hot like a spotlight, and the area they illuminate is a smaller area than that from a comparable HID. For simply extending the photoperiod in a natural-light garden, any type of lamp will do. The new, low-wattage MH and HPS lamps in self-contained horizontal fixtures are cheaper than mercury-vapor lamps in the long run and actually, they're more effective in terms of plant growth. These self-contained minihorizontals are highly recommended for both minigardens and as supplemental lights.

CIRCULAR AND "U"-SHAPED FLUORESCENTS

Circular fluorescents need no special fixture to operate. They are self-ballasted and designed to operate in an incandescent socket (typical table-lamp socket). Hang them around the garden's perimeter or position them in stand-up lamps in standard light sockets. The wattages range from 20 to 44 watts and you should use the highest

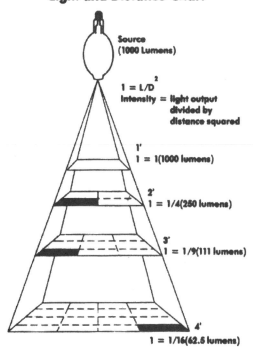

Light and Distance Chart

Source
(1000 Lumens)

$1 = L/D^2$
Intensity = light output divided by distance squared

1'
$1 = 1(1000$ lumens)

2'
$1 = 1/4(250$ lumens)

3'
$1 = 1/9(111$ lumens)

4'
$1 = 1/16(62.5$ lumens)

HIGH TECH, HIGH LIGHT
BY JORGE CERVANTES

One question that has been on the minds of indoor growers since they first saw HIGH TIMES' photographs of greenhouses and grow rooms from Holland is: How can the Dutch use 400-watt lamps and get the same results as American growers using 1,000-watt lamps? The answer is simple: horizontal orientation of the bulb and a small reflector. This setup is just that much more efficient.

Light is one of the five basic necessities a plant needs to grow. The other growth-inducing factors—air, water/nutrients, heat and a growing medium—are generally easy to learn about and easy to control. But only marginal information is available about light for the hobby gardener. Until recently, there was not much need to study light, but high-intensity discharge lamps have made the study of artificial light very popular.

How much light do plants need? Seedlings, clones and vegetative plants thrive at low-light levels: 500 to 1,500 footcandles. One grower uses a MS 1,000-watt super-metal-halide hung 4' above the plants in an 8' x 8' room to grow a very healthy crop.

Flowering, however, is another matter. Depending on variety, a light intensity of 1,000 to 2,500 footcandles is needed to produce healthy flowers.
#145, September 1987

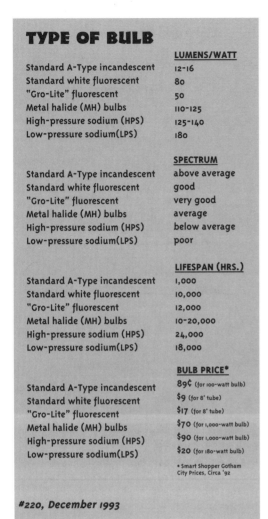

TYPE OF BULB

	LUMENS/WATT
Standard A-Type incandescent	12-16
Standard white fluorescent	80
"Gro-Lite" fluorescent	50
Metal halide (MH) bulbs	110-125
High-pressure sodium (HPS)	125-140
Low-pressure sodium (LPS)	180

	SPECTRUM
Standard A-Type incandescent	above average
Standard white fluorescent	good
"Gro-Lite" fluorescent	very good
Metal halide (MH) bulbs	average
High-pressure sodium (HPS)	below average
Low-pressure sodium (LPS)	poor

	LIFESPAN (HRS.)
Standard A-Type incandescent	1,000
Standard white fluorescent	10,000
"Gro-Lite" fluorescent	12,000
Metal halide (MH) bulbs	10-20,000
High-pressure sodium (HPS)	24,000
Low-pressure sodium (LPS)	18,000

	BULB PRICE*
Standard A-Type incandescent	89¢ (for 100-watt bulb)
Standard white fluorescent	$9 (for 8' tube)
"Gro-Lite" fluorescent	$17 (for 8' tube)
Metal halide (MH) bulbs	$70 (for 1,000-watt bulb)
High-pressure sodium (HPS)	$90 (for 1,000-watt bulb)
Low-pressure sodium (LPS)	$20 (for 180-watt bulb)

* Smart Shopper Gotham
City Prices, Circa '92

#220, December 1993

DIAGRAM OF A HALIDE LAMP

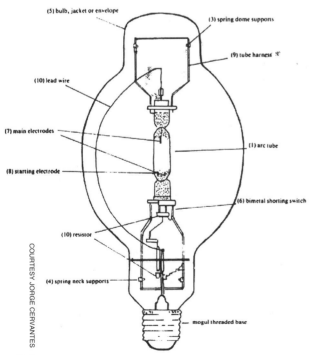

(5) bulb, jacket or envelope
(3) spring dome supports
(9) tube harness
(10) lead wire
(7) main electrodes
(1) arc tube
(8) starting electrode
(6) bimetal shorting switch
(10) resistor
(4) spring neck supports
mogul threaded base

COURTESY JORGE CERVANTES

wattage available (circular fluorescents over 22 watts need a special fixture). Usually growers use these bulbs to increase light during flowering, so the best, most common bulb to use is the Warm White, which is strong in the red band, the preferred light for flowering. Circular fluorescents are excellent for supplementing light or for extending the photoperiod in natural-light gardens, since they require no special fixtures and they shade little of the garden from natural light. Circular fluorescents take up little room and are inexpensive and easy to employ. A 44-watt GE Watt-Miser emits more light (lumens) than a 100-watt incandescent. Circular bulbs are about 16" in diameter for the largest (40 to 44-watt) size.

"U"-shaped fluorescents are much like circular fluorescents, but require a special fixture and ballast. Their only practical use is when the space available is restricted, although some growers use them to illuminate the lower branches in small gardens. Circular fluorescents are equally effective and are easier to set up. "U"-shaped fluorescents come in sizes from 25 to 40 watts; a 40-watt tube is nine inches wide and about two feet long. Circular lamps work better, since they require no special fixture, and their overall cost is much less.

LOW-PRESSURE SODIUM LAMPS

Low-pressure sodium lamps (LPS) are offered by a few distributors that advertise in marijuana publications. The LPS is the most efficient of all lamps in converting electricity to light. However the bulb is monochromatic: That is, it produces light in a single, narrow band at about 589 nanometers, in the orange part of the visible spectrum. Although its yellow/orange light is slightly outside of the desirable red part of the spectrum, its high output versus electrical consumption makes it a good performer as supplemental light. LPS lamps must only be used to supplement natural light, fluorescents or MH lamps. Plants elongate and grow abnormally when cultivated solely under LPS lamps.

The most popular sizes offered to marijuana growers are the 135- and 180-watt sizes manufactured by North American Phillips. These require an LPS fixture that looks somewhat like a slightly oversized four-foot fluorescent fixture. In any halide- or natural-light garden, a supplemental LPS very effectively adds much useful light near the red end of the spectrum to promote flowering.

An LPS has the unique property of maintaining the same lumen output throughout its lifetime. The bulb gives no indication of age before it suddenly ceases working after about 18,000 hours of use. Because the bulb contains sodium, be particularly cautious when using water near either an operating or a discarded bulb. Sodium explodes when it contacts water.

STANDARD AND PLANT-GRO INCANDESCENTS AND SPOTLIGHTS

Incandescents are the standard screw-in bulb that we're all familiar with. They are inefficient lamps, produce an unbalanced spectrum (mostly red, orange and yellow), are very hot and can burn the plants. Their advantages are that in a pinch, before you can set up other lights, they are cheap, easily found, and easy to set up on the perimeter of a garden.

Spotlights are actually focused incandescents. The spectrum is a slight improvement on incandescents. They also are very hot and can burn the plants.

"Plant-gro" versions of both incandescents and spotlights are available in garden shops. They are coated to improve the light spectrum for growing plants, but they still burn hot and are inefficient. Replace them with other supplemental lights, such as self-contained mini-HlDs, LPSs, circular fluorescents or mercury vapor lamps in any extended operation.

WHERE TO USE SUPPLEMENTAL LIGHTS

Use supplemental lights to extend the natural day length or to increase the light in natural-light gardens. Their advantages (except for "U"-shaped fluorescents and LPSs) are that they require no special fixture other than an ordinary light socket; they don't have a bulky fixture that shades natural light; they are lightweight and easy to hang or position around the perimeter of any garden. All of these lights work well enough as supplements, but MHs or HPSs and fluorescents work much better as sole sources of electric light.

TYPES OF BULBS AND THE LIGHT SPECTRUM

The white light of electric lamps consists of all the colors (wavelengths) of the visible spectrum (colors of the rainbow). Electric lights differ in the amount of light radiated in each color band: This gives them their characteristic color tone or degree of whiteness. For example, an incandescent bulb (common table lamp) generates mostly red, orange and yellow light but very little blue light; hence it appears orange/yellowish. White fluorescents have a more balanced spectrum, so they appear white. You can trust your eyes to tell you whether a bulb predominates in blue or red because it will have a bluish-white color or a softer, pinkish tone. A glance at a metal halide (MH) tells you that its spectrum favors blue because of its blue-white color. High Pressure Sodium vapor lamps (HPSs) appear pinkish-orange; their spectrum is much richer in the yellow, orange and red regions of the light spectrum.

Plants use light energy primarily in the blue and red regions of the light spectrum to carry on photosynthesis and chlorosynthesis, the two life processes that plants use to transform light energy into biochemical energy for growth. For healthy, normal growth, plants need adequate amounts of radiant energy in both the red and the blue regions of the light spectrum.

FLUORESCENT LAMPS (TUBES)

There are innumerable fluorescents manufactured for plant growth, vision and for special lighting effects. Since white light contains all the colors of the light spectrum, plants get some red and blue light from any white-light source. Plants actually use light of all colors to some degree, except for green light, which they reflect or transmit (this is why plants appear green).

To take advantage of the use of red and blue light by plants, Gro-Lux, Agro-lite and similar purple-looking "Plant-Gro tubes" were designed to emit primarily red and blue light. Much of the manufacturers' talk of plant growth and tube type (or spectrum) is simply hype. There are several less-expensive regular fluorescents manufactured by many companies that work at least as well as, if not better than, these Gro-tubes. Don't be swayed by manufacturers' claims. In practice, as long as the lamp produces sufficient red and blue light, the higher overall output (lumens) of white lamps more than compensates for their lesser output in the blue and red regions. Gro-lamps work well enough, but given the choice, choose those

AFGHANI STASH BUD

These buds were grown under a 175 MH and a 150-watt HPS. A variety of skunk, they were grown in about 5-1/2 months in a mix of potting soil, vermiculite and perlite. The seeds came from stash bud. They developed nice resin along with a stinky smell and killer buzz. I am not sure of the total yield because I kept snipping buds every few days and microwaving them.

Plants by Zigmond
Photo by Kerry S.
Eastern Massachusetts

#196, December 1991

FISHING FOR BULBS

MH and HPS light fixtures can be purchased at electrical-supply stores (if purchasing them at your local grow store poses problems). Look under "Lighting Fixtures—Retail" in your Yellow Pages.

To check soil acidity, pH 7.0 is neutral. pH meters may be purchased at pet stores or in the pet sections of some department stores. They are used for aquariums.

In addition, sterile aquarium gravel works well to add texture and break up heavy soil mixes.
#224, April 1994

ADAM'S INDOOR GARDEN

Pictured here are about 35 high-quality but unstable Kush, Northern Lights and Hash Plant crosses, growing under three 1,000-watt HIDs. It's a nice variety of potent ganja, and a great way to make use of attic crawl space.

High & Blind
New Hampshire

#221, January 1994

HOW TO TAKE PERFECT CUTTINGS

When I take cuttings I place them in small pieces of Styrofoam that have holes punctured in them for the stem to slip through. Then I let the stems and Styrofoam float in water and light them with 24 hours of fluorescent. After five days in water the cuttings are dipped in Rootone and gently placed in a medium of 75% fine vermiculite and 25% perlite.

After three days I apply a half-strength solution of Ortho Up-Start. In about two weeks the clone is ready for transplanting. I've rooted cuttings with one node and 1/16th-inch stem diameter.

I can also root clones from a mother plant without leaching high-nitrogen fertilizers. This method has given me a 100% survival rate with 60 clones.

Jim
Central Iowa

#138, February 1987

lamps recommended here since they'll work at least as well, are easier to find, last longer, and are usually much cheaper.

Manufacturers use standardized names, such as "Daylight" or "Warm White," to designate a fluorescent tube that has a certain degree of whiteness. Each name corresponds to a tube that emits a particular combination of light in each of the color bands. For example, "Daylight" emits more blue than red light, and appears blue-white. By matching a tube that predominates in blue light with a tube that emits more red light, the tubes complement each other and produce better plant growth than if either is used alone.

HIDS—METAL HALIDES (MH) AND SODIUM LAMPS (HPS)

Once you decide to use MH or HPS lamps, the next consideration is what bulb to buy. There are some small but noticeable differences in growth when comparing an MH, a super-MH or an HPS. MH bulbs may be coated, diffuse or clear. The coated bulbs have a slightly more natural light spectrum than clear bulbs, but the coating reduces their output by about five percent. For an MH garden, a clear super-MH gives the best overall results, because the plants grow slightly faster than under regular, coated or diffuse bulbs. The light output (total lumens) is far more important to the rate of growth than the particular spectrum.

HPS lamps emit more overall light (lumens) than any other bulb, but most of the energy is in the yellow, orange and red bands. Despite their unnatural light spectrum, HPS lamps give the best return for electrical and bulb costs. They're also relatively safe to use compared to MH lamps, and the initial set-up and the ongoing care of plants is easier under an HPS when compared to fluorescents. HPS lamps sometimes give inexperienced growers problems when starting seedlings, because the abundance of orange and red light causes seedlings to stretch or elongate toward the light. If this is a problem, position the lamp closer to the seedlings or use a small fluorescent system to start the seedlings, then move them under the HPS after about two to five weeks. The combination of a small fluorescent system to start seedlings and an HPS for growth and flowering is the best overall light setup you can buy. HPS bulbs emit about 25 to 50% more lumens of light than MHs, promote excellent flowering, and last about twice as long as MHs. They also can be mounted in the new horizontal reflectors, which increase the light directed to the plant by 20 to 45%. Overall, HPS lamps are your best buy and are your best performers except for starting seedlings and rooting clones.

HPS bulbs are less trouble if you are growing in an outbuilding that is susceptible or open to insect invasions. The yellow-orange color of an HPS does not attract night insects, whereas all white lights (all MHs) attract insects in droves.

Growers using several HID bulbs often balance the light spectrum by mixing HPS lamps and MH lamps, or by using HPS lamps only for flowering in rotating gardens. Preliminary scientific studies in England support this balancing. During foliar growth, the spectral distribution best for growth decreases in the following order: red, blue and yellow-green. During flowering, the decreasing order should be red, far-red, blue and yellow-green. The combination of an HPS with an MH gives additional red and far-red light to the overall spectrum for flowering.

KEEPING THE ELECTRIC BILL COOL

by D. Gold

Many indoor growers are justifiably concerned these days with keeping their electric bills as low as possible. This can be difficult with a growing operation utilizing multiple metal-halide or high-pressure sodium lights. A 1,000-watt light puts out almost as much heat as an electric space heater drawing the same amount of wattage. In many cases, the costs are not just reflected in the electricity to run the lights, but in the electricity necessary to keep the air temperature down within acceptable limits. This has usually meant that growers need to install expensive-to-operate air-conditioners. There are many solutions to the heat problem. Like the air-conditioner, some are simple—and expensive to set up and operate—and others are complicated, but inexpensive.

CONSTANT VENTILATION

If the grower is not providing CO_2 enrichment to his plants, heat build-up problems can usually be handled by leaving the exhaust fan running while the lights are on. This will remove the air that is heated by the lights before the temperature has a chance to rise. The air intake, of course, must receive air that is cooler than the desired temperature in the grow room.

In hot climates, the air outside the house may already be higher than the desired temperature. This situation can usually be overcome by running a reverse light-cycle—the plants receive their light during the hours when the sun is down, and are given their hours of darkness during the heat of the day. Another method is to draw the air into the grow room from the coolest room in the house. This is usually the basement or the first floor in a two-story house.

When CO_2 enrichment is added, the situation becomes much more complicated. No practical form of CO_2 enrichment will allow the grower to achieve and maintain the desired CO_2 levels when the air is being constantly exchanged for fresh outside air. Providing the high levels of CO_2 and keeping the air temperature within the desired parameters can get difficult and expensive for growers utilizing HID lights.

Installing an air-conditioner is a quick and simple fix for many heat build-up problems. Simply put one in the window, set the vent on closed position so that the CO_2-laden air is recycled, and set the thermostat to turn the device on at 95 degrees. Most larger growers don't seem to mind the initial cost, considering the benefits. But those monthly electric bills can become real worriers.

SENSIBLE USE OF THE AIR-CONDITIONER

There are some climates and conditions where an air-conditioner is just about the only method possible to keep the temperature down to desired levels. Even so, there are a number of steps that can be taken to keep the conditioner's electrical use to a minimum. Here's a few of them:

1. Run a reverse light-cycle. After ascertaining that the grow room is absolutely free of light leaks during the daylight hours, set the lights to

GROW-ROOM VENTILATION

BY PROFESSOR AFGHANI

In many grow rooms, ventilation systems are vastly deficient. A good supply of fresh air is a prerequisite for any Victory Garden, so installing the right-capacity ventilation system is essential to growing a quality indoor crop.

All systems require intake and exhaust, as well as automated controls. The materials needed to install the system may be purchased from indoor garden centers, electrical supply houses and hardware stores. Dayton™ exhaust blowers, axial fans, switches and air circulators are rated for continuous duty and, in my opinion, are the best bet for any serious growing operation. Items such as roof ventilators and shuttered-gable fans are occasionally used as exhausts in remote or private areas. A thermostat and a humidistat are used for atmospheric control.

In most designs, air intake is located at the floor level of a room corner, and the exhaust is found at the ceiling level of the diagonally opposite corner. Within many grow chambers is a smaller, enclosed propagation room, which is continuously lit for cloning and vegetative growth. In such cases, a pair of 5" or 8" axial fans are deployed in the same fashion so the atmosphere of the smaller enclosure is the same as that of the larger flowering room. The latter discharges the old air outside. However, separate controls are needed.

Intakes can be either passive (unpowered) or active (fan-driven). Active is the more efficient method and usually accomplished with an axial fan wired to run simultaneously with the exhaust fan. Clothes-dryer exhaust hoods are very discreet intake ports. Ideal locations are under staircases, crawl spaces and behind heavy hedges. Some applications allow drawing fresh air from the interior of the house. If the light from a grow lamp noticeably beams out of the intake port, then a shadow box should be installed on one side or the other, preferably inside. It can be crafted from a cardboard box. Additionally, attaching a disposable filter to the intake will help control unwanted pests.

A squirrel-cage-type industrial blower fan is often used to power exhaust. The ultimate in discretion is an existing or new roof-level chimney, because it provides an outlet for odors that is clear overhead. The odor-control aspect of overhead exhaust makes it really worth the effort. If structural design or costs prohibit placing the exhaust outlet in a chimney, then crawl spaces, attics, casement windows, under stairs and even garages, cellars or other rooms can be substituted.

A final word on odor control: Incorporate multiple negative ion-generators, time-dispensed aerosol fragrance and scores of plug-in style air fresheners.

#221, January 1994

BLOOMING TECHNIQUES

BY JORGE CERVANTES

There are five basic blooming techniques common indoors: perpetual harvest, short plants, tall plants, pruning to a central bud or into a bush and second harvests or rejuvenation. Timing is essential to a successful "perpetual harvest." Every day one or more clones are taken and one or more plants are harvested. There is never a bare spot underneath a lamp. If you want to go on vacation, or plan to be away from home for more than three days, a perpetual harvest is not for you. In the "short plant' flowering technique, also referred to as Sea of Green, clones are induced to flower when they are 6" to 18" tall. The "tall plant" technique is the same as the short plant, except that the plants are induced to flower when they are about three feet tall. Lazy and busy growers appreciate this productive method because it requires less care. Huge "central buds" are easy to grow on short or tall plants. Simply prune off lower or spindly branches. This will concentrate flower growth on the central branch. Pruning into a "bush" or "pinching back" promotes more and smaller buds. Snipping off growing tips diffuses floral hormones and may retard flowering somewhat unless done two weeks before moving the plant. Producing a "second crop" is inexpensive and convenient, but not as productive as starting with a fresh crop of clones. The mature buds of the plant are clipped off and the lower leaves are left on the plant. There are two variations: lower branches are left unshaded to grow larger flowers for a couple of weeks, or, remove almost all foliage and set back the photoperiod to promote vegetative growth. It will take about a month for the female to rejuvenate and produce leafy growth.

#134, October 1986

go on when the sun goes down, and go off when the air heats up in the morning. This schedule permits the use of the cooler night air to help cool the grow room.

2. Try running the air-conditioner in the "fan only" cycle during the night. Make sure that the air being circulated by the fan is being drawn from inside the grow room, and not outside. The air loses heat when it is drawn through the conditioner's cooling fins, and the CO_2-laden air in the grow room is not diluted with fresh air from outside. Most conditioners provide a "closed" cycle which will permit this type of operation. Even without the compressor running or the exchange of any outside air, this technique can be very effective in removing a lot of heat from the air.

3. Increase the frequency of exhaust/CO_2 injection cycles. For example, a grower who regularly exhausts for seven minutes once each hour found that his air-conditioner came on about 20 minutes after the completion of the exhaust cycle. The air-conditioner bounced off and on until the next exhaust cycle.

Simply by changing to three shorter exhaust/injection cycles per hour, the grower was able to keep the temperature low enough that the air-conditioner never came on again. Although the amount of CO_2 use tripled, the savings in electricity was considered to be well worth the extra CO_2 cost and effort, and the lowered humidity caused by more frequent exhaust/injection cycles was a real bonus.

4. Increase the internal circulation to a virtual blast with strong fans. (Trellis and add supports to the plants if necessary to hold them upright. The additional support may also be needed in the fruiting or flowering phase.) Pay special attention to vertical (floor-to-ceiling) air circulation.

5. Consider drawing the air from a cooler area. In a two-story house, the first floor remains much cooler during the day than the air in the upstairs. The basement or crawlspace below the house has the coolest air of all.

6. One grower buried a network of four-inch sewer pipes and drew his incoming air from these pipes. The air was ten degrees cooler than the air entering the intake. (Be certain to screen the intake to prevent against dust and pests. There could also be a mold problem with this arrangement.)

7. The location of the outside air intake can be very important in determining the temperature of the air that comes into the room. A cool north side of a house shaded by trees will provide much cooler air than an intake just under the roofline on a side that remains in constant sunshine.

SWAMP COOLERS

No, not Bartles & Jaymes's newest concoction designed to bring back those steamy nights by the Black Lagoon, a swamp cooler is a name for an *evaporative* cooler. This is a device that cools the air by circulating water over cedar pads and drawing a high volume of air through the wet pads. The evaporation effect draws a lot of heat from the air. The problem is that some water is put into the air.

Swamp coolers work best in dry climates. That is where they are most often used, in lieu of air-conditioning. In dry areas the humidity occasionally stays down in the teens during the hot months. The cool air coming from the swamp cooler can be quite low in humidity if the air entering the cooler is relatively dry.

"BROKEN" AIR-CONDITIONER

An air-conditioner that has the compressor unit broken or disconnected can still be of considerable benefit to the grower in a heat-overload situation. The warm air of the grow room is circulated through the cooling fins of the air conditioner's refrigeration unit, just as in normal operation but without the compressor operating. Although the fins are not as cold as when the energy-sucking compressor is operating, the outside air keeps them much cooler than the grow-room air that is circulating through them, and they remove a good bit of heat from the air. By operating the conditioner in the unvented position, no CO_2 is lost to the outside air, and no outside air is drawn into the grow room to dilute the CO_2-laden air.

The effectiveness of this method has been demonstrated by a 180-cubic-foot grow room running two 1,000-watt HPS horizontal lights. (The ballasts were placed in another room, and did not add to the heat in the grow room.) Despite a Californian location, the air conditioner never had to actually run—other than the fan. And this was in an upstairs apartment, during the summer months.

In the case of an air-conditioner with a broken fan, as well as an inoperable compressor, the unit can still be used in this manner, simply by directing a squirrel-cage blower into the air-conditioner's normal intake. Remember, the air outside the window in which the air-conditioner is sitting must be cooler than the incoming air in order for much heat exchange to take place. A fan directed over the conditioner's cooling fins will help the process. A method for misting or dripping water on the conditioner's cooling fins will help even more.

REMOTE CONDITIONING

The "broken" air-conditioner concept can work well in a situation where the air-conditioner is located in a window, but some distance from the grow room. In one particular case, the grow chamber was a small cubicle built against an inside upstairs wall in an apartment. The air-conditioner was placed in the window in the normal manner, and a wooden enclosure was made for the front of the conditioner. Four-inch insulated tubing was used to direct the air to and from the air-conditioner to the grow room, which was about six feet away. The only power supplied was a small squirrel-cage fan, which provided a positive displacement of air through the cooling fins. The temperature usually dropped about 10 degrees after the air was run through the cooler.

COOL THE LIGHTS—NOT THE ROOM

It is a simple matter to separate the lights themselves from the growing area. One grower using a three-light Sun Circle in a small room simply installed a plate-glass partition right below the lights and above the plants. This, in effect, created two separate microclimates within the room. Constant ventilation cooled the area above the glass using a small squirrel-cage fan, and the area below the glass was exhausted for several minutes each hour and immediately re-injected with CO_2. Before installation of the glass "heat barrier," it was necessary to run an air-conditioner almost constantly. The cost of installing the glass false ceiling and running the small vent fan used to cool the chamber housing the lights was far less than the previous cost of running the air-conditioner.

Another method of cooling the lights can be adapted to stationary

JAMAICAN INDICA

This plant is six weeks old and is grown with two metal halides in an 8' x 10' room in a trailer. Some *indica* and Jamaican.

John of Kentucky

#106, June 1984

WATER QUALITY

I have read a number of articles on grow rooms. They seem thorough for the most part, covering lighting systems, air, temperature and humidity controls and growing mediums. However, most of the articles do not address water quality.

Both city and well water often contain contaminants that affect plant growth. Grow books often suggest letting water sit to remove chlorine. But what about the other impurities, such as organics and chloramines, phosphate complexes and undissolved solids?

I use a water-filtration system that removes them all. First the water is run through a roughing cartridge called an ion-exchange absorber, then through the filter. My small system can purify water at the rate of five gallons per hour. The cartridges last about six months and are disposable. This assures me high-quality water by removing all the impurities and leaving the water with a pH of 7—neutral.

With these systems it is wise to use a reservoir to hold enough water for the system. The container should be made of dark plastic so light does not filter through, which would encourage the growth of algae.

A Satisfied Grower
Rockford, Illinois

#138, February 1987

THREE INDOOR TIPS

Roll-up reflective walls. Flat white window shades, when mounted on frames, make very nice reflective walls that easily roll up out of the way for viewing or spraying of plants. They can be purchased inexpensively at resale or thrift shops.

Seed-germinating aid. Poke a one-inch hole in soil, fill halfway with vermiculite. Place seed in hole and fill hole with vermiculite. It helps retain moisture and is a light, porous surface for the seedling to break through.

Soil mixer. A large round garbage can with trash bag placed inside. Roll the can back and forth to mix the soil.

SH, Des Plaines, IL

 # 103, March 1984

horizontal lights. Simply by mounting a sheet of glass over the bottom of the reflector and attaching a small computer-cooling fan and an intake and exhaust duct made from any type of flexible or rigid tubing, the air surrounding the bulb can be constantly exchanged for cool fresh air from outside the grow room, without affecting the CO_2-laden air in which the plants are growing. It takes only a couple of watts to run the small computer fans, and sometimes several thousand watts to run an air-conditioner. Some growers may want to hook the intake or exhaust tube up to a larger squirrel-cage blower or other type of fan. Any type of reliable fan or blower that will pass a constant flow of fresh air through the reflector will do the job. Note: Until someone places a unit such as this one on the market—which shouldn't be long after this is printed—home inventors should engage in careful monitoring of the temperatures created by the alterations to the lighting system. Remember that fire can be the indoor grower's greatest threat.

D. Gold has been known to regular readers of this magazine since its inception—his classic book on alchemy has been advertised in virtually every issue. Numerous references to the book have appeared in HIGH TIMES over the years, the most recent in the series of vaporization articles by Dr. Lunglife. After having briefly lapsed out of print, this classic is once again available.

The above article was excerpted from D. Gold s new book entitled CO_2, Temperature, Ventilation, Humidity, & Odor Control *from a new series entitled* The Maximizer/Problem Solver Series. *Unlike other books which concentrate on the science of indoor growing, the books in this new series concentrate on applications—ways to put the science to practical use.*

EXTRA-HEAVY BUDS

By using a lower-phosphorus (P) flowering formula, or by mixing a percentage of growth-nutrient formula in a high-P nutrient formula, one gets a midbloom formula. Hydro-grown plants will take an extra two weeks to mature, but will have a heavier yield and pistil formation growing in layers, rather than forming and then dying back.

Another way to use P control is to use the lower-P mixture when the clones are first placed in the flowering room, until the crop is the desired height. Then switch to a formula such as 3-35-10. Then include calcium nitrate for extra calcium: extra calcium for extra-heavy buds and the nitrate for continued good health of growing older growth.

High Tech Party Hot Line
Rochester, New York

#144, August 1987

PART 4
OUTDOOR CULTIVATION

GUIDE TO INDOOR-GROWING PRODUCTS

HIGH TIMES

MARCH 1984   USA $3.25
                                                    CANADA $3.95

THE EMPIRE STATE
STRIKES BACK

Look Out, California,
Here Comes New York's Finest!

IS IT HER OR IS IT HER COKEAROMA?
HARVARD'S FIRST POT PARTY·COCAINE NAZIS ON TRIAL
SECRETS OF THE UFOs REVEALED

COMPACT GROWING FOR HIGHEST YIELD

HIGH TIMES

Field of Dreams
SWEET HOME MARIJUANA
BY GENE CHRISTIAN

Would
YOU
lick this
toad?

AMAZONIA
Shamanic plants
& medicines
BY PETER GORMAN

CLINTONGATE
Guns & Coke in Arkansas
BY BILL WEINBERG

GREEN DAY These kids are alright

THE FIELD OF DREAMS

BY GENE CHRISTIAN

As I rolled into Jack "The Dirt Farmer's" driveway, I was greeted by a mad assortment of dogs, cats and chickens, all grunting and yelping for my attention. Nature and open space are two things we don't get in the Big Apple and I immediately was put on the defensive. I imagined at any moment some grizzly bear eight feet tall was going to emerge from the woods and beat me over the head with a blunt object. I rang the bell, and before I even had a chance to say "hello," Jack grabbed me and gave me a big bear hug. This is it, I thought, this guy's gonna have me squealing like a pig before sundown.

Jack must have noticed the desperate, road-weary and underpaid look in my eye because he steered me straight to the plants.

Sometimes enlightenment can be the product of years and years of concentration, experience and meditation, and other times it comes to you in one blinding, emotional second. When I saw those plants, I felt like Ben Franklin must have as the lightning traveled down the string of his kite and lit his balls up like Christmas ornaments.

"Forgive me Father, for I have sinned!" I cried out, seeing the folly of my cosmopolitan ways. "I have seen the promised land!" Hundreds and hundreds of green and purple *indica* plants stood before me, all lined in rows, imparting upon the air the sweet smell of purple lollipops. Now maybe I'm just stupid, but suddenly my fear of imprisonment vanished. I felt as though I were standing in a sanctuary, a little piece of Eden that God spared for himself and then forgot about.

#233, January 1995

THE SECRET GARDEN

by George Lassen

Violence is the last refuge of the incompetent.
—Salvor Hardin

In order to succeed in growing pot, you must carefully plan for the security and concealment of your garden. You must make it a secret garden. The trouble with many secret gardens is that the people who have them do not keep them secret. The one rule to follow is, "Don't tell nobody nothing nohow—no matter what!" Time and time again I have seen one too many people told about a garden and then about one day before the harvest some rip-off artist gets the plants. Your hard work goes up in somebody else's smoke. You have to be content with the deep inner satisfaction that comes with growing good plants and a successful harvest. So don't talk about it. Keep it a secret.

A good way to handle the secrecy is to keep the information between you and your spouse or partner, and do all the work yourself. Now, in some cases this is not possible. For example, if you did everything right and you have a bumper crop, you might need to get some help drying and trimming. In a situation like this you still do not need to let anybody know the location of the garden, because you will want to grow there next year. You can farm out some of the trimming or take it to another location.

If an outside partner is necessary, be careful. Problems with partners are the rule rather than the exception, the most common being laziness. There are more stories about nonperforming partners than any others. Resolve all differences early, and be very clear about any sharing of the harvest. You cannot easily put this type of agreement into writing, but that is about the only way to keep things straight. A growing partnership is like a marriage. If you don't genuinely like or respect your partner, it's going to be a long time until harvest. More partnerships fail than succeed.

After you see how much work it is to set up a garden, you will probably want to be able to use it for several years. There are many days of work involved in setting up a proper garden. Also, it usually takes a year to work the bugs out of a new garden, or learn the ropes if you are a new gardener.

SELECTING A SITE

Secret gardens can be almost any place. An outside garden is very tricky. The spot must receive adequate sun for the plant to grow well, and you must be able to get water and fertilizer to the location, but must be almost totally invisible from the air and difficult to stumble across by accident on the ground. I say "almost" because it is very difficult to be completely invisible from a helicopter.

Sunlight may be the most important element in growing large, robust plants (assuming adequate soil and water are provided). Of course, the lack of any key element will limit the size of harvested plants. Similar gardens, differing only in the amounts of sunlight, consistently show the garden with more light producing bigger, bushier plants.

It really pays to spend some time walking around looking for all aspects of your location. For security reasons you must pay particular attention to the air. If you have 100 degrees of clear view from any direction, you are likely to be busted or ripped off. Less than 50 degrees is much better.

Surveillance aircraft look mostly on south-facing slopes and along naturally occurring streams. Their logic is correct. These places are the most desirable and will produce the largest plants with the least work. Think one or two steps ahead of the law and rip-offs. Avoid these likely spots, or use them with care.

For just a minute close your eyes and think of yourself as a lawman flying over the countryside, looking for pot gardens to bust. You have been doing this for five years, and you know exactly what you are looking for... OK! Did that scare you a little? Now when you go out there, keep that in mind with every step you take. Go the lawman one better. Dress up a little so you look neat, rent an airplane, load up the Pentax with high-speed film, and take about 50 (or more) photos of the area. Before seeking a pilot, get a map of the area nearby and locate your property. Then mark out some land that is nearby, but not touching yours.

Tell the pilot that you are thinking of buying some property and want to look at it from the air. Take out your maps and show the pilot the premarked area. Then direct the pilot to fly all around the area. Do this only in the winter or very early spring or you run the risk of upsetting other growers. They may even shoot you.

I know a couple of honest growers in my local area who will scout out and photograph an area in ultralite aircraft for their customers. They charge for this service, and it is well worth the price for the extra piece of mind.

Now, if you really want to scare yourself, fly back over your spots in the fall when the crop is mature and see what the plants are like when they are six to 10 feet tall.

There are almost as many ways and places to grow as there are growers. In the last few years the law has been increasingly successful at finding marijuana gardens. As they refine their techniques, they will probably do even better.

Smaller gardens are harder to find (and hopefully not worth the trouble to bust). Many growers have taken to setting up plots that have only 10 to 20 plants. They may have several of these small plots scattered over a large area to keep a low profile.

Another approach is to scatter one- and two-plant minigardens over the countryside, taking maximum advantage of all natural cover. This is becoming increasingly popular and highly successful. There is a lot more work to it with fencing and water lines, but the results are worth it. A single plant with natural cover all around is extremely difficult to see, and this has proven to be the best method of concealing a garden.

Many growers who want only two or three plants for their own use will plant in their vegetable gardens. They surround their marijuana with corn, sunflowers, staked tomatoes and pole beans. Then they bend and tie down all the branches of the marijuana plant to make it look like a low bush. It works. People don't see it.

Then there are the somewhat more unconventional ways. One grower filled the bed of a tired old pickup truck with a high-powered soil mix and planted in the truck. He had a two-way radio, and whenever he heard that the law was in his area, or when he heard low-flying

HAZE HYBRID

After growing 'ghanis for so many years, this Haze hybrid is a refreshing change. This plant yielded a half-pound indoors.

BC
Jackson Hole, WY

#216, August 1993

GERMINATING SEEDS

First, find a place to plant, preferably a few miles from town. Don't plant in your backyard. I've known too many people busted for growing there. Till the ground, add nutrients and soak it with water. Plant the seeds and cover with clear plastic. Hold down the plastic edges with rocks, branches or gravel. Cover the plastic lightly with leaves or other foliage to keep the plastic from being seen from the air.

The plastic becomes a mini-greenhouse. It keeps the seeds moist so that watering is required less frequently. It also keeps birds from pecking the seeds. In 7-10 days the seedlings are up and going, remove the plastic and pack it out.

Chief Little Buzz
Brighton, Colorado

#163, March 1989

GERMINATING SEEDS

BY DARYL

Go through the seeds and pick out the strongest, healthiest looking ones. Put the seeds into a ziplock baggie with a clean white wash rag that has been soaked in warm water and treated with Nitron A-35. Do not squeeze water out of the rag. A 6" sandwich baggie is large enough for 100 seeds. A 10" baggie is good for up to 300 seeds.

Blow air into the baggie and seal. (If you smoke cigarettes or have a cold, do not blow air into the baggie—your seedlings will die. I've also experimented with putting pure Co2 into the baggie, but this killed seedlings.) Place the baggie in a warm spot. The top of a refrigerator works well. Do not place the baggie in direct sunlight. It will be too warm and the seedlings may rot. Most will germinate in two or three days, but there are strains that take up to two weeks.

After the seedlings have germinated, let them grow for a few days until they are one or two inches long. Open the corner of the baggie, suck all the air out and reseal. The seedlings can now be placed in your refrigerator, where they will stay in suspended animation until you are ready to plant. Seedlings can be stored like this up to two months without any harm. However, if germinated seedlings are not stored in a vacuumed baggie, they will continue to grow. My experience has been that seedlings placed in the refrigerator for a few days grow better than plants not given this treatment.

#172, December 1989

aircraft, he moved the truck from the full sunlight that the plant normally enjoyed to a very secluded spot. His vigilance paid off in a successful harvest.

Other growers have planted their entire crop in trees. They put a container in a tree or find a hollowed-out stump, fill it with high-powered fertilizer and let Mother Nature take over. Tree planting has one big plus: Almost no predators can climb up here to eat the grass. This system does work, but it is more work than most people want to do. Watering seems to be the biggest problem.

Whenever possible it helps to plant your crop with evergreens to the north and sunlight to the south. This helps to hide your garden and still provides good sunlight for growth. The fact that these trees are of a similar color and big enough to break up the view has helped hundreds of growers. I know one fellow who crawls through acres of manzanita and clears a spot for each plant far away from any other. These plants are hidden so that they are almost impossible to see. Many growers are hiding their crops in young oak forests with regular, but not dense, coverage.

These people do lose a little in production because of reduced sunlight, but they more than make up for it in peace of mind. They will cut down a few trees and trim selected branches to let in the required light. The freshly trimmed stumps and branch ends are painted black so they will blend into the natural cover and be hard to see. This approach has been very successful. Planting in this way can still yield a half-pound per plant—more if it is well tended.

Some growers have been experimenting with locating their plots on other than south- or southwest-facing slopes. This seems to work if you are not too far down a slope. It is important that the plants get at least eight hours of sun each day. Note the location of the sun in the early part of November. If it is still a few degrees above the horizon on about the 10th of November at 4:00 PM, you probably have enough sun for a successful crop.

Water lines are a dead giveaway to any secret garden. There are no statistics on how many gardens have been busted because of water lines seen from the air, but it is one of the easiest things to spot, and ridiculously easy to follow on the ground. Most growers will bury their lines if they plan on using the same patch for several years. Another, more time-consuming, method is to move the lines each time the crop needs to be watered.

No matter how you deal with this problem, remember that your water lines must be as secret as your garden. This goes double for your water tanks. A water tank will almost always be visible from the air. Careful placement is a must. If the tank can be located near a regular garden or dwelling or some other structure, it may look like it belongs there and avoid unnecessary attention. On the other hand, if your garden is spotted and the water lines are followed back to the tank by your house, you might find yourself in a bit of a bind.

Look for heavy natural camouflage and add to it. The only real way to take care of hiding the entire water system is to plan months ahead. All of the digging and hiding should be done early in the rainy season. That way Mother Nature will help to cover what you do by dropping more leaves and twigs. In the spring new growth will jump up all around, covering whatever is there. Use anything that is lying around to hide the system: broken tree limbs, dead brush, and rotting logs, whatever you can find. Be imaginative. Avoid straight lines and clumps of things mounded together. Make everything blend with nature.

Keep in mind that some rip-off artists are just as sophisticated as the law. They fly their own planes for spotting and come in with four-wheel drives, bolt cutters and semiautomatic weapons. I don't say things like this to scare you, but unfortunately they are part of reality. If you don't know about them and plan accordingly, you may be in trouble. I know many growers who keep a full-time armed guard on their crops the last few weeks before harvest. They disappear if the law shows up, but they shoot at thieves.

It truly saddens me that this wonderful and useful herb has taken on such a disturbing cloak of violence and greed. In the last two years, in the Great Northwest alone, there have been at least three deaths directly connected with the growing of marijuana and a number of other beatings and shootings. Remember, the bigger the crop, the bigger the problems.

SECURITY

Security must be one of your major considerations in selecting your garden site. One little slip to the wrong person and your garden is gone forever! The first principle of security is to keep anyone from finding out about your garden. The second is to keep animals from destroying it.

Do not protect your garden by booby-trapping it! I believe that it is wrong to hurt people who may accidentally stumble across your secret garden.

If you are growing on public land, or huge private timber holdings, the risk of discovery just goes with the territory. The act of hurting someone while you are growing on land that does not even belong to you is not acceptable. In fact, violence of any kind should be avoided. I do believe that it is right to take steps necessary to stop a thief from ripping you off. But it's best to exercise caution.

A dog is one of the best security devices you can find. A *big* dog! Two dogs are even better. One at each end of the garden. Dogs make a lot of noise, strike fear in the hearts of all animals and send most two-legged predators on their way.

I know one grower who has dogs staked throughout his garden. They are chained in such a way as to overlap. He uses no fences and has no deer problems. People stay away, too. I heard of someone who built high, strong fences all around their garden and put in some big cats—three full-grown Bengal tigers and a leopard. That's fine, but imagine the food bill. The law had no trouble finding them because the operation was so big.

Another popular security device is an item called a Ripstopper. This is a commercial item that uses a radio transmitter to send out a wireless signal to a beeper device carried by the grower. The item uses a trip-wire switch and/or a motion sensor. The alarm will sound even if the wires are cut. The Ripstopper will send an alarm in a line-of-sight transmission of up to half a mile (or more if the power supply is modified). This may not seem like much, but if it frees you to do other things within that range, it's worth it. A grower told me that, after sitting in his garden with a gun for two weeks, he could not stand it. He bought a Ripstopper. It sells for about $250 and comes with one motion sensor. You provide the batteries.

Some people build their own with greater range and much reduced cost.

Sometimes good karma alone will get you through. I heard a story about a grower with 15 plants way out in the middle of nowhere. This person went out to check his garden one day during the fall when his

BACKYARD BUDS

This first generation Mexican produced 1-3/4 lbs. the first harvest and three-quarters of a pound the second harvest, a month and a half later. This plant was never transplanted or pruned, nor did it have its green sun leaves removed. The leaves received full sun and the benefits of wind protection from an eight-foot walled-in backyard. Plastic tarps were erected to protect the plants from the three rains we had in the fall.

The plant grew in well-composted, aerated soil which was enriched with pumice, rabbit and chicken manure, bloodmeal, bone meal, egg shells, dolomite lime, worm castings and worms—all added the previous winter. A small helping of rabbit manure, blood meal and bone meal was added three weeks before planting with an inch of sandy top soil layered on top.

I started the garden with roughly 1,500 seedlings, thinning down to eight main females and a few transplanted females to fill in around the perimeter. Favorable males were put in pots and stunted for use in hand-pollinating. Ground growing area was 12 by 15 feet. Except for a couple of sprayings with diluted liquid seaweed to keep the bugs in check during the vegetative stage, there were no organic or chemical fertilizers added after the plants were started. I watered slow and deep only when plants showed first signs of wilt, ideally the day before.

Around the Wild Animal Park
San Diego, CA

#117, May 1985

DEER PATH TIPS

I've planted outdoors for a couple of years near well-traveled white-tail deer paths. To keep the animals away from my plants I use a 3-4' stick with a bar of Irish Spring soap tied to it for each plant. It's scent is long-lasting. I haven't lost a single leaf. I also urinate near the plants to give the area a human smell.

Mr. Enjoy
Weirton, West Virginia

#167, July 1989

DURBAN POISON

This is one of three tops on a pure Durban plant. It's my second-generation seed purchased from the Dutch.

This plant was started under lights, then sexed and rejuvenated. It was planted outside in the second week of June. The plant never completely reverted to vegetative growth as did its sisters. It matured small floral clusters all season, and was harvested the first week of September.

P.T. McBud
Monmouth, NJ

#191, July 1991

AVOID TRANSPLANT SHOCK

To prevent transplant shock, use peat pots for starting plants. They are available at department stores in the garden section. Made of peat moss, the pots are available in 10 compartment trays and 2-1/4" and 3" diameter pots. You simply grow the plant in the peat pot until you are ready to transplant, then plant the pot itself. Peat moss is biodegradable, and the roots grow right through it while the pot eventually disintegrates.

J. B.
Michigan

#235, March 1995

garden was in full flower but still three to four weeks away from harvest. He was shocked to the point of panic when he saw fresh horse poop and two sets of horse prints within ten feet of his plants. He spent the next 48 hours guarding his plants with a borrowed .357 magnum and 50 rounds of ammunition, all the time freaking out, thinking that there was no way he could ever shoot someone, and wondering what he would do if a thief showed up...armed?

After two days of this justified paranoia, he went home and went to bed for a much-needed rest. He let go...and, beyond belief, he harvested all 15 plants. This person obviously led a charmed life, and the odds of that ever happening again are beyond calculation.

Harvest can be a nerve-wracking time. However, often just the signs that "somebody's home" will be enough to stop rip-offs. With gates, fences, dogs, people, etc., you must stop other people from seeing the garden. If it is not seen, it will not have to be defended.

Camouflage

Keeping your garden hidden means making the maximum use of whatever natural cover you have available, and supplementing it where necessary. Always consider the need for camouflage with each step you take in developing your garden. Strive to maintain harmony with the surrounding environment.

Black plastic bags are highly visible from the air. If this type of container is used, it must be painted with earth-tone colors. Black plastic is shiny and reflects light as well as being a solid color that is not in harmony with the environment. There is a company in Northern California that makes a camo sleeve to fit over a 15-gallon plastic bag, but spray paint is cheaper, faster and more reliable.

Many farmers wear clothing that blends in with the environment. They avoid bright solid colors that stand out and are easy to spot from a distance. Some growers even go so far as to buy special camouflage clothing and hats from army surplus or specialty stores.

Trails in the woods need special consideration. Do not make obvious trails that lead directly to your garden. Tramping over the same path carrying hundreds of pounds of amendments will beat down vegetation and become highly visible from the ground or the air. Paths that run along forest edges or through the forest itself are hard to see. Go out of your way to avoid open spaces. Use rocks or fallen trees to walk on whenever possible. Trails that go up and down a hill are more difficult to see from the ground than trails that go laterally along the contour of the land. One grower goes downhill to about 100 feet below and off to one side of the garden and then makes a kind of sharp V-shaped turn back up the hill to the plot. If you have a fence, place the gate in an obscure location. Somewhere in the shade or surrounded by high bushes is best.

There is a type of camouflage netting, made out of nylon, that some growers have used. It is very light-weight and lets a lot of light through the mesh. Unfortunately, from the air this stuff stands out like a sore thumb. The idea was to copy the tactics used in warfare to hide the crop. Forget it! Those people were not interested in letting in light, and their methods were much different. This stuff only fools ducks.

There is one use that has worked. Hiding trails. The camouflage material is rolled out along a path. Dirt, leaves and twigs are then scattered along its length.

When talking about growing marijuana at our local fertilizer store, irrigation equipment company, etc., many growers will talk about

tomato plants instead of pot. Nobody is fooled by this ploy, but you will quickly find out if the other person is sympathetic to your cause by the way they act. And tomatoes (except for the fact that they are acid-loving) have many of the same biological needs. Many store owners and clerks love to play this game with you, so take advantage of the situation if it comes along. Some of them may even have a plant or two out on the south 40.

Do be careful of the other possibility, that the clerk may be an agent of the DEA. I have never heard of this happening, but there is always a first time. Sting operations are not new. I know of two or three suppliers who carefully screen all prospective employees before hiring just to reduce the chance of this happening. Most suppliers want to protect your privacy because it means dollars in their pockets. And dollars are dwindling with the increased success of the law in finding gardens and growers getting out of the business. One nonagricultural businessman told me that his business has dropped off 25 to 40% due to reduced marijuana farming. He does not like marijuana and has never used it, but he likes to make money. Marijuana does have a positive impact on the local economies in the areas where it is grown, especially where there are many small growers. One clerk was arrested for selling seeds after repeated requests from an agent posing as a grower.

BUD IN THE SUN

This picture was taken in the late afternoon and I could feel the energy that the bud absorbed from sitting in the sun all day. Needless to say, this was pretty powerful, with a real high high!

Anonymous, USA

#104, April 1984

COVERT CULTIVATION:
Outdoor Growing Hints From A Confirmed Sneak

by Dr. Lunglife

Hidden, unexplored wooded areas are great for hiking and planting. Here are a few tips on how to select a location for a secret garden.

Whether I walk, cycle, drive or fly, I find likely spots or secret gardens on almost every trip. There are many remote locations where cannabis can grow to her full glory—but consider that if you keep your plants no taller than shoulder-high, they'll be difficult to detect in a multitude of places, many within walking distance of your home.

It gives me hope to see that it is impossible to end our freedom to grow cannabis. American ingenuity will always overcome oppressive laws, although many people continue to get hurt by marijuana prohibition. It makes sense to grow it yourself. You may not get the best sinse, but the price is right.

In this article there are six types of outdoor locations suggested for covert cultivation: deep woods; vacant semiwooded land by roads, power lines, railroad tracks or gas lines; lakeshores and riverbanks; among swamps or wetlands; and by vacant buildings or abandoned city land.

WHY PLANT OUTDOORS?

As you are well aware, the current law prohibits the growing of cannabis for either hemp or marijuana purposes. The penalties for growing

MR. BUD

The setup that I have outdoors now gives me total control of watering without me being there to do the work. I use a gravity flow system from a creek. An irrigation pipe is placed in a creek that is at least 15 to 20 feet higher than the garden area. A transistor battery-operated water controller is programmed to turn the water on once a day for two hours. Each plant has drip-irrigation emitters so that the medium becomes fully saturated. A fertilizer mixer, which injects water-soluble fertilizers, is connected to the irrigation line.

Last year I watered by hand and had to go up to my outdoor gardens in the mountains every other day whenever the temperatures were 80 degrees or more.

This year I had peace of mind, knowing my lady friends up in the hills were getting all the water and nutrients they needed. I found that there is a direct correlation between the amount of water the plant gets and the size or vegetative mass of the plant. When the plants have the optimum amount of water, it makes all the difference in the world.

#110, October 1984

GUERRILLA GROWING IN THE BIBLE BELT

BY SERENUS

One should put himself in the mind of his enemy in planning and concealment and access strategy. Mao writes, "The best method by which a guerrilla unit can maintain its own security is through agility of action."

Here is the guerrilla grower's greatest advantage. He is not bound to a shift schedule and hourly wage. He is never "off-duty." Furthermore, he is the moral superior of his adversaries as he works to produce, to support his family by honest and upright labor. The law, on the other hand, is merely trying to seek out and destroy and is frequently underpaid, dishonest or both.

The chance for profit, and to stay out of prison, gives the guerrilla grower a kind of initiative unknown to law-enforcement types (except crooked ones). This initiation motivates one's agility of action. The successful grower varies his approach route and watering schedule. He never advances on his plot unwarily, and is always prepared to bolt and run. My own method of moving bread racks of gro-bags to transplant sites employed a pickup truck with a cane fishing pole sticking out of the bed. I used this method only between ten and noon on Sundays and then only once or twice each season. The religious proclivities of the community were such that great safety was afforded me. The entire populace was at the local church.

#156, August 1988

(manufacturing) hemp can range from a moderate fine to imprisonment and loss of one's home and property. This, of course, is an outrageous punishment for a nonviolent act; but, until cannabis is legal, it is dangerous to grow it in your own home or on your property. Although most grow rooms remain undetected, the snoops are looking hard. New efforts include infrared heatdetection from helicopters looking for the extra heat generated by grow lights. (Be sure to vent and insulate your grow rooms!) Another recent police method is to seize the customer lists of indoor-growing supply retailers. Outdoor growing, although a lot more time-consuming and tiring, may be a safer alternative to the otherwise more preferable method of home-growing, which does yield more consistent crops.

WHERE TO PLANT A SECRET GARDEN

To choose a hidden growing location, first select a place where you would normally be hanging out without arousing suspicion. It is common and healthy for people to take walks and explore, especially with a dog, a camera or a boy/girlfriend. Enjoy walks, perhaps carrying a canteen and lunch. During your walks, look for a place that is hidden from view and then go further. Go where nobody would normally walk—like a place you have to cross wet ground, slip through vines, crawl through thorns or walk far into tall weeds to find. The more maze-like your entrance path and the more you stoop or climb to find it, the better. The idea is to make detection difficult, if not impossible. Try not to disturb the natural vegetation, and don't scuff your shoes. It is best to pick a place that will receive southern sunlight for much of the day. Using garden shears, shorten small trees so that more sun can reach your plants, but don't cut them down unless you have to. They can help hide your plants. In deep woods, you may wish to fell a moderate-sized tree for use as a barrier, to create a sunny spot.

After you've started work on a small plantation, be careful to minimize your visibility and not to follow a rigid time schedule. That is, work on the garden in the evenings, but don't do it often. Don't limit your visits to the same day of the week. If the area is fairly open, you can work in full moonlight. Wear clothes that will blend in with your surroundings. Have a cover story prepared ahead of time in case you are questioned. If questioned, be cheerful and friendly and be very apologetic if you accidentally trespass on private property. Bring along a large canteen, as thirsty hikers (or plants) need water. If a water source is handy to your secret garden, paint a five-gallon bucket in camouflage and leave it hidden near your plants instead of carrying it in more than once.

One method of sneaky planting is to space your plants hundreds of feet from one another, on a winding trail. I have found it more efficient to have at least four different locations that each contain five to 12 plants. Gardens this size are hard to spot, even from the air, if you don't plant in rows or a circle. Expect to lose half of your crop to hungry animals, lack of water, insects (usually not a big problem, as THC is the plant's natural defense) or other people. You can't do much about the last problem other than good hiding, so don't get angry or even think about hurting someone. Them's the breaks. Nonviolence is essential if we are to gain public support.

Many losses cannot be prevented, but there are many things you can do besides camouflage to increase your yield. It is essential for young plants to have water, especially in the first critical month. A moderate amount of fertilizer also helps. But before you begin planting, you must consider how to get to your hidden plantations—car, motorcycle or bicycle. There are countless locations where, if you park at the side of the road and walk in 10 or 20 feet, there is undeveloped land no one ever visits. Even a 10-foot barrier of small trees and bushes will protect medium-sized plants from being noticed.

Do not park off major highways—you may be questioned. Stopping there is usually only done in cases of car trouble. However, if you can get to the highway from an outside road, the strip of trees at the side of the highway may be an excellent place to find a rarely-visited, isolated spot. Be sure to leave plenty of cover on both the highway and outside road sides. You can stop at the side of smaller country roads with fewer questions, because everybody has to empty their bladder on occasion.

Other locations include the strips of land accessible from railroad tracks, power lines, gas lines, telephone lines and logging trails. These paths crisscross the land, and provide access to many areas from roads. Few people ever visit these right-of-ways, but they are usually fairly easy to travel, especially if you use the dirt paths that company trucks use when doing maintenance. Be sure to plant far enough off the strip so that workers on these access routes will not see your plants.

If you own a canoe, a small flat-bottomed boat or even a rubber raft, you will be able to get to interesting sites—like an island, a peninsula or a riverbank. A small boat can get you to land far from roads, where very few people go. This has the additional benefit of allowing you to enjoy the natural beauty all around you as you check in on your garden.

If you live in a rundown city or town, you can use this to your advantage as well. There may be abandoned buildings, such as old factories, that provide hidden southern exposure. If tall weeds are growing beside an old building, you could always break another hole or two in the pavement to plant a few more weeds, if you won't get caught.

More relatively unused locations are swamps, or land between ponds. It may be messy getting there, but if it is difficult for you, it also will discourage less purposeful explorers. Rubber boots are a good idea here due to snakes. A work-saving advantage to these locations is that they do not require watering after the first few weeks.

There are many pieces of land that used to be farmed, but are now vacant and overgrown with weeds. Many will be developed in a few years, as suburbia expands. For now, they might make perfect spots for your secret garden.

A fun thing to do is leaving one plant in a location that's clearly visible once the plant matures in mid-summer. It's very enjoyable to drive to work, looking off the road to check out one of your plants. This quick eyeballing from a distance can give you an idea whether your other plants need watering, because a dry cannabis plant will droop. But remember: Be extra sneaky when harvesting a plant that is not totally hidden.

A political action that can be fun is seeding or transplanting in a place that will be seen eventually, like next to an advertising billboard or police station. Choose a location that's hard to weed, so the plant is seen before eradication. Attach a card to the stem demanding the freedom to grow and consume cannabis. This way, if the plant is taken prisoner, the political statement might make the news.

OUTDOOR PLANTING: WHEN AND HOW

Cannabis is very similar to tomatoes in the amount of cold that they can tolerate. Tomatoes are a good guide. They are widely grown, and many people can tell you when is a safe time to transplant outdoors. For most

ALOHA HAWAII

I grew this Hawaiian plant in the summer of '92. The plant was bent over, so it grew these vertical branches. I used a 23-19-17 during vegetative and foliar-fed with fish emulsion during flowering.

Bill
Grand Rapids, MI

#220, December 1993

BACKYARD STASH

I started using stash seed behind my house in the first week of June. Several days later, the seeds sprouted. On July 16, I chose 24 plants from the 32 that sprouted and dug up the remaining eight to give to a friend (who killed them). You're probably wondering: What about the neighbors? Well, I have a lot of old people living on both sides of my house without sons or daughters as well as a high wooden fence separating yards on one side.

My next-door neighbor asked me what the plants were, and I told him some sort of tropical flower that I ordered through a mail-order company. The neighbors next door to him—a mother and daughter—were really a trip. They wanted to know what "those nice tree-bushes" were.

On August 31, I realized that 21 of my plants were male. I cut them down and got 4 lbs of impressive smoke. I had two large females and one 12" plant left.

My interested female neighbors asked me what had happened to my plants, and I told them there were too many and they were killing each other so I had to thin them out.

On September 8, I clipped the top off the largest female. Five days later, I applied a fertilizer that promotes flowering. On October 15, after about 80% of the buds' hairs had darkened to a deep red, it was harvest time! I cut the plants off at the base and hung them to dry for five days. I ended up with 1 lb. of manicured, bagged bud. I played the odds and won and can laugh about it now. My friends and I are very happy with the harvest.

Mary Jayne
Northeast OH

#202, June 1992

ZIGGY MARLEY

BY STEVE BLOOM

Ziggy Marley twists open a bottle of ginseng extract and chugs it. Upstairs in New York's Academy Theater, where Ziggy Marley and the Melody Makers will take the stage in a couple of hours, Bob Marley's oldest son is making himself comfortable. He slices open a mango and picks at a bowl of raw cashews. "Urb-an Music" is ganja music, Ziggy says. "When we play music, we smoke herbs. So it's herbal music, ya know?" Born David Marley on October 17, 1968, "Ziggy" (his nickname from birth—it's Jamaican slang for a good play in soccer) cut his musical teeth at Nyabinghi prayer rituals, where drums and chanting connected him to the Creator, and on his father's stage, where he gravitated to the trap set. Ziggy would eventually strap on a guitar and strum the six strings. After initial lessons, he borrowed books and began the self-learning process. When he was just 11 years old, in 1979, the Melody Makers—consisting of Ziggy, Stephen, Cedella and Sharon (Bob Marley's four children with his wife, Rita)—were formed. They recorded "Children Playing in the Streets," a song written by Bob to benefit the United Nations' International Year of the Child program. Raised and coached by Rita, Ziggy and the other children regrouped as the Melody Makers in 1984. *Play the Game Right*, the first album from this young brother-sister act received a Grammy nomination. Four years later, a more mature and politically aware Melody Makers took the prize for *Conscious Party*.

of the country, this is at the beginning of May. Most tomato growers start their plants indoors a few weeks before transplanting them outdoors to their garden. In the case of cannabis, I recommend starting indoors three weeks before transplanting. Start the seeds between wet paper towels, and once the roots sprout a few days later, put them in small peat pots filled with soil of the type in which they will later mature. You might want to add a trace of peat moss. Don't fertilize seedlings until they have three sets of leaves. Transplanting will probably be successful after the plants are six inches tall. There are two good reasons not to wait too much longer. One is to avoid root-bound peat pots, and the other is that taller plants can't be easily hidden during transplanting in a grocery bag or other closable container.

When you take your young plants out to be transplanted, all you need to carry are the plants, water and a pocketknife or trowel for digging. I suggest going to a grocery store, and in the section where you can buy disposable aluminum cookware, find a pan that is approximately the size of the bottom of a large paper grocery bag. Six 2-1/2" peat pots fit perfectly, and the high sides help keep the wet and weakened peat pots from splitting.

PROTECTIVE CAGES FOR SMALL PLANTS

A common disappointment for outdoor growers is the loss of plants due to animals like deer, rabbits and mice, who like the taste of hemp. The most effective way to protect new plants is to surround them with iron cages made of hardware cloth. (Hardware cloth contains strong iron wire joined in 1/2" squares.) Buy a roll of hardware cloth 24" high and 10' long. This will cost between $6 and $12, and will make 10 protective cages once the roll is cut in foot-long sections. After cutting the sections with a snip, bend the wire cloth straight, then bend it across your leg so each piece is one foot high and makes a circle about 7-1/2" in diameter. It can be held in a circle by using one piece of strong wire that is bent to form two hooks. Place one hook in the center of one end of the barrier, bend it to form a circle and hook it together so there is no opening for small animals. I suggest painting all the galvanized metal with a dull brown paint to avoid detection. This barrier will allow a plant to grow out of the open top, but will stop low-level nibblers.

Dr. Lunglife must make a confession here. After constructing these cages and gloating over protecting my plants so well, I returned to find that a mole had dug a tunnel under the barrier, pulled a plant underground and eaten the roots and stem. I did manage to salvage the leaves for a midsummer smoke, but was humbled by the genius and power of Mother Nature.

TRIMMING YOUR HIDDEN PLANTS

Cut off the tips of your secret plants when they reach knee-high. Make the cut just above a node. This will force two or more main shoots. A month later, when the plant approaches waist level, pinch off the tallest tips again. This will force the plant to become bushy rather than tall. Although tall plants do produce larger buds, the more numerous smaller buds on a trimmed plant will be almost as good—especially if there is a better chance of avoiding detection and actually getting to enjoy them. These trimmings may not be great, but will get you through the summer. Don't trim after the middle of July. Most plants will be developing buds by then and won't grow much higher. It's a good idea to harvest by the end of August, as most other plants will be losing their green by then. The hearty cannabis plant will stay a deep green and may stand out too much.

HARVESTING

When your buds are ripe—or when you start sweating too much about losing your crop to a near-freeze or discovery—it is time to harvest. This is also a good time for extra precautions, so as not to get caught with the goods. Your first job is to remove all the buds and put them in one bag. Then strip each branch of leaves by holding the tip of each branch and running your pinching fingers down toward the main stalk. This easily pulls off the leaves and separates them from the stems. Put the leaves into another bag. The best kind of bag to use is a cotton pillowcase with a camouflage print. This can be hidden easily and allows moisture to escape.

If you have a small crop, you can simply lay it out on a table to dry. If you have a large one, you must give some thought to drying methods. One that worked well for a seven-pound crop was putting it in a cardboard box. A round hole was cut near the bottom of the box and a clothes-dryer duct inserted in the hole. The duct carried hot air from a small electric-heater fan.

While the dried buds are ready for vaporizing (see the Dec. '89 issue of HT), the leaves will be of poorer quality. To inhale less non-THC material, extract the oils from the leaves. This can be easily done by boiling batches of leaves in denatured alcohol inside of a pressure cooker for safety. After 20 minutes, drain the now-green alcohol off, and add some fresh alcohol for further boiling. Continue this until no more color can be leached from the leaves. Then boil off the alcohol to leave an oil rich in THC. After further refinement, this will be perfect for vaporizing. To learn more about extraction and refinement, read David Gold's *Cannabis Alchemy*.

Due to lack of water, weather vagaries, soil or nibbler problems, outdoor weed may not match the quality of carefully cultivated indoor sinsemilla, but overall it isn't bad, and sometimes it can be great. The price is largely your own time, and you may find that it is fun to meet the athletic and mental challenges of covert cultivation.

ORGANIC OUTDOOR GROWING

by Elmer Budd

Although this grower didn't have the world's greatest seeds, he more than made up for it with his organic approach and knack for proper pruning. The result? A bountiful crop of sticky green bud.

It all began in February 1989 with a purchase of weed, an ounce of *sativa* from Wisconsin. I was pissed off. No grass should cost $300 an ounce. More importantly, I was suddenly tired of smoking potentially poisonous plants. I'm an organic vegetable grower. I wanted my pot to be organic, too.

So I decided to grow my own. I've been gardening since the age of

WEED WONDER FROM DOWN UNDER

We Down Under look to our American brothers and sisters in awe of their achievements, but after 15 years of guerrilla farming I have come to the conclusion that some of the best weed in the world grows in the southeast of South Australia. I feel it is time to set things straight. The "Pine Tree" was grown in straight sand and fed numerous nutrients; the large head was grown 4' away from the Pine Tree; the purple head is a cross between a Vietnamese and a local strain. I submit these photographs as definite proof of the ability of Australians to strive for the highest-quality cannabis known to man.

The Quiet Achiever
South Australia

#218, October 1993

HIGH PLAINS HERB

This little sinse plant was grown indoors using natural outdoor light at over 7,000 feet elevation.

High Plains Herb
Wyoming

#224, April 1994

SUPERTHRIVE

In the Best of HIGH TIMES #12, there was an article titled "Goin' For Growth" by Bob Ireland. In that article, Bob mentions several products which contain hormones that may help cause plants to become female. I tried "Superthrive."

I grew two crops from the same batch of seeds—a fine purple *indica* that has been growing in the Hudson River Valley for over ten years. I grew one crop with Superthrive, the control without.

The crop that was grown with it showed males at six weeks with 18 hours of light. Out of 60 plants, 12, or 20%, were male. The females did not show sex until light was reduced to 12 hours.

The control was grown identically to the first except I did not use Superthrive. Out of 60 plants, I got 39 males and they did not sex early.

The quality of the buds was excellent from both crops, except the buds from the first crop were slightly better and more numerous.

Harvey Hemp
Fishkill, New York

#227, July 1994

five, so I felt pretty confident. I felt that if I could grow sweet potatoes, peanuts and okra, I could grow the wacky weed. I purchased several books from the HIGH TIMES Bookstore and read them cover-to-cover several times over.

Then I started looking for seeds. A neighbor had a bag of weed that was great—and it was really seedy. I figured that if the grass was excellent, the seeds had to be good.

I germinated the seeds the same way I do my veggies: in plastic flats on top of the refrigerator with fluorescent light. I put them in organic garden soil from my quarter-acre garden, which has been worked for over five years. It's a fine black loam. Over the years I've been adding all sorts of organic goodies to it: dried leaves, grass clippings, horse and cow manure (from organic farms only), lime, peat humus, composted chicken manure (from chickens fed only organically grown corn).

My seedling soil mixture was one part soil, one part peat humus, one-part vermiculite, one part perlite and one part charcoal. The flats were filled with the mixture. Quarter-inch-deep furrows were made. The seeds were planted every inch and then covered lightly. The flats were sprayed with a mister (one teaspoon of fish emulsion 5-2-2 to one gallon water) and covered with plastic wrap to keep the moisture in.

Within three days the seedlings popped and the plastic was removed. Germination was 90%. The seedlings stayed in the flats for the next five days until the first true leaves developed. I then transplanted them into 8-oz Styrofoam cups with the same soil mix as before. I added a teaspoon of HIN bat guano 10-4-1 and a teaspoon of fish emulsion 5-2-2 to a gallon of water and fed the plants every other day. The cups were placed in flats and lined up next to the baseboard. The temperature was set at 76 degrees.

Fluorescent Vitalight was used at 18 hours for the next four weeks. The seedlings really took off. Most plants had developed four nodes. At this point, I transplanted half the seedlings into black plastic bags that hold approximately 32 oz. Two days later, I started to clip the tops in order to make them more compact and bushy.

After another 10 days, the plants split at the top into two heads, and I clipped those, as well. Two weeks went by, and the tops split again. By now it was time for transplanting. Three-gallon plastic pots were used. The soil mix was basically the same, except for small stones placed at the bottom of the pot for drainage, and the addition of one part worm castings to two parts of soil mix. Of the 96 original seedlings, the plants that were transplanted earlier into 32-oz bags were much bigger and fuller than the ones in the 8-oz cups. I chose 40 of the healthiest ones. The rest were distributed to friends and neighbors. A decision had to be made about their location. I split them into four groups.

I placed three groups on neighboring state land and one group on the roof of my screened porch. Each garden was within a five-minute walk from my home.

The plants were now nine weeks old and averaged about one foot high and about the same in width. At this point I changed their diet some and gave them one teaspoon of HIN bat guano, one teaspoon of fish emulsion and one cup of liquid kelp per gallon every four days. Every day I gave a half-gallon of water to each plant by hand. All watering and feeding was done early in the morning. Each plant was in full sun all day long. I was lucky to find good south-facing locations with good cover.

I also continued to clip the tips of the tops for the next four weeks. The plants really spread out; some had as many as 20 to 25 tops. At 14 weeks, they averaged two to three feet high and were very bushy. In late June I stopped clipping.

I still couldn't distinguish the males from the females. But in the second week of July, the males started to pop. With each new day, I spotted more and more. By the 20th of July, I had 24 males, and the females had started to flower a little. I cut down all the males except for one. He was a real stinker: only three feet high and real bushed-out. I saved him for his pollen and put him in the house in a south-facing window.

I then changed the plants' diet to one teaspoon of HP bat guano, a teaspoon of HP fish emulsion and one cup of liquid kelp per gallon of water every five days, with a cup of liquid kelp for side dressing. At this time I decided to move all 16 girls to my roof garden. The second week of August, I noticed two hermaphrodites and cut them down. Two days later, I found one more. Now I was left with 13 gorgeous ladies to attend to. For the next two weeks, the plants really gained in height and width, and the flowers were getting heavier and smellier. I was also starting to notice heavy resin production.

In September, the nights started to get cooler. The roof garden proved to be a perfect microclimate. It would get full sun all day and the house roof, which is asphalt shingles, would store the heat from the sun and keep the plants warm at night. As the days went by, the smell got heavier. It's a good thing I always grow at least five 50-foot rows of onions. At this time of the year, the smell of onions fills the air around my property. Only when I set foot into my outlaw garden could I smell the skunky sweet aroma of the blooming flowers.

The second week of September, the rains started to hit my area. Fearing bud rot, I moved the plants inside the porch and added an oscillating fan and small electric space heater.

I pruned a lot of the bigger sun leaves to improve air circulation. Some of the plants started to show signs of rot anyway—we had gotten almost five inches of rain in the last week, with temperatures reaching into the low 40s.

I pruned off all of the afflicted buds. About half the plants were ready to pick by the third week of September. I started to selectively harvest some of the top flowers, which had lots of red and brownish hairs on them with some phony pods and plenty of resin on them. I couldn't wait to taste them.

I popped a few in the microwave for 90 seconds at high temperature. For a flash-cured bud, it tasted excellent. I was surprised, but the buzz surprised me even more. I had succeeded in growing primo bud. Now I had to wait for the rest of them to mature.

Then came a very uneasy time for me—paranoia was really setting in. Every night when I came home from the office, I expected that the *federales* would be in my driveway, waiting for me. This was the toughest part of the cultivation process. I cured the plants by hanging them on lines in a dark, dry walk-in closet. It took from seven to 12 days to finish.

On the 25th of October, I still had one female indoors under a 1,000-watt high-pressure sodium lamp, on a 12-hour dark cycle, and one female which was fertilized for seed. The last girl is a very late strain. The buds are finally starting to get some amber hairs in them. She is also a true dwarf, only two feet high and three feet wide, with close to 30 tops, and the leaves are real tiny. Another week and she's finished.

Editor's Note: Last December, after reading about Operation Green

LYON'S SHARE

This plant was grown from Super Skunk seeds bought at Amsterdam's Sensi Seeds. It was grown outdoors last summer in Lyon, France. The seeds were started indoors under lamps and then placed outdoors in early June. The plants were harvested in September. The high is strong; the taste smooth.

Delacroix
Lyon, France

#225, May 1994

NITRON

I am writing to tell you about the most effective new growing aid that I have ever seen. It is an enzymatic soil-conditioner sold under the brand name "Nitron." The manufacturers claim that it is a totally natural product, and totally safe to use. Nitron makes all the nutrients in the soil available to the plants. You need only use a fraction of the fertilizer you would normally use. It is available for both soil and container growing.

In my current garden soil I use commercial potting mix, bone meal, bat guano, seabird guano and perlite. Some three month old plants were only a foot tall due to late transplanting. After using Nitron twice in a week there were three new sets of leaves on the plants. Color and vigor improved immediately. After three weeks the growth rate has become phenomenal. The plants are filling the greenhouse to overflowing. My vegetable garden has reacted the same way. I have giant irises and roses now.

R.M.
Kansas

#136, December 1986

ONE WEEK BEFORE HARVEST
The plant was six feet tall.

Animal
Salem, Ohio

#118, June 1985

LET THEM EAT FERTILIZER

BY KAYO

At this time there are 16 chemical elements known to be essential to plant growth. Three of these—oxygen, carbon and hydrogen—are processed from air and water through photosynthesis. The remaining 13 nutrients are made available through the decomposition of organic matter in soil.

There are three primary macronutrients: nitrogen (N), phosphorus (P) and potassium (K).

There are three secondary macronutrients: calcium (Ca), magnesium (Mg), and sulfur (S).

There are seven micronutrients: zinc (Zn), iron (Fe), manganese (Mn), copper (Cu), boron (B), molybdenum (Mo) and chlorine (Cl).

#106, June 1984

Merchant, Elmer converted his grow room and garden to vegetables only. At the end of April, he was visited by four armed agents of the DEA and local sheriff's department. Since they had a search warrant, Elmer allowed them inside. They left without finding a thing.

ORGANIC NUTRIENTS FOR YOUR PLANTS

by Tom Alexander

MIX:

1 cubic yard of redwood sawdust
1/4 cubic yard rice hulls or cocoa bean hulls
1/4 cubic yard ground peat moss (Canadian milled sphagnum moss is best.)
1/4 cubic yard easily composted lawn clippings and nonpoisonous leaves, weeds, coffee grounds, washed beach seaweed, wood ash, eggshells, kitchen scraps, green vegetation, etc. Fresh-cut or saved weeds, plants, etc. are important to add life to a pile. Important: Don't include eucalyptus leaves or pine needles.

The raw uncomposted sawdust will suck nitrogen from the soil. To break down the sawdust, etc. into rich fertile humus, you'll need to compost the above ingredients with the ones below for approximately three months, depending on the materials and your particular situation (temperature, humidity, aeration, pH, carbon-nitrogen ratio, etc.). With more sawdust, use more nitrogen.

Now add 1 cubic yard of fresh, hot manures (fresh cow manure can take too long). Best fresh mixture is 1/4 cubic yard each of horse, chicken, rabbit and goat manure plus 10 pounds of fishmeal and five pounds of bat guano.

If no fresh manures are available, then add instead:

50 lbs bagged steer manure
50 lbs fishmeal
20 lbs hoof and horn meal
20 lbs bloodmeal
50 lbs bagged chicken shit
5 to 10 lbs bat guano

If you are a vegetarian and don't like using bloodmeal and hoof and horn meal, try 50 lbs each of fishmeal, steer manure and chicken manure. Also, 20 lbs each of cottonseed meal, linseed meal, soybean meal and bat guano. In all of these formulas add more nitrogen if you think it is needed. No matter which nitrogen combination you choose to add to the sawdust mixture, you need also to add 10 pounds of sodbuster (humates which break up heavy soils and make nutrients available) and five to 10 pounds of any good biodynamic compost starter.

Mix all the above sawdusts, nitrogens, sodbusters, etc. very well and turn the pile with a pitchfork once or twice a week for about one month. Keep the pile covered with a sheet of plastic which will keep the rain from leaching away valuable nutrients. Keep the pile moist but not soggy. The pile should start heating up in a few days and be too hot to stick your arm in comfortably. A garden thermometer can give you accurate temperature readings.

If it is not getting hot, and as long as it is not too soggy or too dry, which will delay composting, then the pile probably needs more nitrogen. If it smells like ammonia, then the pile has too much nitrogen. Add a little, one or two cubic feet, of peat moss and turn very well. Repeat if necessary. Turn the outside of the pile into the inside. All the sawdust should be turning black, with any lumps of sawdust broken up.

STEP 2
Finished in approximately two to four weeks.
Next add to the pile:
20 lbs of greensand (trace elements and potassium. If unavailable, use granite dust.)
20 lbs rock phosphate (phosphorus)
20 lbs bone meal (phosphorus)
20 lbs powdered and unsalted kelp meal (potassium and trace elements)
10 lbs ground oyster shells (lime), which raises the pH slowly
1 lb trace elements (micronutrients) such as agricultural frit, chelated minerals, azomite or TMI

Mix all of the above very well, turning once a week for one month. Keep covered and moist. Make sure all the ingredients are well mixed, especially those on the bottom next to the ground. Be sure all sawdust is fully composted and well distributed.

STEP 3
Finished in approximately two to four weeks.
Next add:
1 to 2 cubic yards of sandy loam topsoil
1 cubic yard of compost which is already well composted. Use either a high-quality store-bought compost or use your own.
2 cubic yards of worm castings (Worm casts have five times the nitrogen, two times the calcium, seven times the phosphorus and 11 times the potassium as the soil they're raised in.)
25 lbs plant charcoal (sweetens and purifies the soil)
25 lbs perlite (to lighten the soil and help conserve water). Add more if needed.
5 to 10 cubic feet horticultural sand (coarse, sharp, clean, washed and unsalted). Untumbled mountain sand is best.
10 lbs dolomite (lime to raise pH)
10 lbs Ringer's Spring Garden Soil Builder
50 lbs peat humus (black)

Mix all the ingredients well and let them sit for several weeks, turning occasionally. Then measure the pH. You'll want a pH of 7 to 7.5 (slightly alkaline). If pH is below 7 (neutral), add 10 lbs dolomite lime for each point under seven. Mix well. Test again in one week. If soil is alkaline, add coffee grounds, cottonseed meal or sulfur (sparingly). The finished mix should have a fresh, woodsy, mushroomy, earthy smell—not rotten or shitty-smelling. You should test the pH of your water and make any necessary adjustment if it has a pH above or below 7. Water often changes pH during the season, so test often.

Finished compost, like rich soil, has a 10-to-1 carbon-to-nitrogen ratio. Carbon is higher in materials like sawdust (500-1) with a high cellulose content. Nitrogen is higher in materials like manures (15-1) or

THE AVAILABILITY OF NUTRIENTS INFLUENCED BY PH

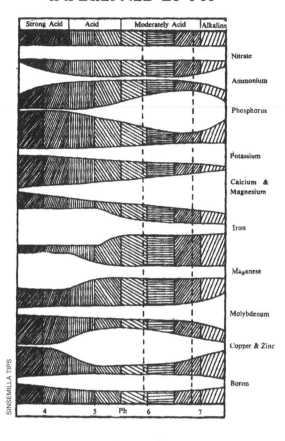

NITRATE OF POTASH
In Ulysses S. Jones' book, "Fertilizers and Soil Fertility" he makes a statement that may be of interest to marijuana growers and I thought I'd pass it on to you:

"Potassium is needed in large quantities for the growth and nutrition of the tobacco plant, and a relatively high content of potassium in cured tobacco is desirable for good smoking quality...Because of the pronounced effect of chlorine on the burning characteristics of tobacco, some states regulate the percentage of chlorine permissible in tobacco fertilizers."

The author recommends nitrate of potash because it contains no chlorine or sulfur and its nitrogen is available in nitrate form. Tobacco performs poorly when the nitrogen is in the ammonium form.

Sagamour
North Carolina

#129, May 1986

bloodmeal (5-1). An active compost pile should be approximately 30-to-1. Less than 25-to-1, and the pile wastes nitrogen by making ammonia. More than 50-to-1, and the pile will take too long composting.

Yield: approximately four cubic yards for 25 to 100 plants.

Cost: approximately $100 to $500 depending on ingredients...how many you can scrounge up and how many you pay for.

SECOND-YEAR SUPPLEMENT

The following mix makes a good second-year soil supplement for approximately four cubic yards of soil:

20-100 lbs fishmeal; bloodmeal; hoof and horn meal; bat guano; and rabbit, goat, chicken or steer manures. Don't use manure that is too hot or too fresh unless it has at least three months to break down before planting.
20 lbs greensand
20 lbs rock phosphate
20 lbs bone meal
1 lb trace elements
20 lbs kelp meal
20 lbs Ringer's Garden Soil Builder
10 lbs sodbuster humate
10 lbs oyster shells (if needed to raise pH)
Compost

First printed in *Sinsemilla Tips 5*, #1: 16.

POT ON THE EDGE:
The Art of Sneaky Gardening
by the Bush Doctor

Once upon a time in Humboldt County, seeds were sown in agricultural geometries. The marijuana marched in rows and columns growing high in the sky. But this made easy pickin's for the helicopters. "Don't paraquat 'til you see the whites of their eyes," the men with badges would say.
And so guerrilla gardening began in Garberville. Plantations underwent linear transformations. They began sprouting up along edges—between forests and fields, fields and streams, roadsides, railways and powerline right-of-ways....

Growing on the edge can mean many things. But here we're talkin' very literally about edge. The secret to "edge success" is simple: Think like a weed and plant a seed. Cannabis, of course, is a weed, which makes it a natural creature of the edge. It was probably discovered growing at the edge of some Central Asian Cro-Magnon latrine pit. The Cro-Magnon man, finding the plant's properties invaluable, began seeking better ways to grow this weediest of weeds. Hence, the genesis of the "weed mindset."

Although outdoor cannabis cultivation has undergone many technological developments since primitive times, it has also been disadvantaged in recent

ORGANIC FLOWERING

BY KYLE KUSHMAN

Overwatering and overfeeding (fertilizing) are the most common ways to kill your plants. Watering cycles should go from very wet to nearly dry. A good way to judge is to poke your finger down into the soil. If you feel no moisture, it's time to water. Being able to judge the weight of the container will also tell you when it's time. You can even squeeze the sides of the bucket to make sure there's no freestanding water at the bottom. Use fortified water and add some Squanto's Secret. Remember that your pH shouldn't exceed 6.0.

You want an NPK ratio of 4-8-8. After a week, increase to 5-10-10 and then to 5-15-10. Gaining precise control of temperature and humidity levels is crucial to maximize potential yield and potency. Unanticipated swings can lead to root rot, stem rot or bud rot. Numerous fans, both oscillating and box, as well as a flow of fresh air, can dissipate heat and lower humidity. An air-conditioner may be necessary in larger gardens or warmer climates. There are visible signs to tell you that ripening has begun. First, you'll notice the stigmas turning colors and then withering. A good gauge of when it's time to harvest is when 75-85% of all stigmas have changed. If you desire precision, you should use a magnifier. Look at the crystals or "sugar" on the tiny leaves protruding from the buds. You will see tiny clear stalks growing on them. If the stalks have a cap on them, they'll look like mushrooms. This is peak harvest time.

#236, April 1995

years by over-zealous prohibitionists riding in helicopters. The need for a good guerrilla garden spot is now more important than ever.

INVISIBLE PIONEER

For protection, think invisible. Seek abandoned land where pioneer forests crop up. Your site needn't be inaccessible, but it should be ignored. Most folks don't know cannabis from asparagus, but, nevertheless, idle eyes should be avoided. "So obvious, it's invisible" is a valuable concept for guerrilla gardening.

Nature can aid invisibility. Pick spots secluded by inconvenient topography, such as cliffs, swamps or lakes. Also, I've never lost a plant set in the midst of a nettles or brambles patch.

Weeds love nitrogen and light. You can add nitrogen to the soil, but you can't add light. It is essential to pick a site with clear southern exposure to the sun. Also, weeds need moisture, but not too much. Don't get discouraged by your local environment—seek microenvironments. I've found perfect little low spots in the Bakersfield desert, and nice dry hillocks in the midst of Jersey swamps. Evaluate the water table of your area by taking a "vegetation survey." I look for ragweed, burdock or other taprooted weeds. If these plants are still healthy and green in September, then the water table never dropped below root reach and, just as important, the plants never got too wet.

FIND IT, MAP IT, LEAVE IT

Once you find a good spot, map it. Don't rely on memory. Of course, don't mark all your separate sites on one map. If you somehow get caught weed-handed at your site, hopefully you'll only have the one map to that site in your pocket. Then you may want to ask a friend to harvest your other sites for bail money. (Only kidding! If you have less than five plants in one spot, the coppers might not jail you.)

INDOOR EDGE

In early spring, I start my seedlings indoors under lights, weeks before the final frost. That way, my plants get a big jump on competing weeds. My potting soil comes from K-Mart. I make small plastic pots by cutting the top three-quarters off 1-liter pop containers and piercing the bottoms for drainage.

Month-old seedlings are ready to transplant. They can still fit in a tall container, so I tape the tops back over the pots. Thus protected, I load six pop containers at a time into my rucksack, like mortar shells ready for launching.

SOIL HEMISPHERES

I usually prep soil in autumn, during my vegetation surveys. Alternatively, you can work the soil in early spring, but the ground is often too wet then. I backpack a small spade, fertilizer and soil conditioner (vermiculite, perlite). Good sites are covered with weeds and require some sodbusting. For each potential plant, I loosen a soil hemisphere at least 3' in diameter, mixing fertilizer and conditioners as needed. (I use lightweight chemical NPK at long-distance-hike sites, but indulge in organics for plants close to home.)

An old friend of mine from *Sinsemilla Tips* magazine, to whom all guerrilla growers owe a debt, was a master hole-maker. For conserving rainwater, he used to line the bottom of a hole with a water-barrier, mix water-retaining conditioners into the soil, and then construct a moat and berm around the plant.

NOCTURNAL MISSIONS

Transplanting is to be done at night. Actually, twilight (dawn and dusk) is the best time. Wear dark, unrestrictive clothing. Run like hell under radar. Mrs. Bush, my wife, always gets anxious waiting back home, because I always take

OUTDOOR ELVIS

This sativa was started in late March and harvested in early September. The plant was heavily pruned to maximize the number or bud sites, and ended up yielding about 4 oz of sweet sinsemilla.
Grow Your Own Club
Southern California

#194, October 1991

POTTING SOIL
BY DENNIS R. PITTENGER
Select mixes high in bark, forest materials or sphagnum peat plus vermiculite.

Thoroughly leach any potting soil at least three of four times before placing seed or plant material in the mix. Leaching will reduce soluble salts to acceptable levels in most mixes.

Fertilize with a soluble fertilizer according to the manufacturer's directions within two weeks after plants are growing in new potting soil to replace leached nutrients and those taken up by the plants.

#146, October 1987

GROWING WITH MOUNTAIN BIKES

We start our seeds in a vermiculite, perlite and potting-soil mix sometime in March and raise them under fluorescents until they're 12-14". Then we load them into coolers and, under cover of darkness, drop them off at their new homes. There are patches I have laboriously hacked out of thick underbrush, often very close to the road. We also drop off shovels and a duffel bag of vermiculite.

The next day, we ride our mountain bikes back out there, wait until no one is coming and duck into the bushes. We turn over the soil and work liberal amounts of vermiculite in. Then we pop our babies in, pack everything into the coolers and ride back home. Often we are so close to the road that we can hear cars whizzing by. Later that night, we go retrieve our supplies. From then on we pray for timely rains, stupid cops and stupider thieves.

Every two or three weeks, preferably when it's raining like hell, we go out and sprinkle liberal amounts of Miracle-Gro around the bases of our plants. I would like to be more organic, but this just isn't practical, given our guerrilla method of growing. We also put mothballs and deodorant soap around them to keep animals at bay. This year we had a problem with slugs, which we addressed with liberal administrations of Dragon snail-and-slug killer. Often we tie our plants down to keep them from being too visible.

Around the first week of August, the males begin to appear, necessitating more frequent, nerve-wracking visits to our pungent plants. Sexing them first would eliminate this, but that always seems to stunt our plants.

About the second week of September, the first colas are ready. Once again, we ride our trusty mountain bikes out to our "buddies." I prefer to harvest in the afternoon after a nice sunny day, when the buds are dripping with resin. We pack a lunch and do most of our manicuring right there in the field. Then we stash our manicured buds and leaf, packaged separately, and wait once again for night to come. My partner drops me off and drives down the road a piece. I dash in and grab the stuff while she comes back to pick me up. From there we head to the drying room.

Sir Smokesalot
Long Island, New York

#237, May 1995

longer than expected. But I have fun. For accessible sites, carry water for the transplanted seedlings. Carry out your plastic.

The rest is up to Mother Nature and the other forces that be. Sometimes my yield is 100%, like in '86. But in '87 only one plant in 50 survived. I got wiped out by floods, highway maintenance and a new housing development. Last year, I lost six African stink fingers when Con Ed decided '91 was the year to clear a long-neglected power line. Guerrilla growing requires a lot of seeds, and you can't get too attached to your plants.

EDGE CAVEATS

Expect more insects and critters nibbling at your plants. Edges amplify pests. For instance, in a forest break you'll find species of the forest, species of the field and species of the edge itself intermingling with your plants. But species diversity also spells relief à la bio-control: The pests rarely eat much of your plant before natural predators eat them.

Site selection can also influence your pest problems. Planting adjacent to cornfields will bring on European corn borers. If you plant near grass or sod, then expect white grubs and certain caterpillars. Shade will exacerbate gray mold but protect against sun-loving flea beetles. Low-lying, heavy soil will predispose to root rot.

Guerrilla gardening suffers other problems common to all outdoor gardeners. In the Midwest, growing sinsemilla used to be impossible outdoors. Pollen blowing from wild hemp ruined my buds, and the hemp/ganja-hybrid offspring made better rope than smoke. Thankfully, the DEA has spent millions of dollars over the last 10 years in an effort to eradicate wild hemp. But you still have to worry about the weather.

It pays to visit your garden a few times per season. Prune the plants for bushier growth and cut back the surrounding vegetation. Later in the season, rogue the male plants. If your tall ganja sticks out like a green thumb from the surrounding weeds, pull the tops sideways (gently!) and stake them down. Add camouflage as your garden grows but don't visit it too often—you'll make a trail.

Harvest spells paranoia time. I try to grow plants at the edge of town instead of the wilderness, so I can walk my dog past the garden without attracting attention. If the coast looks clear and the bud stinks big, I "cut'n'stuff" and book home with my doggie bag. Happy trails!

BARRELS IN THE SUN
Maintenance-Free Outdoor Cultivation

by Buddy Hemphill

In this outdoor adventure, cultivator and nature-lover Buddy Hemphill shows how to grow super-sticky pot outdoors for a full, nine-month season with as few as two visits to the garden. His secret? Fifty-five gallon, food-grade "honey barrels" and wicks.

Like many of my good brothers and sisters out there, I enjoy fine herbs—and what better way to enjoy the profound healing and awareness effects of herbs than to grow your own? Sharing the cannabis flowers of your labors with friends can be very special.

There are as many ways to grow herb as there are people to smoke it, so I will only explain the way that works best for me.

MATERIALS REQUIRED FOR FEBRUARY STARTS:

1 sunny greenhouse
4"-6" pots (or 4"-6" rockwool cubes)
Compost (if not using rockwool)
Old braided rug (ones with more synthetic fiber last longer)
Plastic tub or plastic-lined wooden tub
2" square mesh galvanized wire to fit inside diameter of tray

MATERIALS REQUIRED FOR OUTDOORS:

55-gallon plastic food-grade drums
55-gallon metal food-grade drums (for buried water reservoir)
Wicking material
Compost
Rechargable drill/screwgun
6-millimeter plastic and padding (necessary if I dig a hole for a reservoir)

Each year I select seed from the top 10 or so varieties of the previous year's crop. The seed is planted as early as the first new moon in February or as late as the new moon in July. (Consult your almanac for lunar cycles.)

I prefer starting during each of the new moons from February until May. I know the seeds will presex under the natural sunlight in February and March, the best months to start in, and even into early April. Seeds started later are backups...just in case. I can always find a loving home for any extra seedlings.

Germination takes place in wicked containers as opposed to between cloths. I've tried other methods, but this one best provides the undisturbed sprouting conditions needed for a good start.

The wire-mesh trellis is raised at least 4" from the bottom of the tray and the containers are filled halfway with fine, rich compost. In each pot 1-2 seeds are planted. After a seedling is 1"-2" above the surface, the container is filled the rest of the way with compost, which improves the stability of the seedling and makes it less likely to fall over. I've noticed that seeds started in wicked containers are much less likely than those in nonwicked containers to get root-bound or experience transplant shock.

PRESEXING

At this time, it is helpful to have a 10x photographer's loupe to determine sex. Last year's presexing experience was typical: Although the seeds started in February and March were showing quite plainly, a few started in April were not, but had to be checked every week until they did. With the help of the lens and a sharp eye, they eventually become apparent. Enough males are kept so I have a good variety from which to choose, then they are weeded down to the top three or four, transplanted and kept at close hand for easy pollen-gathering.

SELECTING AND PREPARING THE SITE

With this style of planting, the forest is literally my canvas. Painted with

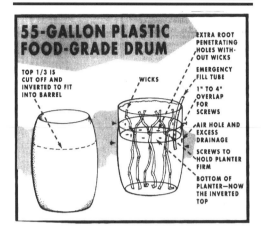

BARRELS IN THE SUN

55-GALLON PLASTIC FOOD-GRADE DRUM

TOP 1/3 IS CUT OFF AND INVERTED TO FIT INTO BARREL

WICKS

EXTRA ROOT PENETRATING HOLES WITHOUT WICKS

EMERGENCY FILL TUBE

1" TO 4" OVERLAP FOR SCREWS

AIR HOLE AND EXCESS DRAINAGE

SCREWS TO HOLD PLANTER FIRM

BOTTOM OF PLANTER—NOW THE INVERTED TOP

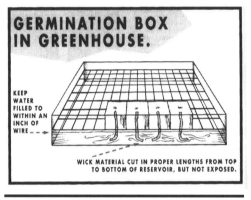

GERMINATION BOX IN GREENHOUSE.

KEEP WATER FILLED TO WITHIN AN INCH OF WIRE

WICK MATERIAL CUT IN PROPER LENGTHS FROM TOP TO BOTTOM OF RESERVOIR, BUT NOT EXPOSED.

BRIAN SPAETH

OUTDOOR WATERING TECHNIQUE

I have been a guerrilla farmer for 15 years and have discovered a few techniques that have served me well. After carrying water for a few seasons, I started storing water from a seasonal creek in a queen-size waterbed mattress placed in a hole in the ground. Once filled, a drip system can be fitted to the filler hole. Covering the mattress with dirt will keep constant pressure on the contents, which flow downhill to the garden.

Deer are a constant threat. A friend of mine showed me a method devised at a tree nursery. They used a dilute solution of egg whites to keep the deer from eating the young shoots. I have used this method and have never had a problem with deer.

E.W.
Lebanon, TN

#238, June 1995

WATER PUMPS

BY CAPTAIN DOMESTIC

A lot of energy is required to move water uphill, and if you have ever hauled water in five-gallon buckets from a creek, up a hill, you know just about how much "poop" we're talking about. The three power sources we will consider will be gas, battery and human. All three pumps push water far more effectively than they can suck water; therefore, get as close as possible to your water source with the pump. Suction hose should be flexible, but it is very important that it not collapse.

GAS ENGINES

Gas engine water pumps are very interesting. Ratings vary between 50 and 300 psi for a lightweight (17 to 50 lbs) Flow delivery varies between 8 and 100 gpm at open discharge. Remember: the greater the altitude you have to go, the less volume of water you will have at the delivery end. The one main problem associated with gas pumps is noise.

BATTERY PUMPS

Twelve-volt battery pumps offer a unique opportunity. The major consideration with them is: The more water you move the more energy is drawn. There are 12-volt submersible pumps that can move 26 gpm and develop 20 psi (40 feet of head) but it takes a lot of battery power to do it. Low-draw (4- to 7-amp) pumps can achieve 100 psi (200 feet of head), but can only deliver 1 gpm at the delivery site 200 feet straight up in elevation. New lightweight (17 lbs) and leak-proof 12-volt batteries have been introduced and they can power a low-draw pump for four or five hours—that's roughly 250 gallons of water, a real bonanza in some places.

HAND PUMPS

Usually these are small, lightweight marine bilge pumps that move a lot of water fast. They are great for starting siphons and can possible eliminate dragging all those five-gallon buckets. Their greatest drawback, however, is their inability to create much pressure—3 to 4 psi (10 feet of head) is okay before breakfast. At open discharge these small pumps can move from 10 to 30 gpm, but when you start pumping up a hill, its efficiency drops off radically.

#107, July 1984

ribbons of green, gold and purple, the hills come alive and become manifest with the brush of my thoughts!

Selecting and preparing the site is the next most important step, besides the quality of the seed. For this, I allow my entire being to become that of the herb. Is this a safe, harmonious place for me to be? Will I be loved and nurtured throughout my existence? Will the sun shine long and strong for me? Is there enough cover so that I may blend in well with my surroundings? Will the air, the earth, the wind and the fire allow me to achieve my highest good, for the highest good of all?

When all of these things come together, the feeling is very warm, and I feel grateful for having been guided to the correct place. Cannabis can grow anywhere and everywhere—high, low or anywhere in between! However, the places on steep hills with no water in sight, the edges, are my preference, for the simple reason that very few sane people go so far out of their way. I select the most obvious but least-traveled path so that supplies (i.e. extra water and nutrients) may be brought in easily from the road without making a trail.

Reservoirs are dug in late fall/early winter to allow them to fill. I cover the plastic-lined, hole-in-the-ground reservoir with recycled corrugated tin to keep critters from falling in and the lining from becoming damaged. The 55-gallon drums also work well as reservoirs. Having a dry tank when you most need a wet one can lead to a very interesting experience called water panic, which is no fun at all for a plant.

Next, I dig in each 55-gallon, food-grade honey barrel at a place where the plants will be well camouflaged. (See diagram, which shows how to convert a honey-barrel into a 17-gallon planter, 38-gallon reservoir, all-in-one unit.) No more than 1' of the planter should show above ground. The wicks are then placed within each one, allowing them to run the height of the barrel from top to bottom. Next, I fill the planters with high-test compost, which is prepared at least a year in advance. Writhing with red wigglers and a base of all organic materials, the planter is almost ready! A top dressing of locally gathered forest moss, 6"-thick, is the final soil component added.

I never used the tin to cover the reservoirs and barrels until curious critters started investigating these "funny" holes, but I have had no further problems since I've started using it. First, a layer of plastic is stapled to the top of the planter. Then a piece of corrugated tin with a rounded-down, 6" middle hole covers the plastic. The edges of that hole must be smooth, so when planting time comes the tin will not cut into the stalk. The tin should be just big enough to "dog ear" and cover the edges of the top of the barrel, so that it may be folded down and kept securely in place. It is then camouflaged to closely match the ground colors. Some of the tin may be removed when the plants start growing.

By now, it is mid-April. The next step taken is the first true adrenaline rush of the season: transportation of the young, nurtured plants to their future homes. Everyone who has ever done this knows what I mean! For convenience's sake, I use 4" wicked pots which allow for easy, compact transportation. Plants started in February are already in 6" pots because they are more developed than seeds started later. For extra discretion, I like to go out in the early evening. For others it may vary, depending on local circumstances as to what time of the day is most discreet. Some of the plants are placed in the barrel at an angle parallel with the hill to allow them to be tied down later with less stress on the stalk, for better concealment.

Once, the barrel is planted, visits are made only when I want to.

Further into the season, more water is added as required from the storage reservoir, not letting the water level in the barrel get below half-empty. The water level can be easily measured with a straight stick inserted through the tube in the top.

Come mid-July/August, I am already looking at prospective females to bear the seeds of change. Past experience allows me to know the various characteristics of the varieties, so I can choose the ones with the most desirable characteristics. With each successive breeding season I become more familiar with the subtle changes that are happening to each variation. What beautiful varieties they are!

Male pollen is carefully chosen from the ones with the most desirable characteristics. Branches are cut and placed in water immediately, and then brought inside to a wind-free environment. It is very easy to gather pollen on a sheet of glass and, once collected, it should be placed in a clean film canister for easy accessibility. With a small, soft brush dipped in pollen, a few taps over the desired pistils assures me of the next generation. Each pollinated branch is then labeled with the information of what cross it contains. That way, if it ever gets separated after harvest, I still know exactly what it is!

Pollination takes place over the period of a few weeks depending on the development of the female pistils.

AUGUST TO EARLY OCTOBER

Now is the time when the most dramatic changes happen. The seeds go full circle and all of the beautiful variations not present earlier are now in evidence: the different qualities in size, structure and fluorescence. It is now harvest time for some, while others wait their turn. Each week, starting with the first wave, there is something to be harvested until mid-October, weather and mold permitting, of course. Since the top third of each plant is three times stronger than the bottom, it is left whole. All the other branches are then cut from the main stem and fashioned as a bouquet. Black tape provides the essential binder at the bottom, holding colas nicely together and allowing for shorter, denser colas. (It is much better to have compact colas if curing space is a consideration.) Each plant label is then included to allow for instant recognition later. The next high adrenaline rush comes at this time: transporting the herb to the drying facility.

Several months earlier, locations were scouted for a drying area. It is much easier on myself and those around me when I can dry and cure the herb away from home. It takes place out in the woods in a wooden-pole structure with a tightly stretched skin of army canvas. A layer of black plastic over the canvas on the roof allows it to be very waterproof. Camouflage netting is then placed over and around the "Sugar Shack" to make it blend in completely. It takes me a good part of one day to build, all under the cover of the forest. Since fall/winter weather makes good drying difficult, I use a small, two-burner propane stove, with a five-gallon propane tank to help keep the environment within a nice, dry 65 to 70 degrees, the temperature at which I am able to achieve a very high quality cure. I allow the herb to hang upside down (untrimmed except for the large tan leaves) for two weeks before they are manicured. I then allow the herb to dry a little more, if need be, on the branch. These branches are then laid lengthwise in a cardboard "flat" until the bud is dry enough to be trimmed from the stem and placed in a gallon glass curing jar.

Each plant's colas are stored separately to allow me to sample each one for the final qualities that will determine the varieties for the "Next

GANJA GROWING
BY JOEL BARREN

Truly, one of the traditions of Jamaican culture is found in its ganja production. Brought to the island by East Indians in the early 1800s, ganja is actually a Hindu term for the finest female cannabis plants.

Jamaicans consider the smoke an herb and not a drug. In the days of slavery, slaves would get together in groups and smoke their ganja. Slave owners thought that these people might be plotting to overthrow them so, to break up the gatherings, they would take away their pipes and herb.

Present-day ganja farmers learned traditional growing techniques passed down through many generations and have acquired new ideas mainly from US growers. The old style of farming left the plants free to breed among themselves. Harvest followed when the seeds were popping out of their pods. Not much attention was paid to selective breeding of various varieties. Farmers in the mountains got their seeds from the commercial grade of lowland marijuana. These growers began to raise seedless ganja around 1976 and have been fine-tuning their cultivation skills with each succeeding crop.

To produce primo ganja requires labor-intensive effort. The growers select a location, in this case on a mountain ridgeline. They cut down the trees and drag them off to the side in order to fully expose the plants to the sun. Stumps are left in the patch to prevent helicopters from landing. They clear the remaining wood for use in building drying sheds for processing the herb.
#168, August 1989

Generation of Change."

Go, now, to the forest and into the hills and sow your "seeds of change." May all the people of this earth be blessed and rejoice in joy, love and light with the profound effects of this healing herb!

INDICA VERSUS SATIVA

Sativa is usually thought of as a tall lanky plant with long distances between the budding sites. On average they are late to maturity and have been here in the USA for several hundred years. Of course when *sativa* was introduced into this country, it was in the form of hemp.

Virtually new to the USA is cannabis *indica* which was brought into the US from the mid-to late '70s up until the early '80s by various hippies and smugglers visiting, working, or living in the Afghanistan area.

Pure cannabis *indica* is a stout bushy plant. Grown outdoors it is no more than 3-5 feet tall, although there are certain exceptions to this rule. Cannabis *indica* has been bred for hundreds of years by the Afghanis for hashish production. To smoke a dried "bud" of cannabis *indica* seems stupid to Afghanis. They would want to know why someone would smoke such a crude unfinished product—the finished product being high-quality Afghani hashish, to them the product of choice.

One of the first places that *indica* was being grown by a substantial amount of people was in the Pacific northwest. More specifically Seattle, Washington, which is actually the home of indoor indica growing. Some smart individuals in the early '70s were probably wondering what those bright lights used in stadiums would do inside on the new strain of seeds. Well, by now the rest is history. Eventually, the *indica* strains walked their way down through Oregon and California.

#163, March 1989

PART 5
ADVANCED TECHNIQUES

SUMMER INSECT CONTROL

by Mel Frank

An indoor greenhouse garden is an artificial habitat. For this reason, your plants may never experience the insect infestations that outdoor plants naturally undergo. For this same reason, once contaminated, indoor plants are particularly susceptible to the ravages of almost any infestation, since they do not have wind, rain, cold and natural predators to help them withstand the onslaught.

The insects that infect marijuana indoors do best in a warm, stagnant atmosphere. A constant stream of moving air that draws fresh air from inside and vents air to the outside helps immeasurably in preventing initial infestations. Adequate and continuous ventilation also helps prevent the establishment of fungus and rot diseases.

Never cultivate houseplants in your marijuana garden, and never go from caring for houseplants or garden vegetables to your marijuana garden, because you or your pet may transport the problem—insect or disease. Whiteflies and spider mites—the two most devastating insects—are extremely contagious. Mites may gain entry to the garden on your hands or clothing, or on your pet's fur. Pests may float through open windows or they may crawl through cracks in walls or floors.

Young marijuana plants are most vulnerable to pest attacks before the plant has begun strong production of the cannabinoids, which are natural deterrents to disease and insects. The younger the plants, the more devastating an infestation might be, not only because the plants are small, but also because an infestation may stay with the plants for the rest of their lives. Even though mites and whiteflies won't kill the plants outright, they do weaken them, and the plants become more susceptible to fungus and rot diseases. If you discover mites or whiteflies, you may choose to induce flowering immediately so that the plants ripen before the infestation does serious damage.

Once a grow room has had pests, before starting any new crop, employ foggers or bug bombs intended for fleas and roaches (available from any supermarket or veterinarian). Foggers kill just about everything that crawls, and since no plants are yet in the room, they're safe to use according to package directions. Siphotrol, from a veterinarian, works very well and has residual killing power that lasts for up to 17 weeks.

Prevention is the best policy, since after infestation you might only contain the attack rather than completely eradicate the pests. Most insecticides that promise to rid your garden of pests rarely destroy all of the pests and eggs. You'll probably notice that after a few weeks, pests are still present. Special problems occur near major farm areas. After years of ever-increasing applications of pesticides, insects develop resistance to sprays that would be effective in other locales. For example, whiteflies and mites are very difficult to treat effectively in cotton-growing areas, such as California's Imperial Valley and in Louisiana, because years of constant spraying have left only the resistant strains. Prevention or containment measures will prove more effective

THE MYTH OF POT POTENCY

BY JOHN P. MORGAN

In February 1994, for the third time in 14 years, a *New York Times* reporter "discovered" the new, highly potent marijuana. The narrative of all three articles is the same. The reporters—Jane Brody (1980), Peter Kerr (1986), and Melinda Henneberger (1994)—discuss some group of former pot smokers (beats, hippies, baby-boomers) who, recalling the nonconsequential smoking of their youth, do not understand that today's marijuana is 10 or even 20 times more potent than the lame ditchweed of old.

This fixed narrative is a fiction. It wasn't until 1967 that delta-9-THC was firmly established as the most important psychoactive chemical in marijuana, and prior to 1970 there were few attempts to assess potency—the percentage of the weight of the plant made up by THC. PharmChem Laboratories of Menlo Park, California analyzed approximately 800 specimens obtained between 1972 and 1975, and found a range of potency between 2.0 and 5.0%. However, throughout this period, their samples contained a number of specimens in the 5 to 10% range and an occasional specimen that exceeded 14%.

#226, June 1994

than insecticidal sprays.

There are several insecticides recommended to control the pests described here. All of them require that you spray regularly and repeatedly to have any chance of actually ridding your garden of the targeted pest. Repeat the sprayings at the recommended intervals several times, even if you don't see any more pests, because egg and certain pupae stages are resistant to any insecticide; otherwise the pests soon reappear in abundance.

It's also a good idea to add a drop or two of liquid dishwashing DETERGENT to each quart of insecticide spray. Detergent is a wetting agent which helps the insecticide penetrate marijuana's "hairy" leaves, and the insecticide better contacts the underlying leaf surfaces and the pests. There are other sprays not listed here that might be effective against a particular pest. When you are searching for an appropriate spray, notice that the insecticide package lists the pests controlled. Make sure that the spray is intended for vegetables (human consumption), and note the number of days after spraying to wait before you can safely use your product. Don't use a spray that is intended solely for ornamentals, since the ingredients may never break down into harmless substances. Whenever you spray, plan a major attack. Wear old clothes, goggles, a painter's mask, a hat and gloves. Turn off the lights and fans and give yourself room to move. Raise the light system as high as possible out of the way of the spray. Allow time for the bulbs to cool before spraying, and make sure the bulbs are dry before turning them back on.

First, discard heavily infested leaves and remove them from the garden. Close all doors and windows and start at the back of the garden so you work your way out to the exit. Spray thoroughly, and spray enough to drench all parts of the plants. Pay special attention to the undersides of leaves, where insects and larvae usually congregate. Remove clothing for washing, and shower. Repeat the spraying at least two more times at the intervals recommended on the pesticide's directions. Thoroughly spraying at the recommended intervals is the only chance of eliminating pests or at least curtailing a major infestation. Any pests that survive may reproduce a new population that's worse than the first. A haphazard spraying leads only to frustration and claims that the spray doesn't work. Follow the manufacturer's directions.

Aphids, mites and whiteflies are the most common, and potentially devastating, of pests indoors. You should be able to eradicate or at least reduce the population of these insects to the point that they no longer pose a serious threat.

APHIDS

Aphids are the most common, especially outdoors or in greenhouses. Fortunately, they're also easy to kill and eliminate. Aphids are soft-bodied, ovoid insects with antennae, and they may be from pinhead to match-head in size. They may or may not have wings. Aphids may be pink to black, but on marijuana they are usually green or black. Infested leaves or shoots might be distorted, curled or crinkled. Aphids are parthenogenic (they can produce offspring without fertilization from a male), and proliferate in enormous numbers if left unchecked.

Aphids initially congregate on growing shoots and on undersides of younger leaves, where they're easily visible and accessible. Start your eradication program by simply running your fingers over the shoots to crush the aphids. Or, take each plant outside or to a bathtub and wash

GIANT BUSH

This giant bush was ten months old at harvest and yielded eight ounces of superior smoke. It stood about six feet tall and had a five-foot diameter. The buds were densely covered with red, brown and white resin glands, which smelled and tasted very minty. The main stem was about two inches wide at the bottom.

King of Budeola
Chicago, IL

#110, October 1984

THE POWDER BUG

I have been growing for eight years. This summer I came across a particularly nasty insect pest called the powder bug. This pest bores a hole in the stalk of a plant and leaves a fine powdery dust behind, which is how it got its name.

The pest lays eggs in the 1/8-1/10 inch hole and then the trouble really starts. The plant is eaten from the inside out and does not recover. Plant symptoms are:

1. Swelling in the stalk, usually where the plant stems connect.

2. Leaf and stem wilting; leaves turn yellow and brown, followed by eventual death. (These are virtually the same symptoms as fusarium wilt.)

Powder bugs are very resistant to insecticides, and once inside the plant they are well protected. They ruined one-third of my crop, but I was able to save the other two-thirds. The only safe biodegradable insecticide that could control them was Raid Garden Fogger, which is found in most supermarkets and garden stores.

The insecticide contains 0.2% pyrethrum, which also kills all manner of mites, aphids and white flies. It also keeps away insects too numerous to mention. Pyrethrum kills on contact and was the only thing that drove the pests away. I sprayed weekly in June and July; that's when the borers first appear in this area.

Mr. T.
Philadelphia, PA

#131, July 1986

HOW TO GROW MUSHROOMS

BY MATIAS ROMERO

Attention all you dedicated seed-sowers out there! Growing your own edible and/or magical mushrooms need not be more fraught with failure or technical complexity than the average home hydroponic setup. While home flower-cultivation has steadily advanced in technique and popularity, mycogardening (myco is Latin for fungi) remains shrouded in mystery, the domain of relatively few enthusiasts. Many people have purchased mushroom-growing kits only to find themselves so intimidated, they abandon the project altogether. Here's hope for the disenchanted.

Growing your own fungal philosopher's stone and growing your own fine herb have a high potential to work together, because the fungi we're interested in are efficient generators of CO_2 and require oxygen to grow, while the plants require CO_2 and generate oxygen. So the possibilities are bountiful.

The following is a brief overview of a typical home fungi-cultivation setup with the popular and easily grown species strophoria (psilocybe) *cubensis*. In general, these guidelines may be adapted for growing other culinary or psychoactive species with only slight modifications. Any good mushroom-growing guide would be an excellent source for in-depth discussions of the methods we look into here.

STEP 1: GETTING STARTED

Spores are the "seeds" of the mushroom. When germinated they produce a fungal growth known as mycelia. Mycelial cultures are commonly available for a wide variety of edible species. However, those who wish to cultivate the more psychoactive species must usually start from spores, owing to the delicate legal situation with which the noble fungi find themselves inanely associated. (Mycelia may contain trace amounts of scheduled substances, while spores do not.) Spore prints may be purchased from a variety of sources (see source listing), some of which are regular advertisers in HIGH TIMES. Or, if you have access to fresh mushrooms, you can make your own spore print.

Spores are usually transferred onto a sterilized agar medium for germination. This is easily accomplished with a pressure cooker and a clean work area. Thirty grams of premixed agar nutrient powder will mix with 3/4 of a liter of water to fill a sleeve of 20 petri dishes. Using a narrow-necked, one-liter

→

the aphids away with a forceful stream of water before spraying with an insecticide.

If a column of ants is running up the stem, then the aphid population is well-established and is being managed by an ant colony. You must rid the grow room of both the aphids and the ants, because ants use aphids like we use milking-cows. Ants carry aphids to other plants and harvest their honeydew excretions. Set out standard ant traps or other ant-control concoctions from any supermarket. These contain a poison sugar solution that the ants transport back to their nest. It will take a few days to a week, but soon they'll disappear, since the whole colony dies from eating the poison (commercial ant poisons are usually arsenic or very slow-degrading organic toxins). Don't put ant traps in your pots. Don't ever let the poison wash into your soil. Place the traps near the ants' entrance to the room, or as far from your garden as practical. Eliminating the ants stops them from further spreading the aphids and from bringing new aphids into the garden and reinfecting the plants. Follow the column of ants and seal their entry into the room. Or place cardboard collars around the stem of each plant and spread Tanglefoot (a sticky substance sold in garden shops) on the collars to stop the ants from spreading the aphids. You might also circle each pot with masking tape and cover the tape with Tanglefoot. This prevents almost any crawler from reaching other plants.

Aphids are one of the few insect problems that soapy water treatments reasonably control. A thorough washing with a soapy solution of Ivory soap reduces the population to acceptable proportions on seedlings. A better, nonchemical control is a spray made from three hot peppers (or cayenne pepper), an onion or two and a couple cloves of garlic. Grind, pulverize or mash the ingredients. Let them sit in two quarts of water for a few days, and occasionally shake the mixture. Filter the solution through a very fine mesh screen or several layers of cheesecloth. Use a coffee filter if the solution clogs in your sprayer. Add a few drops of detergent and spray as you would an insecticide. This spray works very well outdoors, and the aphids seem to gladly seek greener, or perhaps cooler, pastures. This spray also helps with almost any other pest. Try it if you want to avoid using chemical pesticides, but don't use it close to harvest.

Supermarkets, nurseries, and plant shops carry a number of sprays that eliminate aphids. Pyrethrum is a natural insecticide produced by plants in the chrysanthemum family. It's not toxic to mammals (you), and it quickly degenerates to harmless natural compounds. Pyrethrum compounds are the insecticides of choice for many growers because of their safety, natural origin and effectiveness. Ortho, Chacon, Attack and many other brands of pyrethrum sprays or general insecticides for vegetable gardens should be very effective for a wide range of problem insects.

Malathion, orthene, diazinon, nicotine sulphates and other safe-to-use insecticides are also effective against aphids. Safer Insecticidal Soap, sprayed every 10 days, controls aphids well. Make sure you repeat the sprayings and thoroughly saturate all of the plant at the recommended intervals.

Mites and whiteflies proliferate quickly, and both have a life cycle that makes complete eradication difficult. If you keep their populations under control, you have succeeded in your main objective.

MITES

Mites are tiny (about 1/100th to 1/16th of an inch) crab- or spider-like creatures that may be black, red, green or yellow (usually they're part black and part transparent). Probably you'll first notice that the top surfaces of lower leaves have speckles—tiny white or yellow specks caused by the mites sucking plant juices. Look up to the light through a damaged leaf, and you might see transparent specks from mite damage, or black specks, which are the mites. Poke them with your finger, and they'll run away (you now know that, sadly, you have a problem). One mite, the eriaphyid mite (Acrilopos *cannabicola*) is specific to cannabis. If the infestation is well-established, you'll see spider webbing at the crooks of branches and leaf stalks. By this time you're in real trouble, and if the plants are nearing maturity, just try to keep the damage to a minimum before harvesting.

Orthene is the most effective; it and diazinon, malathion and pyrethrum sprays are the only reasonably effective and safe sprays to use. Kelthane, which works well against mites, is harmful to the environment and to you, and is not recommended. Diazinon, pyrethrum and malathion sprays might work if you are not in a major agricultural area. In such areas, where the mites have become resistant, they're useless.

Spray at seven-day intervals at least three times. Don't spray if you're within three weeks of harvest. Washing the plants with soap is not worth the hassle. Soapy sprays work well for some plants, but with mites on marijuana, they don't help much at all. Mites are protected by marijuana's hairy or cystolith-covered leaves. No soap or water remedy for mites on marijuana seems to work effectively, even when used with detergent penetrants.

To prevent mites, periodically spray your plants with fresh water. Mites like a dry, stagnant environment. In several grow rooms, a twice-weekly spray of fresh water to the undersides of all leaves helps significantly in preventing mite infestations to all plants, including marijuana. A vent-fan or directed fan also helps prevent initial contamination. Spraying the undersides of leaves periodically with water and keeping the air in your room moving are the best noninsecticidal procedures to use if you anticipate a possible mite attack.

For infested gardens, lowering the temperature slows down the mites more than it affects the growth of the plants. Lower the temperature at night (open windows) to slow the mites' life cycle. Lowering the temperature and spraying with water are both helpful if you're nearing harvest and don't want to use insecticides.

If you discover that only one or two plants have mites, remove them from the garden or move them to the garden's periphery so that their leaves don't contact another plant's leaves. Encircle all pots with a band of masking tape or surround the lower stem with a cardboard collar. Cover the tape or collar with a layer of Tanglefoot or heavy-weight motor oil. The sticky barrier captures mites and stops their spread to other plants.

One worthwhile treatment for mites, and almost any other insect, is a fogger generally used for fleas and roaches. These "bug bombs" are very effective, but possibly poisonous on plants you intend to ingest. In fact, use them only in the seedling or vegetative stages of growing if other insecticides haven't worked.

Holiday Fogger seems to work the best, probably because its concentration of active ingredients is mild compared to other foggers, such as Hartz, Ortho or Germain's and other concentrated foggers which can damage the plants. Close all ventilation to the room and

container, sterilize the mixture in a pressure cooker for 30 minutes at 15 psi. Seal the top of the one-liter container with a loose twist-top or a cotton plug wrapped with aluminum foil. This allows for steam penetration. After cooking and when cool enough to handle, pour the still-warm agar into the petri dishes. As it cools, the agar gels and becomes the perfect home for spores to grow in, when transferred quickly and cleanly from your spore print with a sterile scalpel. Baby-food or other small jars may be substituted for petri dishes; cook the agar directly inside the jars.

Follow the manufacturer's instructions for safe operation of your pressure cooker. Inexpensive models may be purchased at department stores in the kitchenware section. These usually have a small capacity and a "rocker" regulator rather than the preferred visual pressure gauge. When you can, move up to a nice "All-American" 21-quart unit or larger.

Presterilized agar dishes may also be purchased from a science or chemistry supply source.

A week or so after transferring the spores to agar, mycelia should become evident as pure white colonies of growth. If any color other than white is noted, transfer a small piece of mycelia to another petri dish. This process may be repeated until only the desired white mycelia grows on your plate.

Those who wish to avoid this stage will be happy to know that Psilocybe Fanaticus (see source listing) offers an innovative method of spore transfer via a liquid spore solution. This streamlined technique has definite advantages for those who may be intimidated by sterile lab work.

STEP 2: SPAWN PRODUCTION

Once you have your mycelia in hand you will use it to inoculate or "infect" a spawn medium. The most common is rye grain. A standard spawn recipe for rye grain is: 200 ml water, 200 grams rye and one gram of ground gypsum (optional) per quart jar. This formula is soaked overnight before pressure-cooking at 15 psi for one hour. The lids of the petri dishes should be loosened slightly or drilled with a 3/8" hole and fitted with a filter disk for breathability. When finished cooking, tighten the loose lids as you pull them out of the pressure cooker.

Successful inoculation of grain is not difficult, especially with a little practice. Basically, a small piece of mycelia-covered agar is quickly transferred into each of the sterilized and cooled grain jars. Close the lid quickly and shake the jar thoroughly to distribute the agar throughout the grain. This helps speed the growth of the mycelia.

Using an ion generator/air cleaner is an

inexpensive way to keep your workspace clean. Ultimately, those who get serious with their hobby will want a sterile air-flow hood, which makes sterile work literally a breeze. These units create a sterile airstream, in which transfers may be performed with considerable ease.

STEP 3: SPAWNING

Once the grain is thoroughly infested with pure white mycelia, it is either fruited directly in the jar (a popular method in the late '70s) or broken up into individual grains and used to "seed" or spawn compost, straw or a similar medium.

Fruiting mushrooms on grain has the advantage of convenient access to all required materials, even in an urban situation. Country or suburban folk may choose the higher production capabilities that a compost or straw medium offers. Shredded, pasteurized straw in particular makes a clean, easy-to-work-with medium that is enjoyed by S. *cubensis*, the potent panaeolus *cyanescens* and the highly edible and nonpsychoactive oyster mushrooms, among others.

To pasteurize, soak the shredded straw in 160° F water for 30-45 minutes and drain well. A simple way of accomplishing this is in one thick, or two thinner, plastic garbage bags. If your hot-water system is equipped with a thermostat, set it on high. Use a candy thermometer to monitor the water temperature. When finished, simply poke holes in the bag and allow to drain. The whole procedure is easy to accomplish in a bathtub or shower. Those without hot-water thermostat controls may heat water in which to soak the straw on a stove. (Straw in an open container needs to be weighted down to be fully submerged.)

The grain spawn is then thoroughly mixed with the drained and cooled straw or compost—about one cup of spawn per square foot of substrate—and placed in bags or bins 4"-6" deep. The mycelia will grow through the new medium in a week or two, depending on temperature and species. 80-84° F is perfect for maximum growth of S. *cubensis*. Slightly cooler is fine, but warmer temperatures may harm the cultures. Allow the straw to breathe but not dry out. Note that you are now working with a clean but not sterile process.

STEP 4: FRUITING

Mushrooms are the fruit of the underground mycelia. Once your grain, compost or straw is fully infested with the white fungal network,

→

place the fogger so that it doesn't directly contact the plants. Raise a bedsheet or newspapers above the plants to protect them from direct contact with the spray (these foggers actually spray the insecticide rather than creating a fog). Don't enclose the plants; just position the protective sheet so that droplets don't land directly on the plants, then follow package directions. One or two deployments of foggers can completely eliminate mites and anything else that crawls in your garden. After seven to ten days, repeat the fogger treatment for best results. Foggers and systemic treatments may be your best options for dealing with mites. They're useful for seedlings, but don't use them if your plants are flowering.

WHITEFLIES

Whiteflies are white (you probably guessed that), but they're not flies; they're small moths about one-tenth-of-an-inch long. You'll see the adults fluttering erratically about the garden anytime you disturb the plants. Eggs, pupae, nymphs and tiny honey-like balls of adult excretions dot the undersides of leaves. You can eliminate many of the larvae by running your fingers along the undersides of the leaves and by disposing of heavily infested leaves altogether. Whiteflies also attract ants, but ants don't "cultivate" whiteflies like they do aphids. As with all insects, if you want to "search and destroy" them, lower the temperature in your grow room, which makes any insect sluggish.

Control whiteflies by spraying with diazinon, malathion, orthene or pyrethrum sprays. Spray at six- to eight-day intervals, particularly on the undersides of the leaves. Wash the plants with soap (Ivory flakes) to help lower the general population, but this is a pain if the plants are beyond the seedling stage. Try one of the other treatments suggested here. If you don't want to use a chemical insecticide, maintain population control by spraying weekly with Safer soap, by hanging sticky attractor cards that are available at nurseries and by vacuuming the adults.

Whitefly Attack is one commercial brand of attractor card that captures the adults. These sticky cards act like flypaper, and the color of the cards attracts whiteflies, gnats, leaf hoppers, and flying aphids. Bright yellow-green or yellow-orange colors attracts whiteflies. The yellow-orange color is similar to the color of Kodak film envelopes and boxes. Cover any facsimile (Kodak slide boxes, cardboard painted yellow, etc.) with either a very heavy motor oil or Tanglefoot. Hang the colored cards or flypaper near the plant tops and periodically shake the plants. Adult whiteflies land on the cards and stick to the tacky surface. These cards won't eliminate the problem, but they do help to curtail a population explosion.

Also very helpful for whiteflies and any other flying insects is a vacuum cleaner. Yes, vacuuming does help. Simply shake each plant vigorously, which should force the adults to take to the air, and you can suck them up like an undersea monster out of Yellow Submarine. Then, vacuum the undersides of leaves. You won't completely rid the garden of pests, but especially if you're nearing harvest, this is a worthwhile control.

MEALYBUGS

Mealybugs are white, about 1/8" long, and look like small, fuzzy, white sowbugs. Once mealybugs are well-established, you might see cotton-like or woolly materials or "tents" at the crooks of branches, or where a leaf stalk meets a branch. Marijuana is not a mealybug's favorite plant, and it's easy to eliminate them, or at least reduce their population to nondetrimental proportions.

Kill mealybugs with a cotton swab dipped in standard rubbing alcohol—seek and saturate each bug or cottony mass. Diazinon, nicotine sulphate, orthene, and malathion are all effective and safe insecticidal controls for mealybugs if the "search and destroy" procedure with alcohol doesn't control the pest.

SCALE

Scale insects encase themselves in a waxy or hardened protective covering in the adult stages. They're about 1/12" to 1/6" long. The adult females are brown and stationary, and they establish themselves along stems and large branches, but the larval stages move about the plant. Check along the stems, where you may see a hardened, brown protrusion, or what looks like a blemish or raised node clinging tightly to the stem, which contains an adult.

Scale infestations are seldom serious, but if they appear when the plant is young, you'll want to eliminate them. Diazinon, malathion orthene or a number of oil-based general plant sprays should eliminate the pests. Scale insects proliferate slowly, making control or elimination with alcohol on a cotton swab touched to each pest a leisurely task. You can also scrape them off with a sharp knife. The hand-scrape or alcohol method works well enough for minor infestations if you watch carefully and keep after them.

LEAF HOPPERS

If you've ever had an outdoor garden, you've probably seen leaf hoppers. Usually they're green with red stripes and about one-half-inch long, although they also come in other colors or color combinations. Leaf hoppers shouldn't be an indoor problem, but if you see many of them, take the time to spray with pyrethrum, malathion or diazinon before any serious problem occurs. Two thorough sprayings with any of these insecticides should eliminate leaf hoppers. Yellow hanging cards with a sticky coating or vacuuming also helps in small gardens.

FLEA BEETLES

Flea beetles are tiny black beetle-like creatures that jump like fleas. They generally attack only flowers, and rarely appear on marijuana. One treatment with a diazinon or malathion spray should rid the garden of flea beetles.

THRIPS

Thrips are speck-sized insects which shouldn't be a problem. Thrips are more insect-like than flea beetles, and with a close look you'll see their wings. To check for thrips, spread white paper below the plant and jar the plant repeatedly. You should see tiny, shiny, black specks if thrips are present. Orthene or malathion sprayed twice, one week apart, should eliminate all of the thrips. Flea beetles and thrips only occasionally invade a marijuana garden, and neither pest should be a serious problem.

CATERPILLARS

Caterpillar is a general term for many larvae of moths and butterflies. They have enormous appetites and the first sign of their presence is that portions of the leaves will be eaten. Some caterpillars take on the color of the host plant, and therefore are hard to spot. The "hunt and destroy"

---

you're ready to produce mushrooms. Most species react to cooler temperatures, fresh air and light to initiate the sexual, spore-producing stage of their growth cycle. At this point, most growers cover the mushroom mycelia with about an inch of peat-based casing soil. This provides a moisture reservoir in which the mushroom pinheads form. (The methods developed by Psilocybe Fanaticus also bypass this final casing step and fruit the cultures directly.) Casing-soil recipes vary from grower to grower. Typically, peat is brought up to a more neutral pH by the addition of a crushed limestone or chalk buffer (4-8 parts peat to 1-2 parts buffer), possibly adding vermiculite or perlite for texture. When kept moist, the mycelia grows up and into the casing layer within a few days.

Provided with high humidity, fresh air, cooler temperatures (70-75° F) and light, mushrooms will appear as tiny dots in the casing layer within a week or two after its application.
#238, June 1995

DO'S AND DON'TS FOR THE NOVICE MICROGROWER

...Keep a clean work area when making transfers. Personal hygiene scores you points here.

...Sterilize your transfer scalpel on a small butane or alcohol flame. Quickly cool the scalpel in agar or sterilized water before making transfers.

...Read a good mushroom-growing book to familiarize yourself with the concepts and techniques of spore and tissue culture.

...Cover your face with a bandanna or surgical mask to prevent breathing into the sterile work area.

...Keep a respectful and positive attitude. You are working with a living, breathing organism that requires sensitivity on your part.
DON'T...

...Over-disinfect (chemical warfare). Remember aerosol disinfectants and rubbing alcohol are flammable. This is very important, especially when working with a flame in a small space!

...Be discouraged. The mistakes you make will teach you as much as your successes.

...Mention legally questionable species when ordering supplies.
#238, June 1995

TERMITES

We have found that old dead roots from other trees attracts them. So does fresh cow manure. Our solution is simple. Mix a moderate amount of cedar pine chips into the planting mix or throughout the planting bed. Termites can't stand cedar pine and will avoid it. It has worked for us for over ten years.

A Skunk Grower
Missouri

#140, April 1987

GROUNDHOG PROTECTION

I had tried dusting, spraying, and even woven fence wire cages to stop groundhog damage. None of these seemed to work. They would even get into the wire cages and continued to strip the plants.

This year I tried using dry chlorine, which gives off vapors for quite a while. I have not seen one sign of the groundhog since.

Another thing I stumbled upon that I believe has really paid off during the past summer which was really dry, was that when I started my plants indoors in peat pellets, I unintentionally let them get very stemmy. I would say that they had six inches of bare stem.

At first I kicked myself for allowing this to happen. But now I think I did something right. I placed the plant so just a little stem was above the ground, the rest of it was buried. They were my most vigorous plants.

R.C.
Iowa

After trying to shoot groundhogs and woodchucks out of existence, I met an old lady who told me how to get rid of them. I just plant a marigold next to each plant and the animals stay away. For three years I haven't lost another plant to groundhogs. If you still run across a groundhog, find his hole, cover the ground with lye and he will get the stuff on his feet, lick it off and die.

Big Uke, the Mountain Man
Hyden, Kentucky

#129, May 1986

method is effective if you take the time to search them out. Some caterpillars naturally gravitate to the more succulent shoots, so first look along the stem of the top-growing shoots. Orthene and diazinon are effective killers of most caterpillars. For long-term control, repeated spraying with bacillus *thuringiensis* (a beneficial bacteria) prevents and eliminates caterpillars and many other larval or grub problems. If you find leaves with portions eaten but can't find the caterpillars, wait a few hours after the lights have gone off. Turn the lights back on, and you'll probably find these nighttime feeders near the tops of the plants.

ANTS AND TERMITES

Ants and termites are major problems only when the plants are rooted in the ground. Any decaying matter such as composts or manures attracts both pests. If they are a problem, avoid the use of composts, humus and manures in future crops. Pull out any old stumps in the planting bed. The best preventative is to mix some cedar chips into your planting mixture, or, for outdoor growers, to mix the chips throughout the planting bed. This procedure works very well in repelling termites, which may eat into the main stem. Simply flooding the bed repeatedly may drive termites away. Or buy Arab termite control to rid any garden of termites. It's safe to use, and doesn't harm the plants. Ants also present problems by damaging roots or woody parts of the stem. Ants also may encourage aphid problems.

Standard ant traps, ant stakes or ant poisons are completely effective in eliminating all ant problems indoors. Or surround the base of the stem with a cardboard collar. Cover the collar with Tanglefoot or a heavy-weight motor oil.

EARWIGS, SOWBUGS, GNATS AND OTHER INSECTS

Earwigs, sowbugs, gnats and other insects living in the soil can be controlled by a rotenone soil drench. Two applications should eradicate all pests. All of these soil-borne insects prefer and thrive in soils rich in composts, humus and other organic materials. Usually they're fairly harmless and only a moderate nuisance. However, earwigs and sowbugs may eat and kill germinating sprouts, and many soil pests eat roots. Get rid of them unless you're nearing harvest.

ANIMALS AND OTHER PESTS

Mice and rats may eat seeds and shoots and hence devastate a newly planted garden. Most problems with mice and rats occur in autumn or winter, because rodents come indoors to escape the cold.

If you've had a problem, the surest protection is to surround the plants with window screening or another barrier. Once plants are past the seedling stage, mice are not a problem, but rats may eat shoots or strip away layers of the stem (cambium layer), which can kill the plant. Repellents sold for rodent control and numerous poisons available from supermarkets and hardware stores should work well enough. Be careful with rat poisons. Some can kill pets and people, too. Keep poisons away from the plants; never let water wash over the poisons and run into your soil. Mothballs laid in the perimeter of the garden are purported to repel rodents. Set up a barrier or enclosure for the surest way to protect precious seeds.

Cats and dogs—don't rely on training your pets to stay out of the garden. Dogs may dig or eliminate into the soil. Soil is more natural to a cat's instincts than a kitty-litter tray, and the jungle ambiance of marijuana gardens is irresistible to most cats. Cats and some dogs also love to chew on leaves, and they can easily destroy young plants. Devise a cat-and-dog-proof barrier before you plant. Once the plants are larger, your cats will spend hours in the garden, and an occasional munching of a leaf causes no harm.

In general:

Aphids, mealybugs, mites, scale insects, whiteflies, thrips, flea beetles, leaf hoppers, cutworms, cabbage worms, leaf miners and many other insects and grub or larval pests are susceptible to diazinon, pyrethrums, orthene or malathion. Alternating one insecticide (diazinon or orthene) with another (pyrethrums or malathion) works better than repeated sprayings with only one insecticide. Pests often build up resistance in agricultural areas, and you should try several sprays if the first isn't working.

Liquid Sevin also kills almost any insect or bug, but it's extremely toxic to beneficial insects, bees and fish. Use Liquid Sevin only if other sprays are ineffective.

Rotenone is a general, natural insecticide derived from the roots of the flame tree and other legumes. Although quite effective against a wide range of insects, rotenone is particularly useful against caterpillars in a spray or dust form, and as a soil drench against sowbugs, gnats and other soil-borne insects.

Safer Insecticidal Soap kills and controls aphids, mealybugs and root mealybugs, scale insects, spider mites, thrips, whiteflies, leaf hoppers and many other problem insects. Safer soap is very popular with growers. Use up to one week before harvest. Be sure to protect eyes when spraying!

Systemic insecticides are applied while watering. The insecticide is absorbed and distributed throughout the plant. Systemics are especially lethal to all pests that suck plant juices or chew leaves, and they're an excellent preventative for all the insects described here. Systemics might be your best choice for controlling mites and whiteflies. If you have had previous problems with mites or whiteflies, try applying a systemic when the plants are young, before you see any pests. Repeat the application one month later.

Many systemics are intended solely for ornamentals, since they do not break down into harmless by-products quickly. Make sure that the systemic you choose is intended for use on edible crops, and note the number of days before harvest when you should stop using the systemic. The average time between the last application and harvest is about 30 days. Dexol Houseplant Insecticide is one safe brand among many that you can use.

BEAT THE HEAT
by Zero Kelvin

At the end of a busy day you kick back, relax to your favorite tunes, unwind with a toke of fresh ganja from your high-intensity garden. It's safe and secure in your home.

But beyond the walls of your castle, at a distance in the night, the narco-police may be scanning your privacy with "Big Brother" science. That grow-room temple once so secure may well be a beacon to the

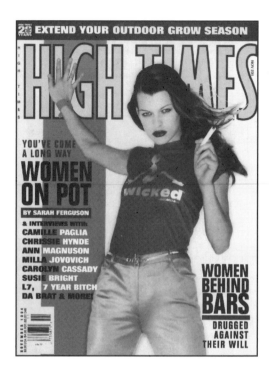

EXTEND YOUR SEASON WITH ROW COVERS
BY BUDD GREENBURG

Row covers or cloches ("cloche" is French for "bell") have been around since the 17th century, helping growers prolong seasons and protect crops from pests. Outside of certain parts of Alaska and Canada, row covers can be used to get harvests as last as the first week in December in most of North America, without any supplementary heating.

This method of growing is also extremely effective for raising late-season sticky bud. The safest way to do this is to be a known gardener and row-cover user in a rural location. I recommend growing vegetable crops for the first few seasons.

The earliest cloches were made from big bell-shaped glass jars and usually covered only one plant. Today's versions are about 100 feet long. I used scrap wood and wire for the frame, two layers of 3mm polyethylene to cover the mini-greenhouses, and big rocks and dirt as anchors for the poly on both sides.

If you start the cuttings in mid-June, they should be well rooted by early July. The young clones then go into the freshly prepared garden beds with no covering.
#231, November 1994

PREFLOWERING: IS IT MALE OR FEMALE?

BY MEL FRANK

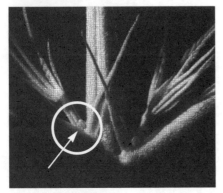

MALE PREFLOWERING

Female marijuana plants are more desireable than males. Females form the familiar flower clusters (buds) that ordinarily make up the marijuana most of us buy.

It is to the grower's advantage to separate the females from the males as soon as possible. Although the male's leaves and shoots are as potent as the female's before flowering, they can't compare to the matured female's buds in potency or in weight.

Male flowers form in abundance when left to grow. The unopened flowers ———➤

MALE FLOWERING

narco-fascists—its excessive heat radiation clearly detectable on their thermal scanners.

This is not science fiction.

But science is a double-edged sword. When scientific apparatus is put to perverted use in an attempt to steal your freedom, knowing how it works and its limitations can give you that "edge" of protection.

Thermal scanning (thermography) measures the radiant temperature of surface features from a distance by sensing the wavelength range 3000 to 14,000 nm (nanometer: There are one-thousand-million nanometers to the meter). Multispectral scanning is sensitive to a wider range of wavelength bands, from visible light (roughly 400 nm to 700 nm), through thermal infrared (light having wavelengths greater than 700 nm).

Temperature is one of the principal factors in virtually all physical, chemical and biological processes. Kinetic temperature is a measure of the average translational energy of the molecules constituting a body. Thus it measures a body's internal energy state. Loose meaning? It is this energy of molecular movement which is sensed as "heat," and when we measure the internal temperature of an object, or the temperature at its surface, it is kinetic temperature that is measured.

Objects radiate energy as a function of their temperature. This emitted energy—infrared light—is an "external" manifestation of an object's energy state and may be remotely sensed and used to determine the radiant temperature of the object. It's the radiant temperature of an object which is the major factor determining which band of wavelengths (think "color") of infrared (IR) light is being emitted by the object. For example, the IR source in your remote-control unit will have a high radiant temperature, even though its kinetic temperature will be only slightly greater than room temperature. Thermal scanning devices detect differences in radiant temperature.

Any object having a kinetic temperature greater than absolute zero —0° Kelvin (K) or -273° Celsius (C)—emits radiation whose intensity and spectral composition are a function of the material type involved and the kinetic temperature of the object under consideration. This emitted radiation is measured over a discrete wavelength and used to find the radiant temperature of the radiating surface. It is this indirect approach to temperature measurement that is used in thermal sensing.

The atmosphere has a significant effect on the intensity and spectral composition of the energy recorded by a thermal system. Gases and suspended particles in the atmosphere may absorb radiation emitted from distant objects decreasing the energy reaching the observer, or they may emit radiation of their own, thus increasing it. Atmospheric absorption and scattering tend to make such objects appear colder than they are; atmospheric emission tends to make them appear warmer. Both effects are directly related to the atmospheric distance through which the radiation is sensed. Even on a clear day, aerosols can cause major modifications to the IR light passing through them. Dust, carbon particles, smoke and water droplets can therefore modify thermal measurements. Fog and clouds are essentially opaque to thermal radiation. Thermal system temperature measurements can easily be in error by 2° C or more at distances of 300 meters.

Surface features emit radiation primarily in the thermal infrared wavelengths. Confusion exists between the terms "thermal imagery" and "infrared photography." Infrared (IR) photography results from the photochemical detection of near-IR energy. "Near-IR" is IR light having wavelengths almost as short as those of the visible light band, thus it may be thought of as "near(ly visible)-IR". This near-IR energy is not directly related to temperature, except in the case of very hot objects.

Electronic detectors must be used to sense the longer-wavelength thermal infrared energy. Their output may be recorded in a variety of ways. For visual analysis, the output is displayed as an image on film and is called a thermogram. The film is used as a recording device, not as the original detection device. Generally, when an electronic IR detector is used to examine a distant object, the process is referred to as thermal scanning.

There are two main atmospheric "windows" used in thermal scanning. The largest window is the 8,000 to 14,000 nm wavelength region of the spectrum. The term "window" simply means that the atmosphere is especially transparent to this spectral range. Most thermal scanning is performed through this window. The "emitting ability" of a material is referred to as its emissivity: the factor that measures how efficiently an object radiates energy. The emissivities of different objects vary greatly with material types in the 8,000 to 14,000 nm range, however, for any given material type, the emissivity can often be considered constant in this range. However, as objects are heated above ambient temperature, their emissive radiation peaks shift to shorter wavelengths. In special purpose applications, such as forest-fire mapping or indoor grow-room detection, systems operating in the 3,000 to 5,000 nm atmospheric window range are used. This offers improved definition of hot objects at the expense of the surrounding terrain.

Thermal sensors detect radiation from, approximately, the first 50,000 nm of the surface being scanned. This radiation may or may not be indicative of the interior temperature. Thermal scanning of roofs is done on cold winter nights at least six to eight hours after sunset to minimize the effects of solar heating. Scans can also be conducted on cold overcast winter days. Wet roofs obscure the scanner readings.

A variety of scanning equipment is in use, which may be ground-based or airborne. Video camera and display units may be used to monitor buildings. This equipment operates in the range of -20 to +900° C and can resolve temperature differences of 0.2° C on surfaces whose temperatures average 30° C.

Thermal scanning equipment is very sophisticated and sensitive, but it is not supernatural. Scanners cannot sense through walls and can only detect temperatures very close to the surface of the object in question. Sufficient insulation will reduce the internal heat being transmitted to the outer wall or roof surfaces and diffuse it. The grow room must first be thoroughly insulated, leaving no gaps where heat can escape.

The biggest problem then becomes venting the hot air from the grow room. If hot air is exhausted directly outside through an auxiliary vent cut into a wall or roof, without precooling it to the outside-air temperature, the vent will resemble a flame thrower on a thermal-scanner display screen.

The simplest way to remove the hot air is to conceal it by venting it into the hot-water heater exhaust-ventilator pipe. Water heaters come on frequently to keep the water supply hot, and gases exiting the water-heater exhaust pipe are much hotter than grow-room air. When splicing into a water-heater exhaust pipe, use a 45-degree tee with the angle pointed up in the direction of air flow, not down toward the heater. If grow-room air flow is vented down toward the water heater, it will create back pressure in the pipe and could prove dangerous. For added safety, mount the 45-degree tee as far away from the water heater as

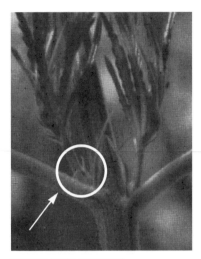

FEMALE PREFLOWERING

look somewhat like tiny bunches (cymes) of grapes. A classic male preflower is flat and spade-shaped with a tiny stalk.

Another form of male preflowers is a teardrop-shaped knob raised on a tiny stalk.

Females form flowers at the tips of branches and the junctures of leaves and branches. The flowers form into progressively larger collections (racemes) known commonly as "buds."
#162, February 1989

FEMALE FLOWERING

VINTAGE 1986

BY OWL

I have been a professional pot farmer for 10 years, growing my first outdoor sinsemilla crop in 1976. My operation was one of several located in a mountain range where, according to Indian legend, the souls of the dead depart this world on their journey to the Great Spirit. The cannabis grown here is powerful medicine.

My colleagues and I shared a wonderfully discreet fellowship. We would celebrate my birthday in mid-September as the beginning of harvest fest. The plants never failed to produce delicious sample buds.

I did all the breeding. Unfortunately, some boastful indiscretions brought night thieves down on us, rip-offs which continued for three years. At the same time, local pot eradication teams increased aerial surveillance.

None of the orginal partnerships survived. Two groups went north to Humboldt and Mendocino counties to diversify. Two groups reorganized here. My team is the only one left. The other team's remote plantation made local news in 1984. CAMP huns hacked up their crop and burned it on a huge pyre, though no one could be found to arrest.

I've seen it all: amateurs bringing heat, CAMP inquisitions, shootouts with psychopathic thieves, betrayal by greed. I survive in this business because I have gone deeper into the wilderness than anemic thieves or pot-bellied sheriffs care to penetrate. Logistical systems contribute to our prosperity.

The 1986 California sinsemilla crop was small. My crop sold out fast. The demand for it was the highest ever. In 1986 every grower I know in Humboldt and Mendocino was raided illegally by CAMP search-and-destroy skirmish lines. No one was arrested—just violated.

#142, June 1987

possible. DO NOT attempt this installation unless the water heater is turned off.

A more complex alternate method of concealing that worrisome exhaust air is to use it to heat other rooms. However, the air will have to be scrubbed of unwanted greenhouse odors first. Of course, removing suspicious greenhouse odors can be just as worrisome a problem as masking suspicious IR emissions. And it should be said: It is possible to detect those odors—using an IR spectrometer—in the air around a house, if they are not scrubbed.

Finally, bear in mind that the Fourth Amendment to the Constitution in the Bill of Rights has no means of enforcement since the Supreme Court replaced the "exclusionary rule" with the "good faith" doctrine. Theoretically, the narco-police can get a search warrant for any house or building with a water-heater exhaust-ventilation pipe by filing a good-faith affidavit stating they believe the water heater is intended to hide the exhaust-air flow from an illicit marijuana grow room.

Unfortunately, there is no guarantee against invasion by narco-police-fascists with (or without) a search warrant—not even if you are willing to live in a cold-water flat and generate no heat at all. So while attempting to "hide the light," don't forget to "stand up for your rights."

Technical reference: *Remote Sensing and Image Interpretation*, second edition, by Thomas M. Lillesand and Ralph W. Kiefer, University of Wisconsin. John Wiley & Sons publisher.

GROWING AND BREEDING SPICE GANJA

by Owl

My crop consists mostly of fifth-and sixth-generation Spice ganja—the result of an accidental cross made in Southern California back in '78. An Oaxacan plant went male and pollinated a grower's early-flowering eighth-generation Afghan females while he was on a short vacation. I was lucky enough to hand-select 40 of those original hybrid seeds. Population closed in on that grower, and he was ripped off the next year, and both parent strains were lost. Fortunately the Spice was in those 40 seeds I was given.

I start Spice seeds indoors under lights in early spring. The 8' x 12' grow room is lit by two MS1000 halides. I use 20-oz Styrofoam cups as pots for each plant and fill the cups with commercial potting soil premixed with bloodmeal, bonemeal and wood-ash organic fertilizers. The seedlings remain on a 1-hour light/6-hour dark growth cycle for three weeks. Then the photoperiod is adjusted to a 12-hour light/12-hour dark schedule to induce flowering.

I make my first serious breeding selections when the males sex out. Males comprise 50% of the genetic material for the next generation, but what useful qualities do I want to breed into my strain from the male side? Earliness is important in any strain, so I group the earliest males into one area in the grow room. Frost resistance is important also. The later-sexing males are put outside into the cold to test for frost resistance. Spice males usually survive temperatures in the low 20s, indicating the first-flowering Spice males grouped in the warm grow room should have nearly the same strain frost resistance as those out in the cold. If any male outside survives a freeze into the teens, I save it for breeding.

When the weather outside has warmed up, I put the early males out to harden off. By then, I have separated enough females to prepare a load for the remote plantations.

I make the final choices for male breeders just before the last group of females in the grow room go out to the plantation. I already know they are the earliest males and are frost-resistant. Now I judge them for physical characteristics. Are the plants hardy? Are side shoots growing? Are the sepal clusters dense or loose; are they skimpy or abundant? Have resin globules formed on any staminate floral buds or bracts? Is varietal aroma present? (If not, I rub my thumb and index finger lightly on the stalk to volatilize the essential oils, then smell the aroma on my fingers, always looking for the plant that stands out from its brothers.) Those males chosen go to the plantation with the last load of females.

We bare-root all plants going to the plantation. This process enables us to carry up to 45 26"-high females in 6"-diameter bundles.

Bare-rooting causes considerable shock to cannabis plants. Over the years I have developed a method with a 99% success rate. Gently remove the Styrofoam cup from the plant's wet rootball. Then lay the plant down on a hard, flat surface. Take a garden hose and spray a jet of water at the rootball. This will dislodge the soil from the root system. Immediately place the plant into a bucket of water containing vitamin B-1 plus growth hormone. I use commercially-available vitamin B-1 with alpha-napthalene acetic acid (ANAA) growth promoter. Make sure the plant roots are submerged into the water. Label every plant with nursery slip-lock tags. The vinyl ones are best. (I once used a color-code identification system, but breeding became more complex. Now I use an alphanumeric code in which letters represent strain names and numbers represent breeding individuals.) Let the loose bunch stand in the solution overnight or for three to four hours to ensure the plants have absorbed the B-1 + ANAA.

When ready to move the shipment, take the plant cluster—while dripping wet—from the bucket and place its roots first into a plastic bag. Then slip the bundle—bag first—into a plastic pipe of adequate diameter and height that has been sealed at the bottom. Stove pipe with the bottom taped also works. Now the bare-rooted plantation bundle is snug, protected and ready to transplant.

Each plant is transplanted into a wet, 10-gallon-size hole at the plantation. The hole contains a 50-50 mixture of forest mulch-humus and dirt. The battery-powered, programmable water valve is on at transplant time, delivering water to each hole's 1 gph (gallons per hour) drip-emitter. The timer-valve is set to deliver water twice a day: 2 gallons in the early morning, then 2 gallons in the late afternoon. The nutrient injector adds B-1 + ANAA to the water. I dust each root system with Ringer Vegetable Garden Restore. It's a commercially-available combination of beneficial soil microorganisms and their nutrients. The soil microbes attach to the plant's microscopic feeder roots in a symbiotic relationship. The plants recover from the bare-rooting process in five-to-seven days, and are rejuvenated within two weeks.

In August, when the males begin flowering again, I cut bouquets

INSIDE SOUTHERN CALIFORNIA

BY CAPTAIN HOOTER

Three stage gardens form the perfect marriage with the sea of green method. The garden is separated into two areas. Lighting in the first area is run for eighteen hours on and six hours off to maintain the plant's vegetative cycle. Cuttings and seedlings are placed in a small chamber under fluorescent lights. The chamber is covered with clear plastic to retain humidity. Cuttings normally take root in a two to three week period. After roots develop, they are placed under a 1,000 watt halide light. It will take three to four weeks before they reach the desired height of 12 inches. Then they are moved to the flowering area until harvest.

A twelve-hour light cycle in this area, with a high pressure sodium lamp, has been found to be most successful. Until this method, yields of nine pounds per 25 square feet per year (the size of an average clothes closet) can be easily obtained.

The same climate of Humboldt is the indoor grower's bane. In Southern California, outdoor summertime temperatures often exceed 100 degrees. With the heat halide lamps produce, this can cause inside temperatures to soar up to as much as 125 degrees. One way to solve this problem is to set the light cycle to begin in the evening, avoiding the hottest part of the day.
#178, June 1990

POST-OPERATION GREEN MERCHANT MEMO

BY NIPSEY AND TIPSEY

A grow system for the Bush Years: The homemade cabinet garden featuring a 174-watt metal halide lamp and exhaust fan. Minimal power draw; no heat profile; locked cabinet; total secrecy and anonymity. No friends know about the garden. The light and fan are turned off when guests are expected. Remote off for "surprise guests."

Bottom half of cabinet will be mother/clone chamber. Upper section for budding. Produces a sweet three ounces every three months.

Growing medium: 1/3 perlite, 1/3 vermiculite, 1/3 sterile topsoil. Fertilizer: only organics—with each watering, use 1 teaspoon bat guano, 1/2 teaspoon fish emulsion, a few drops of Maxicrop seaweed, a pinch of organic wood ash, all added to the water.

Exhaust fan runs 24 hours per day. Bud light—12 hours per day. Clone/mother shelf is light-tight and has its own small exhaust fan. 18 hours light/6 dark.

Seeds: never mail order to your address or your name.

How to buy halide: Go to indoor garden shop in person, with dark glasses on. No names. No "pot" references. Just indoor gardening. If pressed, you should be prepared with a cover crop, like tomatoes or organic gourmet basil. Pay cash only. No checks or credit cards, no delivery of items. Cash and carry only.

#184, December 1990

from each plant before any sepal clusters open. Each bouquet is wrapped separately in paper towels that have been soaked in B-1 + ANAA solution, then transferred out of the plantation to vases containing more of the solution. The male bouquets finish ripening in the vases. (Add more water when the level in the vase drops.) When the majority of the sepal clusters open, I put the bouquet in an open brown paper bag to dry. Male pollen is susceptible to moisture damage. Humidity on the pollen will render it impotent and useless. Male pollen will remain viable in a dry paper bag up to three weeks.

When the selected females are ready for breeding, place the paper bag containing the male pollen and dried bouquet inside a plastic bag. This is to keep pollen from escaping the paper bag while carrying it through the plantation. Open both bags carefully and direct a well-developed lower branch from the breeder female into the paper bag. (It is easier if big shade leaves are removed from the breeder branch beforehand.) Then close the plastic-bag opening around the stem. Lightly tap the bag to stir up the pollen inside; give it 30 seconds, then do it again. Carefully remove the bags from the branch just bred. Tag that branch with breeding information.

Selecting breeder females can be a bewildering process when specimens number in the hundreds. The most important criterion is potency, but potency is the last quality to be tested. Pollination must take place before the plant is ripe, so the potency of each breeder isn't fully realized until after harvest—when samples are smoked to get the overall *feel* of that breeder's potency, taste and aroma.

The first quality I look for in florescent female ganja is the aroma given off by the essential oils on the live *colas*. There is a category of smell I call "Spice"—the name I have given to this strain. Not all Spice plants have it. At one extreme, some are putridly skunky; these are invariably short and leafy Afghan throwbacks. Others have only the faint smell of musk or earth; these are usually tall and airy Oaxacan throwbacks. The majority of Spice ganja (70-80%) falls within the range of fragrance that practically gets me high on smell alone. One quaff and my soul sings, "That's it!"

Once I am hooked by the aroma of a particular plant, I study it for physical characteristics; the most important being an estimate of dry bud weight after harvest. I will not breed a skimpy female unless the aroma is so affecting it won't leave me alone. But if I *do* breed it, its potency must be superior to other, bushier breeders. Even then, I will plant its seeds cautiously, in small numbers, for observation next season.

Spice ganja expresses itself in two ways. The 8' to 10'-tall Oaxaca phenotype produces moderately dense, *sativa*-type buds with thin, pointy bracts and the aroma of steel corroding. The taste is expansive and gets richer with every hit. The high is strong, clear and philosophical. The short 4' to 6'-tall Afghan phenotype produces maximum-density *indica*-type buds with high calyx-to-bract ratio, and carries the penetrating aroma of cardamom-chocolate-allspice. The taste is expansive, spicy and rich. The high is forceful—almost psychedelic. Both Spice variations are multicolored. The bract-leaf veins turn maroon to purple. The calyx is either solid purple or striped purple and green. Occasionally some pistils are pink or magenta.

There is more to variety than the *indica-sativa* controversy. It is essential to preserve old varieties and stabilize new ones. Keep the gene pools pure. Make hybrid crosses cautiously while continuing inbreeding with proven parental strains. First-generation hybrid crosses usually show superior vigor and a flashy new high, then fizzle out three or four generations later. Yet when a successful hybrid is stabilized, a wonderful new variety is added to the list that lifts the spirits of ganjaphiles.

Specimens of a strain still produce subtly-differing aromas and complexities of high and growth habits when in different microclimates. I have plantations a few miles apart and at varying elevations. Each plantation produces *colas* with nuances unique to the location, even though the strain used is the same throughout. And the district where my plantations are located produces ganja with overall characteristics that differ from *colas* grown by colleagues in another district, even though we use the same strain.

Growers operating in a superior district can develop a superior variety unique to that district. The strain will adapt to the local climate and express varietal qualities of bud structure, aroma, taste and effect (high) in response to that environment, including the indoor environment. This will become apparent by inbreeding (selfing) three generations from the P-1 seed-stock or F-1 hybrid.

Another factor added to the complex equation of variety is the personality and temperament of the grower/breeder. The spirit of ganja interacts with the soul of the grower on physical, conscious and unconscious levels. I have spent enough time with my plants over the generations to feel them sensing me. I breed the ones that appeal to me the most.

The birth of a new variety depends as much on good luck at the initial cross as it does on the breeder's skill in developing the next three generations. If you succeed in stabilizing a new strain, growers using your strain in other regions can expect to enjoy its unique varietal qualities for one generation at least. This is why it is important for serious breeders in established superior districts to supply fresh seed from the varieties developed there.

What makes a superior district? Outdoors, it's the test of time in the marketplace. Indoors is one district with many microclimates, depending on the systems used.

The best outdoor districts produce ganja superior to the best indoor systems. An average outdoor climate is inferior to the best indoor system. More stability and standardization can be achieved indoors, but at a cost to gene robustness. Each has its advantages.

OLD MAN & THE SEED

The seed came from some high-priced local weed. The plant was grown in a 4-gallon peat pot using peat moss, vermiculite and cow manure. It was only 30" tall. It yielded about 1-1/2 oz. of dried bud.

The Old Man and the Seed
London, Ontario
CANADA

#173, January 1990

BREEDING FOR BIG BUDS

by Jorge Cervantes

"Look at the size of that thing—I must be hallucinating," said Tim as he stared in awe at the huge six-inch-diameter flower top. "What did you put in this joint to make me see things twice as big as life? I mean, that is the biggest bud I've ever seen!"

"We call her Big Bud. I think she is one-hundred percent *indica*," replied James with a big smile. "I brought her back to Detroit from out West. Here, give her a try," said James, passing Tim a bomber of Big Bud.

Tim put the spliff between his lips and gently drew a few breaths through the unlit joint. "So fresh and minty, it's the best I've ever

FORCED FLOWERING

Recently I saw a show on PBS in which they discussed forcing bromeliads to flower using ethylene. Rather than using commerical preparations, these horticulturists tied the leaves up with string, creating a pocket in the center. They placed a small pouch made of cheesecloth filled with apple peels into the pocket. As the apple peels decompose they give off enough ethylene to induce flowering. I'm planning to place bags of peels all around my garden next time.

Prof. T.H. Custer, Chairman
The Homegrowers of Connecticut
#112, December 1984

CRAZY BUD

Seeds were started in mid-March in a garden at home. When these reached 6", they were transported 50 miles from the city to a forest in rural Virginia. There's a special rush you get while motoring down the highway with 150 seedlings in the back seat. Trust me, you don't want to be pulled over. We put out over 500 plants from April 1 to May 31. Our method of growing is to keep it simple and basic. We feel it is impossible to improve on Mother Nature, and as long as good seed stock is used, no special care is needed. The blend of bright sunny days, above-average rainfall and cool nights couldn't have been more perfect for our project. The photo shows our reward after one of the most beautiful seasons anyone can remember in Virginia. Now in the middle of September, we wait for our colas to fully ripen and then our 20-year dream of growing will become a reality.

Vamped in Virginia
J.W. and the Crazy Man

#233, January 1995

MAGNIFIED POT

BY "T.L."

A very close-up view of cannabis reveals another dimension of the plant's life. Cultivators can use magnification to determine the sex of the plant, as well as to diagnose plant maladies, particularly insect infestations. An 8x photographer's loupe or a 30x self-lighted portable field microscope are inexpensive tools for observation. "Blister" microscopes are inexpensive low-power instruments made for viewing specimens which have depth, such as a single flower petal or a section of a leaf. These 'scopes usually have optional eyepieces which give magnifications of 25x, 50x or 75x.

#116, April 1985

tasted. I take back all the bad stuff I said about indoor smoke," Tim said with a pleased, sheepish grin.

"They've been breeding some incredible plants out on the West Coast. When I was there, indoor growers were talking about the Hash Plant that matures into a 36" tall two-to-three-ounce plant (dried tops only) after eight weeks of flowering: stout, broad tops laden with thick, gooey resin. Or Lime Bud, a *sativa/indica* cross, with long, dainty, lime-green leaves and lightweight buds packed with pistils and glistening resin glands. Or Northern Lights, a mainstay variety in Vancouver, BC that matures into a four-foot, four-ounce plant at the ripe old age of 85 to 90 days. But everyone's favorite is Big Bud because she grows huge buds and has the sweetest, mintiest taste in the world. My last crop weighed in at three-and-a-half pounds—that's better than four ounces a plant!"

All of these varieties were developed by industrious, careful and caring individuals that have kept meticulous, detailed records of plant-growth habits and the offspring that resulted when they crossed a male plant with a female. Indoor breeding is two or three times faster than outdoors. As many as three generations may easily be completed in one year indoors. The breeder controls the hours of light and darkness per day, causing the plants to flower and produce seed at will.

Selective breeding (also known as selective sexual propagation) has completely changed the quality and yield of indoor marijuana crops. The starting point is to collect marijuana seed from well-known pot-growing regions throughout the globe. The various seed strains are grown and studied thoroughly without any cross breeding. Once each is understood, then selective breeding can begin, either to attain a pure seed stock or to improve the strain. Once the ultimate plant is developed through this sexual propagation, it can be cloned to preserve the genetic blueprint created by selective breeding.

Cannabis *indica* seeds are highly prized for their potency and adaptability to the indoor environment. The characteristics of *indica* plants include: squat, bushy, vigorous growth; early, sustained potency; disease resistance; and heavy bud yield. An *indica* plant may yield two to four times the dry-bud weight of a *sativa* at harvest. Thai, Colombian and Mexican are examples of cannabis *sativa*. These *sativa* varieties are tall, lanky and disease-resistant, with narrow, long leaves and light buds that take up to three months to mature. But the high is energetic, soaring and clear.

Ideally, skilled breeders will strive to retain the desirable dominant growth characteristics of both cannabis *sativa* and cannabis *indica* to form super strains. Breeders may cross a *sativa* with an *indica*, hoping to retain the desirable soaring high while keeping the short, stocky growth characteristics and early maturity of the *indica*.

Selective breeding requires the breeder to simply assume the role of Mother Nature once again. In nature, pollen from the male cannabis plant is shed into the wind to randomly fertilize any receptive female plant. A breeder adds precision and control to this process by catching pollen from a desirable male and carefully placing it in contact with chosen female pistils.

Two basic kinds of breeding are: (1) inbred or true bred—plants of the same strain or ancestry that are crossed with one another, and **(2)** outbred or hybrid—plants of different strains that are crossed or cross-pollinated.

The goal of inbreeding is to establish a pure breed to start from.

Selected females are pollinated with male pollen of the same strain, then the resulting seeds are planted and checked for variability. This process may take several generations to produce a strain that actually breeds true. Purebred plants are grown until the fifth to sixth generation, after which negative characteristics, like low potency, legginess and lack of vigor tend to dominate.

This true or pure breed is essential to establish common growth characteristics. Without a pure breed on one or both sides, it is difficult to predict the outcome of a hybrid cross. Ideally, both male and a female are purebred plants, with known ancestry and growth attributes.

A hermaphroditic plant (a plant displaying both male and female flowers) will self-pollinate and produce inbred seeds. Although this is a shortcut to inbreeding, the seedlings resulting from self-pollination may tend to be hermaphroditic themselves. This can be a real headache for the sinsemilla grower or breeder, with unwanted seeds and uncontrolled pollen. Nonetheless, the seed produced by a hermaphrodite that has just a few male flowers on a female plant will be 80-90% female seed. One easy way to produce seeds from an all-female clone crop is to stress one of the female branches by twisting a piece of wire around one of the branches a couple of weeks before flowering is induced. The extra stress will usually cause the plant to produce male flowers.

Outbreeding, or producing hybrid seed, has increased agricultural production more than anything. Farmers, breeders and cannabis horticulturists have found that crossing parents of different pure strains, especially those exhibiting exceptional, dominant, complementary characteristics, will result in a super plant, also referred to as hybrid vigor.

It is possible to cross *sativa/indica*. Some growers swear by the cross, saying you get the best of both plants: vigor and size from the *sativa*, and squat, bushy, early, potent growth from the *indica*.

Choosing from a large and varied plant stock is the key to successful breeding. Since the origin of most seed is dubious, an accomplished breeder waits to see what kind of plant it produces before deciding which plants to cross to form hybrid seed. If the breeder plants only a few seeds, there is no guarantee that they will grow into ideal breeding stock, even if they came from dynamite smoke. If the breeder instead selects the best plants from many seedlings of various strains of cannabis *indica* (and/or *sativa*), he or she will have a better chance of achieving the desired outcome.

BREEDING: STEP-BY-STEP

STEP ONE: Choose male breeding stock exhibiting desirable characteristics.

STEP TWO: One branch full of male flowers is all that will be needed, unless a large crop is desired. Unused branches may be stripped of flowers to help contain pollen and guard against accidental, random pollination. The male can be isolated from the females once flowers have developed, but not yet opened, by placing him in a sunny window or in a vegetative grow room. This will slow flower development and not hurt the male in any way.

A branch of ripe, male flowers may be cut and placed in water. It will remain healthy for several weeks. When the pollen sacks open, proceed with Step Three. The remaining male plant may then be cut back or harvested.

MARIJUANA SEXUALITY

Ethryl releases ethylene (a plant hormone used by plants during flowering) when it is used as a foliar spray. In marijuana, the photoperiod and other factors determine the time when the plant should enter the flowering phase of its cycle. Guided by its genetic blueprint, the plant subtly manufactures the proper hormones that inspire the bud primordia to become either male or female. From there the plant matures to adulthood. When the plant is first forming buds as a reaction to the change in light-cycle, it is especially susceptible to outside influences regarding its sexuality. By applying ethryl, which the plant recognizes as a female hormone, the scales are tipped in favor of femaleness, and the plant itself starts to produce the hormone on its own to maintain sexual stability. Marijuana sexuality is easy to manipulate. It has the genetic capability of becoming either sex, depending on the favorableness of its environment and the necessity for the continuance of the species. Rather than being genetically simply male or female, due to the XX and XY chromosomes, a great many of the phenotypic characteristics that lead us to believe a plant is male or female are not carried strictly on the sex chromosomes, but rather on the other chromosomes (autosomes). Ethryle is available from my company, Plantastic Plant Products. I market the product under the name Sensa-Spray.

Bob Ireland

#103, March 1984

POST-GREEN MERCHANT GROWING

BY THE BUSH DOCTOR

If you want to avoid detection, don't charge it. Pay cash. Also, don't order grow equipment through the mail. People using the United Parcel Service found out too late that UPS handed over all their records to the DEA.

I like growing outdoors. The key to success is to think like a weed. Weeds thrive on roadsides, railways, under powerlines, riversides, backlots and swampbacks. The good ground lies right under your nose but is ignored—so obvious it's invisible. In '86 I lived on the South Side of Chicago and dropped eight seedlings next to Lake Shore Drive. Ten thousand maniacs commuted right past them every day, but I harvested all eight American beauties.

I scope out sites in autumn and look for big healthy ragweed plants. If the weeds are still green in September, then the local water table never dropped below root reach. A spot like this should be mapped. Then you go out and find more of them.

In late winter, I start seedlings under a light about a month before the final frost. That way my transplants get a big jump on the surrounding vegetation. In the spring, I find my outdoor spots, turn over the soil and add conditioners like vermiculite or perlite. This is a nocturnal mission—as is transplanting the next night. Always wear dark clothes and fly under radar. It's fun.

#197, January 1992

STEP THREE: When the pollen pods start to open, place a clean, plastic sack or baggie over the branch to collect pollen. Secure the bag at the bottom with a piece of string or wire tie. Keep the bag over the branch for several days to collect pollen.

STEP FOUR: When enough pollen has been collected, shake remaining pollen off into the bag. Remove spent branch. Pollen may be kept for several weeks by removing all vegetative matter to prevent mold and storing the pollen in a dark, dry container in the refrigerator.

STEP FIVE: Ideally, pistils should be ready for fertilization three to four weeks after the first calyx has appeared. Receptive pistils are white and fuzzy, not starting to turn brown. Cover the selected female branch that has many ripe, receptive pistils with the pollen-filled bag. Shake the bag.

STEP SIX: Use a small paintbrush to apply the pollen from the bag to the pistils if just a few seeds are desired from many different females. Be very careful. Just use a little pollen on each calyx and keep it from spreading to the sinsemilla crop.

STEP SEVEN: Leave the bag for two or three days, to ensure fertilization. Be careful not to scatter pollen on adjacent sinsemilla crop when removing the bag.

STEP EIGHT: After fertilization, seeds will be ripe in three to six weeks. Harvest seeds when they split open the containing calyx or rattle in the pod.

STEP NINE: Let seeds dry for two to three months in a cool, dry place before planting.

For more information on marijuana breeding, purchase the best book available: *MARIJUANA BOTANY, An Advanced Study: The Propagation and Breeding of Distinctive Cannabis*, by Robert Connell Clarke ($12.95, And/Or Press, 1981). Clarke discusses, in understandable, scientific detail, genetics and breeding, as well as cloning, climate, chemistry and much more of interest to the serious breeder.

INDOOR CANNABIS BREEDING

by Robert Connell Clarke

The breeding of improved varieties of drug cannabis adds a rewarding new dimension to one of America's most rapidly growing gardening hobbies. Indoor marijuana horticulture is rapidly gaining popularity across America but only a very limited number of cannabis cultivators consciously select and breed their plants in an effort to create improved varieties. Clandestine marijuana breeders secretly work to improve drug types of cannabis, but the vast majority of marijuana growers practice no selection at all, and continue to use accidentally produced seeds from domestic sinsemilla, seeds from imported marijuana or clonal material from another grower. This chapter gives a short history of drug cannabis breeding, tips for indoor breeders, indoor selection criteria and descriptions of suitable indoor varieties. A few simple breeders terms are introduced in an effort to remain contemporary with breeders of other crops.

DOMESTIC DRUG CANNABIS BREEDING

During the early 1960s marijuana cultivation came to America. Ancient cultivators gave American growers a strong start by favoring and selecting potent varieties for at least 3,000 years. At first, cannabis seeds found in illicit shipments of marijuana were casually planted by inquisitive smokers. Commercial domestic-marijuana cultivators were unknown. Nearly all domestically produced marijuana that lacked seeds was immature, and that which was mature, fully seeded. Tropical varieties from Colombia and Thailand rarely matured to the late floral stage before frosts killed them. However, the subtropical Mexican and Jamaican varieties occasionally did mature outdoors across the southern two thirds of America. Some of the tropical varieties regularly survived until maturity in coastal Southern California, Florida, the Gulf Coast and especially Hawaii.

Since most imported marijuana was full of seeds, many exotic varieties were available. Early marijuana cultivators tried all available varieties in their search to find potent plants that would consistently mature before killing frosts. Early-maturing northern Mexican varieties were the most favored as they consistently matured at northern latitudes. The early-maturing *C. sativa* inbred-line varieties of the early and mid-1970s such as "Pollyanna" and the late-maturing "Original Haze" resulted from crosses between earlier-maturing Mexican and Jamaican varieties and more potent but later-maturing Panamanian, Colombian, and Thai varieties.

Most early varieties were bred for outdoor growing, but others were specially developed for glass houses or indoors under artificial light, where the season can be artificially extended to allow the later-maturing types to finish. Once varieties had been perfected that would mature under these conditions, pioneering marijuana breeders selected for potency (THC content), followed by the additional aesthetic considerations of flavor, aroma and color. Modifying adjectives such as minty, floral, spicy, fruity, sweet, purple, golden or red were often attached to selected varieties and the marijuana connoisseur was born. Continued inbreeding of the original favorable hybrids resulted in some of the "super-*sativas*" of the 1970s such as "Original Haze," "Purple Haze," "Polly," "Eden Gold," "Three Way," "Maui Wowie," "Kona Gold," and "Big Sur Holy Weed." These were the first domestically created inbred lines of drug cannabis.

During the second half of the 1970s marijuana breeders had great success with developing connoisseur *sativa* varieties. More potent and exotic-smelling flowers brought both greater pride and greater profit to the grower. Outdoor purple varieties gained popularity, largely following on the coattails of the extraordinary "Purple Haze" of central California.

Cannabis cultivators both indoors and outdoors wanted a variety with high flower yield and with short broad stature as well. The

STRAWBERRY FIELD

This mixed batch of sativa and indica was grown in a high-nutrient soil under two HPS lamps and dual fluorescent fixtures. We watered the plants with a strawberry-margarita-type flowering solution (strawberries, small dash of confectioners' sugar, water and a 12-50-22 flowering fertilizer). The result was a sweet 'n' fruity crop that was ohh-soo glandy. The key to success is fresh, CO2-rich air, and many visits to the grow-room. End the crazy price wars by growing your own and sharing with your bros!

Eddie da Eagle
Sniffo "Boom Boom" Ali
Joey "Bag O' Doughnuts"
Pittsburgh, PA

#229, Sept. 1994

HAWAIIAN BLACK LAVA BEDS

The plants were started using perlite in Styrofoam cups, then placed in larger containers filled with black lava. Pumps and misting equipment supply irrigation. Natural illumination was used.

We use flowering and sexing greenhouses. Our strains mature in two to three months. We grow 15 to 20 plants, each in a one-gallon bag, for six weeks, then plant the remaining females in the flowering houses.

Nine hours of light makes them bud and grow the least. Nine and a half hours makes them stretch out on top. Eight and a half hours makes them brown out prematurely. A house like this (10 feet by 18 feet) is worth between two and four pounds every four months. The two-month plants are constantly picked, while the three-month plants get really gungy in a few more weeks. We harvest daily, clipping here and there.
#102, February 1984

LIGHT REFLECTOR

HOLE IN CARDBOARD DISC

Cover "dark soil" with white paper 3"x5" cards, or cut a hole in the middle of a round piece of white cardboard. Light is absorbed by dark objects such as the soil. The white surface of the paper will reflect the precious light upwards towards the plant and not into the soil.

Doc
Columbus, Ohio

#150, February 1988

AIR LAYERING

I am surprised at the number of growers who have never heard of nor tried air-layering instead of taking cuttings. With *indica* strains being so good for home-growing and so hard to come by, air-layering is an important technique to learn. Here's my method:

1) Support the branch to be rooted, using thin stick. Use branches that have at least two nodes plus top and are at least one-eighth inch in diameter.

2) Make a long slit through middle of stem, spread halves apart (carefully!) and paint all surfaces with Rootone powder, using a small dry paint brush.

3) Stuff a small amount of peat moss or a vermiculite/perlite/peat moss mix into the cut. All you really want to do is hold the cut open.

4) Cut a two-inch square off a Baggie corner. Notice that this makes a small pocket with two flaps. Cut off one flap, making an envelope. Fill with peat or mix and cover stuffed cut, using tape to close. Be sure before fastening closed that the peat covers the branch all the way around. It doesn't matter if you have to include the support stick inside the envelope and peat; it is still easy to slide out after rooting.

5) Wet all peat inside envelope. An eyedropper works well. Keep wet throughout rooting process. The fungicide in the Rootone keeps things from rotting. Sufficient rooting to cut branch and plant directly should occur within two weeks.

Jim
Rockville, Conn.

#97, September 1983

answer came in the form of an exotic new imported variety. Hashish varieties from Afghanistan provided the perfect solution. Plants of the *afghanica* variety, popularly referred to as "indica" or "hashish plant", are characteristically short and bushy with broad dark-green leaves. Since *C. afghanica* varieties originate from far-northern latitudes with a short growing season they nearly always mature quite early, finishing outdoors between the middle of August and the end of September. Plants often stand only 3 to 6 feet tall at maturity and produce copious resin covered flowers. *C. afghanica* varieties are used to make some of the world's finest and most potent hashish. Smoking the dried flowers provides much of the same aroma and flavor as fine hashish, so connoisseur smokers were willing to pay extra for the exotic *C. afghanica* flowers. Dozens of separate introductions of *c. afghanica* were made during the middle to late 1970s. Since the Russian-Afghan War began in 1979, many additional introductions of *C. afghanica* were made into America from northwestern Pakistan.

C. afghanica spread throughout America very rapidly. Marijuana breeders intentionally crossed *C. afghanica* with sweet tasting but late-maturing *C. sativa* varieties to produce earlier-maturing hybrids. Thai x Afghan hybrids were particularly sweet and potent. Hybrid vigor caused by dominant heterosis or the blending of different favorable dominant traits was usually evident in the early hybrids. Flower potency increased and yields were much higher although the plants rarely exceeded 10 feet in height. Soon the majority of cultivators began to grow various *C. afghanica* x *C. sativa* hybrids. From these early hybrids some true-breeding inbred-line varieties were created.

Since cannabis is wind pollinated, and sinsemilla is usually grown in small, crowded gardens, accidental pollination by uncontrolled males often results in many seeds. Accidental seeds were much more common than intentionally produced seeds, and were rapidly and widely distributed as a contaminant in sinsemilla. Intentionally produced seeds were usually only passed along from one serious cultivator or breeder to another, and their distribution was much more limited. Accidentally produced seeds containing various proportions of the introduced *C. afghanica* gene pool were grown and unintentionally crossed again and again without strict selection. Random outcrossing produced a confused hybrid condition involving several parental lines in which favorable combinations of traits were rarely reproducible. Few of the offspring of F_2 and subsequent generations appeared alike, their gene pools having been formed of randomly collected traits passed along from their assorted predecessors. As the mixed gene pools reassorted they manifested many undesirable as well as desirable characteristics. Many of the original imported varieties that were used as the original building blocks of the inbred-line varieties have vanished and their genes have been diluted into the massive domestic drug cannabis gene pool. Although many of the favorable genes may still exist, it is nearly impossible to retrieve them in combination with other favorable traits.

By the early to mid 1980s, the vast majority of all domestically produced commercial sinsemilla in America had likely received some portion of its genes from the *C. afghanica* gene pool. By 1980 it was already becoming difficult to find the pre-*C. afghanica* varieties that had been so popular only a few years earlier. By 1985 it was nearly impossible to find pure *C. sativa* varieties cultivated domestically. "Afghani#1," "Hindu-Kush," "Mazar-i-Sharif" and "Skunk Weed" were some of the more successful pure *C. afghanica* inbred-line or varieties. Their hybrid offspring have spread far and wide.

It might appear that *C. afghanica* hybrids were perfectly suited for domestic cultivation and received with open arms by all American cannabis growers. Although the use of *C. afghanica* varieties increased nationwide throughout the mid-1980s, owing to its delayed introduction in many areas of the East and Midwest; its popularity began to decline in the West and other regions where drug cannabis varieties were first introduced. Accidental recombination into complex hybrids had brought out some of the less desirable traits of *C. afghanica* that had previously been hidden. Without careful selection and breeding cannabis begins to turn weedy, and as natural selection takes over, drug varieties lose their vigor, taste and potency. Low potency, a slow, flat, dreary high, skunky acrid fecal aroma, harsh taste and susceptibility to mold are traits that soon became associated with many *C. afghanica* x *C. sativa* hybrids.

Many sinsemilla connoisseurs felt that *C. afghanica* had not lived up to expectations. Commercial and home cultivators had quite the opposite opinion. The characteristics of *C. afghanica* such as hardy growth, rapid maturation and tolerance to cold allowed sinsemilla to be grown outdoors in the northern tier of states from Washington to Maine. This revolutionized the domestic-marijuana market by making a potent homegrown smoke possible for those living in the northern latitudes of America and widened the scope and intensity of sinsemilla cultivation in America and Europe. During the 1980s production areas spread from the epicenters of the West Coast, Hawaii and the Ozarks into at least 20 major marijuana-producing states. A little sinsemilla is still grown outdoors in each of the 50 states.

Creating new hybrid crosses between inbred-lines restores vigor and supplies new combinations of genes for further breeding. Serious connoisseur cannabis breeders have returned to some of the older pure *C. sativa* varieties as a source of "new" genetic material for variety improvement. Breeders can enhance the flavor and potency of inbred varieties by crossing the older pure-breeding inbred-line varieties with highly inbred *C. afghanica* x *C. sativa* hybrids. Also breeders are constantly searching for new sources of exotic germplasm. Pure *C. afghanica* varieties are still highly prized breeding stock and new *C. afghanica* varieties from Central Asia are occasionally introduced and tested. *Sativa* varieties from South Africa have gained favor with breeders, as they mature early but do not suffer from many of the drawbacks of *C. afghanica,* such as mold susceptibility and acrid flavor. Imported South African varieties, since they come from so far south of the equator, mature in August but are often very short, not very potent and relatively low-yielding. However, persistent selection has resulted in inbred South African varieties such as "Durban." Crosses with inbred *C. sativa* and *C. afghanica* varieties or their hybrids are usually vigorous and early-maturing and may express the desirable *C. sativa* or *C. afghanica* traits of potency, fragrance, full flavor and high yield within a few select individuals. These select plants are preserved through cuttings for later use as seed parents.

Since the late 1970s several breeders have worked with *C. sativa* ssp. fibrosa sect. spontanea weedy cannabis varieties from Central and Eastern Europe. Most Western cultivators called these varieties "ruderalis." These weedy varieties mature in July or August, which makes them desirable to use in drug cannabis varieties in an attempt to hasten maturity. It is not clear whether these weedy populations are truly wild varieties or merely escapes from cannabis hemp cultivation that have turned weedy. Unfortunately, in either case the weedy varieties are almost devoid of THC, the hybrids are of very low potency and

GREENHOUSE GOLD

Enclosed are some shots of a very special, or maybe the word is "different," strain of *indica* that produces buds sometimes yielding as much as 56 to 60 grams. These Big Rogues are beautiful, and near the end of the cycle will go from a strong skunk smell to a sweet pungent aroma of pine—which spells dynamite. Out of roughly a hundred plants a year, there is a yield of 15 to 20 purple ladies which are without a doubt the premier pot of California. These ladies dress themselves in purple leaves with gold veins, and the resin-rich buds have bracts that resemble kernels of corn on the cob. The bud does not produce a comatose state, but rather picks up the high side and generates action not the "Ass Flopper" that some overpowering pot produces.

John
Sacramento area, CA

#102, February 1984

BILLWEED

This is my first extended period of indoor growing. The majority of plants here are from a strain that a local guy named Bill developed from some Holland seed. We started with 65 Billweed clones last June, grew them vegetatively for four weeks, then took cuttings for our second generation. Immediately after, we put them into the flowering room for eight weeks, until maturity. We root clones in Rockwool, then transplant into an organic professional grower's mixture using a high-N fish emulsion, then a high-P fish emulsion for fertilizer. The pictures are from our third harvest, and I'm out of the scene now to enjoy some skiing while the pressure subsides.

Benier B'vore
Tennessee

#240, August 1995

ELECTRICAL TIPS

Many folks whose growth chambers I've consulted or constructed ask, "What about high electric bills? Won't the cops see the records?" For starters, a few examples of electrically powered devices which use massive amounts of juice are electric pottery kilns (23 to 30 amps), MIG electric welders (which also consume CO_2) and electric space heaters (15 to 20 amps).

As for the law scanning power records, unless you live in Buttfuck, Iowa, population 20, they're not looking for you. It is only when you're informed upon, thereby initiating an investigation, that the police turn immediately to power records. These are usually held in the electric company's computers for three years. If it's the Feds, they will likely use overhead infrared imaging, long-distance directional microphones (to hear pumps, gas, ballasts, etc.) and even nonstatic surveillance.

It all boils down to being ratted on. The DEA, with their five-year mandatory minimum sentences for 50 plants, is going to create a rock-solid criminal case against you before they blast through the front door like the young caffeine-dosed commandos that most of them are. Additionally, search warrants are usually served during daylight hours, between dawn and 10 AM.

And never attempt to steal electricity!

This advice is dedicated to Mr. Rodger Belknap, a classic American patriot and greatest of all anticannabis prohibition activists.

Professor Afghani
New York City

#233, January 1995

SAFETY TIPS

I have suggestions for growers who are gone from their grow rooms for extended periods of time. One reader wrote in suggesting that a GFCI circuit was necessary. I say it is neither necessary nor desirable. The main purpose behind a GFCI circuit is to protect people from electrical shock. If you get between electricity and a wet floor, a GFCI is more sensitive and will trip to protect you. A regular breaker might allow you to fry in a similar situation, but standard breakers do protect against dead electrical shorts—the kind that cause fires.

This is the upshot: If this gentle reader equips his room with GFCI circuits, he is likely to come back to dead plants simply because an electrical storm tripped his GFCIs. They are that sensitive.

Rasta Reader
Oklahoma City, Oklahoma

#151, March 1988

consequently repeated back-crosses to the high-THC parent and recurrent selections must be made to restore potency. These backcrossed lines should be well adapted to far northern latitudes but very few of them have proved to be potent enough to be accepted by sinsemilla growers.

Exotic imported varieties from India, Kashmir, Nepal, Africa and Indonesia are occasionally used in first filial generation or F_1 hybrid crosses to enhance potency or impart particular flavors to the smoke. Since commercial shipments do not often originate in these regions, the seeds are usually collected in small numbers by travelers and are very rare compared to seeds from the major marijuana-producing regions of Colombia, Mexico, Jamaica and Thailand.

Because cannabis is a difficult plant in which to fix traits through selective breeding, and only the female plants are of economic importance, it is advantageous to clone exceptional plants by rooting cuttings. Through cloning, large numbers of identical select female plants can be grown. Besides circumventing the vagaries of genetic recombination, cloning can provide uniform crops of female plants in one generation, rather than through many generations of selection and breeding. No rouging of male plants is required to produce sinsemilla, as no male plants are cloned and no pollen is produced. All of the female flowers mature simultaneously and the entire field can be harvested at once. This is an obvious boon to commercial cannabis cultivation.

Due to continuing governmental pressure against outdoor growers, sinsemilla growing has largely moved indoors. Halide and sodium-vapor light systems are most often set up in attics, bedrooms or basements where space is limited. Under these circumstances there is no room for nonproductive plants and the single best clone is usually selected for all future cultivation.

C. afghanica hybrids have proved to be well adapted to indoor clonal cultivation. *C. afghanica* varieties mature quickly, allowing 3-4 harvests per year, and yield up to 100 grams of flowers on plants less than 3 feet tall. Many *C. sativa* varieties are often too stretchy and tall and take too long to mature. *C. afghanica* hybrids are much easier and more economical to grow than pure *C. sativa* varieties. The tops of the tallest plants, very near the lights, shade the bottom branches and prevent them from producing any flowers.

Modern indoor growing conditions often seem ill-suited for the improvement of cannabis through selective breeding. Grow rooms are small in comparison to the plowed fields that are usually planted for the breeding of open-pollinated crops such as maize or cannabis. Most modern indoor cannabis growers use clones of select female plants for sinsemilla flower production and rarely, if ever, grow a male plant or even plant a seed. Commercial growers try never to have seeds in their product and have little interest in making seeds. Clones provide uniform predictable crops, harvest after harvest. Clones remain consistent and stable through dozens of clonal generations as long as they are not infected by viruses or other contagious pathogens. There are no markedly inferior plants in a monoclonal grow room. However, since all the plants in a monoclonal population are genetically identical to one another, there are also no unique and potentially superior plants. All offspring are identical and only as good as the mother plant from which the cutting was first taken. Grow rooms represent the antithesis of breeding. They rely on asexual reproduction to provide enough vegetative cuttings to grow and mature into a crop and seeds rarely enter the picture. Female clones improve grow-room performance, but preclude the possibility of seed production. Breeding is no longer practiced and variety improvement ceases entirely. It is difficult to say if cloning will have a lasting effect on cannabis breeding and the evolution of the cultivated cannabis gene pool, but it has certainly limited variability in grow-room populations.

Accelerated eradication efforts in America by state and federal law enforcement during the 1980s lowered the supply and the quality of domestically grown cannabis. Shortages fueled the hyperinflation of cannabis prices. The price of cannabis continues to steadily rise, while the quality is rarely as high as it was only a few years ago. This situation has resulted in the increase of home cannabis cultivation for personal use as smokers try to provide themselves with a steady hassle-free supply of consistently high-quality cannabis. The vast majority of personal grow rooms have only one to four grow lights and produce just enough smoke to satisfy the needs of the household in which they are set up.

Increased acceptance of cannabis as an applicable therapeutic agent for the treatment of the side effects of appetite loss and nausea associated with AIDS and cancer chemotherapy is resulting in an increase in the number of small home-growing operations. The afflicted public has learned that cannabis can be effective in relieving their discomfort. It is impossible to buy legal cannabis for medical use in America, so patients are turning to their close friends for their medicine or growing their own closet crop. As more and more patients suffering from glaucoma, AIDS and the nausea associated with chemotherapy decide to relieve their discomfort by smoking cannabis, many will be forced to become closet cannabis growers in order to medicate themselves.

Different varieties of drug cannabis provide the smoker with differing intensities and types of highs. Cannabis varieties also differ in their therapeutic effect. These differences are produced both by the potency and cannabinoid profile of the particular cannabis variety as well as variations in individual patient's physiology and mindset. Individual cannabis varieties specially bred for a particular potency level and particular cannabinoid profile, tailored to the individual medical needs and personal preferences of each patient, can be created by home cannabis breeders. This type of personal selection of the most therapeutically effective varieties could provide each patient with the best possible treatment for their particular condition and circumstances. For instance, it may turn out that a less potent variety could have all the therapeutic benefits of a more potent variety without the side effect of making the patient stoned.

Although the crowded conditions of indoor grow rooms are not ideal for breeding cannabis, the 1980s have shown us that the immediate future for cannabis and cannabis breeders in America is in indoor grow rooms under lights. Compromises have been made to circumvent law enforcement efforts and sinsemilla is still produced. If cannabis quality is to improve, rather than remaining frozen in its present cloned state, then improvements will have to come from the selective breeding of indoor cannabis crops. The illegality and high visibility of marijuana cultivation make it preferable to limit the size of gardens and the frequency of visits to observe the plants. This lowers the total number of potential breeding plants the breeder will have to choose from and limits the amount of time that can be spent with each plant. Indoor grow rooms provide the grower with more privacy than outdoor gardens and allow the grower to concentrate more on breeding.

All gardens and fields are finite. Even outdoor cannabis gardeners tend to make their fields small in an effort to avoid detection. Grow

FORMULA FOR SUCCESS

A few years ago I grew 6'-7' tall plants using fluorescents and large pots. What a waste of time and space. This time no plant is over 30" tall. At 12 weeks from seed to harvest, some of the colas were 6" long and oozing with resin. I built a table using scrap wood in a spare basement room. The bottom was enclosed with black plastic to keep light in; above I hung a 1,000 watt MH on a 6' solar shuttle. Two 4' fluorescent fixtures were hung below that. Here's my simple formula for success: 1) Germinate seeds in 4-oz cups filled with a mix of four parts potting soil to one part sand. 2) Place the pots under continuous light from the MH. 3) Water every 3-4 days. 4) Add nutrients every 3rd watering. 5) Keep a fan on them to circulate air and strengthen the stems. 6) After 17 days transplant to one-gallon pots. 7) Around 21 days take cuttings above the third internode. Put these in 4-oz cups under continuous light. 8) At 45 days change the light cycle to 12 hours on, 12 hours off. 9) Kill the males and their clones as they indicate. My male plants indicated at seven days. The females showed at ten. 10) Forty-five days after turning the light cycle back—Harvest!

Astral Al
Southern Illinois

#168, August 1989

HOW TO HYPE HORMONES

BY BOB IRELAND

Hormones are organic molecules produced by plants and transported to its site of action where, in very small amounts, they control, stimulate, inhibit or alter one another and plants' life processes. There are five classes of plant hormones: auxins, cytokinins, gibberellins, abscisic acid and ethylene.

Auxins are the most common growth regulators available commercially. They include indoleacetic acid (IAA), napthylacetic acid (NAA), indolebutyric acid (IBA) and 2,4, dicholorophenoxyacetic acid (2,4-D), which is also a component of the herbicides Agent Orange and Weed-B-Gone. Dip'n Grow (IBA and NAA), Hormodin IBA), Hormo-Root (IBA), Rootone (NAA and (IBA) and Transplantone (NAA) are some of the brands available.

Cytokinins are sometimes called the cell division factor. Sensa-Soak, containing 6-BAP, is used as a germinating fluid for the promotion of female flowers in cucumbers, melons and cannabis. There are no other cytokinin products currently on the market.

Gibberellins are produced by all green plants. Over 50 different types have been isolated. Gibberellins' most striking action is stem elongation, but they have also been used for seed germination, bud sprouting and to initiate flowering. The most commonly used products are Wonder-Brel (GA3), Pro-Gibb (GA3), and Florel (GA3). When used on female marijuana, GA causes hermaphroditism.

Abscisic acid (ABA) is a naturally occuring phytohormone whose function is opposite to

A) NORMAL PLANT WITH CLOSEUP OF INTERNODES.

rooms are bounded by walls and seem extremely finite and small. However, in America today the total indoor space devoted to cannabis cultivation may equal or even exceed the outside area devoted to cannabis cultivation.

The vast majority of progress in the breeding of improved drug cannabis varieties has been made in small-scale growing situations both outdoors in fields and indoors in glass houses or grow rooms. No domestic cannabis breeder has ever felt as if they had enough space for breeding, and conditions always seemed overcrowded and cramped. Despite the adverse conditions imposed by clandestine crowded conditions, greatly improved drug cannabis varieties have been created both in America and in Holland.

Dutch cannabis seed companies sprang up during the middle 1980s, offering seeds of predominately American sinsemilla varieties along with a few Dutch and assorted foreign varieties. Their breeding lines were established from improved varieties collected in America and elsewhere. Except for making available a wide range of simple multihybrid crosses, the Dutch seed companies, such as the Seed Bank, Super Sativa Seed Club, and the Sensi Seed Bank, have done little to improve the varieties that they initially collected. The Dutch seed companies reproduced established varieties, attempting to clean them up and make them more homogeneous, while preserving their individual character. This is always difficult with open-pollinated plants such as cannabis that suffer from inbreeding depression, especially when there are only small populations to select from.

Inbreeding depression results in a loss of general health and vigor caused by an accumulation of recessive gene pairs. Some Dutch varieties have also proved to be acceptable early-maturing material for sinsemilla production outdoors under natural daylight conditions at far northern latitudes.

Service from the Dutch seed companies was at times slow. Resulting from short stocks, many substitutions were made in orders. Sometimes seeds did not appear dark and fully mature because they were grown under artificial lights. To many growers, the Dutch seeds seemed overpriced. Despite these shortcomings, the cannabis varieties offered by Dutch seed companies met with great acceptance in America. Most of the varieties offered were better than the varieties customers already had, so they were satisfied. The mail-order availability of improved cannabis varieties coincided with the general knowledge of cloning, and much of the material from the individual offspring of the Dutch seeds is still being used for sinsemilla production in America today. The Dutch seed companies that exported seed to America went out of business in 1991. Cannabis seeds are still available at selected coffeeshops and from a few retail seed shops in Amsterdam and other Dutch cities. The cultivation of cannabis for seed and the sale of cannabis seed is currently legal within Holland but the importation of cannabis seed into America is not allowed under American law.

Many of the original improved varieties were derived from dihybrid or polyhybrid crosses between traditionally used land races of drug cannabis from such diverse origins as Afghanistan, Colombia, Jamaica, Mexico, Panama and Thailand. The extreme potency and delicate characteristics of these initial hybrids often resulted from the heterosis condition of hybrid vigor, reflecting the diverse genotypic backgrounds of the original land races incorporated into the hybrids. Today it is nearly impossible to acquire many of the original land races available during the 1970s, and modern breeders must often rely on collections of select domestic inbred lines derived from these original polyhybrid crosses. In some ways the breeder's task is easier, because many previous breeders have already made improvements that will benefit future breeding programs. There is no reason to repeat other breeders' work. However, it may also be impossible to undo some of the unfavorable combinations made by earlier breeders, whose priorities in breeding may have differed from the priorities of the current breeding project. Even if parts of the original gene pools have been carried over into the hybrid offspring, individual genes have surely been lost. It is a tragedy that many of the original varieties are lost forever. The initial easy hybrids relied on the basic genetic building blocks of the land races and can no longer be made. However, it is more important now than ever to preserve what does remain of the original diverse drug cannabis gene pool and use it to develop new and better varieties that meet our current criteria for satisfying smoke and other cannabis products. Further improvement will be another leg in the long uphill climb to higher-quality cannabis, and as always it will be well worth the effort.

BREEDING TIPS

Indoor grow rooms offer several advantages over outdoor gardens. Grow rooms offer easy access and encourage frequent visits, especially when the grow room is conveniently located in the grower's home. Monitoring of male plants for pollen dispersal and females for pistil ripeness and seed maturity requires frequent visits to inspect the plants. This is often nearly impossible in clandestine outdoor gardens where privacy is lacking and visits must be kept to a minimum if detection is to be avoided. Inside a grow room there is a much lower chance of stray pollination from an unselected source than there is in an outdoor garden. Filters can be used to cover the intake vents and then no pollen or dust can enter the grow room.

Usually varieties that perform well under artificial-lights will also perform well outside or in a glass house under natural sunlight. The converse does not hold true nearly as often. Varieties that perform well outside often prove to be a disappointment when grown under artificial light. This explains much of the general success experienced by breeders who have been forced to breed under artificial light conditions. Their varieties have often proved to be acceptable for both indoor and outdoor cultivation. However, there are few varieties that are superior for both indoor and outdoor applications, and most varieties perform best with the same growing conditions under which they were selected and bred.

Cannabis is not a particularly straightforward plant to breed although it produces copious quantities of both pollen and seed. The life history of cannabis presents several obstacles to improvement by selective breeding. Individual cannabis plants are usually either all male or all female and thus individual plants are usually incapable of selfing. Selfing is the most effective means of fixing desirable traits, since the selected genes are more likely to be represented in both the pollen and the ovule if they come from the same plant. In cannabis breeding, the genes controlling a selected trait must be present in two separate individuals, one male pollen parent and one female seed parent. The psychoactive resin of cannabis is only produced by female plants. This makes it very difficult to recognize potentially favorable traits in male parents, especially when these traits must ultimately be expressed in the female offspring. All cannabis varieties are wind-pollinated and inter-cross freely. Perspective female seed parents must be isolated from all male plants to avoid stray pollinations until they are to be pollinated with a

those above since it is a growth inhibitor.

Ethylene is the only gaseous hormone. Its primary role centers about inducing flowering in some plant families and maturation and ripening of fruit in almost all. Ethylene is sold under the brand names Ethrel, Florel Ethepon and CEPA. All are 2-chloroethylphosphonic acid, which decomposes after application to yield ethylene and harmless salts.

#115, March 1985

B) PLANT RECEIVING GA STRETCHES BETWEEN INTERNODES.

C) PLANT RECEIVING GROWTH REGULATORS ARE COMPACT WITH THICK STEMS.

SPECIAL HOLIDAY GROW ISSUE

HIGH TIMES

GOING ORGANIC
KUSHMAN'S COMPLETE GUIDE TO INDOOR CULTIVATION

FDA
APPROVES
MUTANT FOOD

INDOOR GROWING
WITHOUT ELECTRICITY

WOODSTOCK ROCKS
3 Daze of Mud & Music

AIDS & POT
BY PETER GORMAN

DEC 1994

POSTER INSIDE!

GETTING STARTED WITH ORGANICS

BY KYLE KUSHMAN

Every living organism has an optimum pH level. Knowing the pH of your soil is crucial to growing healthy plants. The numbers vary from 1 (very acid) to 13 (very alkaline). For cannabis, the optimum pH range is 6.5 to 6.8. If your soil drops below or exceeds this range, your plants will have trouble absorbing nutrients.

Mixing soil can be messy. A kiddie pool works great. They cost under $10, last a couple of years and are available at any department store. When my pool is filled with soil mix, it fills almost twenty 3-gallon buckets.

Water needs to be drawn 24 hours before use and left in open containers. This will allow chlorine gas to evaporate while the water rises to room temperature. I prefer cold water because it has fewer dissolved solids. I use a clean 32-gallon trash pail for watering. It's important when container farming to use a low nutrient ratio. Don't overfeed your plants or you'll create a toxic fertilizer overload.

The most common organic fertilizers are worm casting, bat and sea-bird guanos and seaweed or kelp meal. These fertilizers can be added to the initial soil mix or mixed with water to make "teas." Organic fertilizers are labeled with three numbers, the NPK, which stands for the ratio of nitrogen, phosphorus and potassium.

#232, December 1994

select male.

The actual strategy for pollinating enough flowers to provide sufficient seed without seeding the remainder of the plants and spoiling the sinsemilla crop can be structured in several ways. The simplest way to make seed is to supply one select pollen source (one male clone or seedling) inside a grow room with a variety of female clones or seedlings as seed parents. This situation is analogous to leaving only the best male plant in a field to pollinate many of the best female plants. Each female parent will provide a different set of offspring from each cross, but the male parent will be the same in each case. Cloning offers indoor growers an added advantage because very small female plants can be produced in very little space that are fully ripe and receptive for pollination and seed production yet large enough to produce sufficient seed for future breeding. More variety of seed parents can be grown on a smaller area. This offers a wider genetic base for selection and increases the number of potentially excellent crosses that a breeder can make.

Each female clone will differ in its ability to make favorable gene combinations with any given male clone. This is the female clone's Specific Combining Ability or SCA. If the percentage of favorable offspring resulting from a specific cross is high, then the SCA of the individual cross is high. If an individual clone is crossed with many other clones and is found to produce high percentages of favorable offspring when crossed with a variety of mates, then it has a high General Combining Ability or GCA. Parents that show high SCA in specific crosses, and especially high GCA in many crosses, are preserved by cloning and are highly valued for further breeding. A clone's GCA is a measure of its reliability as a parent, and GCA can only be measured by repeated crossing with a wide variety of other clones. Determining a clone's GCA requires much space in the grow room. If only 5 female clones are tested with 5 male clones, then 25 crosses must be made. At least 10 female plants should be grown from each cross for evaluation. This means over 500 seedlings must be started to produce 250 females.

The ultimate breeding system would provide an individual isolated grow room for each male pollen parent. Many different female clones could be grown in each room and only one male used in each room to pollinate all of the female clones within. If a reliable male parent is used, common pollination by one male is an especially good way to test a large number of female clones for their crossability. During the early stages of a breeding project, if a male must be used that has not been test-crossed with various females, then it is advisable to use an open-pollinated imported variety with favorable vegetative and floral characteristics, or better yet an improved vigorous inbred line such as "Skunk #1," "Early Girl," "California Orange," etc. This increases the chances that a vigorous male is chosen rather than an inbred male that could produce inferior weak offspring.

Multiple pollen sources can be used within a common grow room without contamination of neighboring plants if certain precautions are taken. The most efficient way to perform multiple crosses within one grow room is to think ahead when the grow room is filled, and remember to make an additional set of both male and female clones for each batch of seeds. In other words for every cross that is to be made with a certain clone, a separate cutting of that clone is provided for each pollen and seed parent. If the grower wishes to cross one female clone with many different pollen sources, then enough cuttings are made at the start so that one cutting may be pollinated by each different pollen source. As the female clones become ripe, they are removed individually from the common grow room and pollinated with a single pollen source.

The pollen is either collected from selected males, dried and stored in a deep freezer until use or a ripe male plant that is shedding pollen is introduced from another grow room. If the female plant is artificially pollinated with stored pollen, it is then left outside the common grow room for three days, allowing time for the pollen to either germinate and initiate seed formation, or die so that it will not be able to accidentally pollinate other plants. After 3 days the female seed plant is sprayed with water to kill remaining pollen and returned to the common grow room. If a living male plant is used for the pollen source, then the male and female plants are left together in isolation until the male releases its pollen. If the male is already shedding pollen, then it is only necessary to dust the female plant with pollen by shaking the male plant over it. The male plant can be returned to its grow room immediately. If pollination is successful within two days, the female stigmatic hairs will wither slightly and darken in color indicating that they have been fertilized. Then the female plant is rinsed with a spray of water to kill remaining pollen and returned to the common grow room. The remainder of the clones within the common grow room remain completely seedless and later serve as perfect controls when comparing the virtues of each variety.

If an insufficient number of individual female clones are available for individual seed parents, and larger female plants with branches are available, then individual branches can be bag-pollinated (see *Marijuana Botany* by Robert C. Clarke, And/Or Press, Berkeley, CA). Stray pollinations can be very dangerous within the confines of a grow room. Great care must be taken to avoid accidental pollination. It is safest to make pollinations individually outside the grow room. The major advantage to producing larger-sized plants indoors is that they ripen more properly than small plants and more fully express their genetic potential. This makes them easier to evaluate in terms of their general worth. Comparative selections can be made between small individuals of the same population, but larger plants are required to judge a variety's general worth.

If male clones are to be used as a direct pollen source, it is advisable to induce them to flower two weeks later than the female seed clones for early-maturing varieties, and four weeks later than the female seed clones for late-maturing varieties. Otherwise the males will mature and shed their pollen before the female stigmas are ripe and receptive. Often it is easier to flower the males well ahead of the females and store the pollen for a short time until the females are receptive. Pollen can be stored in a cool, dry place for several weeks without much loss of viability. If pollen is to be stored for longer, it should be placed in paper envelopes in a cool dark place and dried with desiccant. The dry pollen is then placed in a sealed container with additional desiccant and stored in a deep freezer. Many of the pollen grains will die upon defrosting, but if several grams of pollen were frozen, enough of the pollen grains will still be alive to pollinate many plants. It is best to defrost pollen inside a refrigerated sealed container containing a desiccant or to administer the pollen to the female plants while it is still frozen, as it will not have time to defrost, condense moisture and clump together, making it more difficult to spread around. The simplest way to keep a viable pollen bank is to keep multiple clones of each male in the vegetative state and flower them as they are needed for pollen production.

Male parents should be selected from the most consistent lines

DUTCH SEED STRAINS
BY ROBERT CONNELL CLARKE

AFGHANI#1

Afghani#1 is an inbred-line variety originally developed during the late 1970s by Cultivator's Choice from an imported *afghanica* hashish variety. Afghani#1 is a dark-green broadleaf variety of medium height and produces coarse heavy buds that are covered with resin at maturity. It is a fairly leafy variety, but the small leaflets around the flowers develop plenty of resin. The aroma and taste are thick, greasy and medicinal, and occasionally acrid and unpleasant. Afghani#1 is one of the most potent varieties available and produces a very physical, sedative, and almost narcotic effect. Afghani#1 requires 8-9 weeks to mature under a 12-hour photoperiod.

CALIFORNIA ORANGE

California Orange is a stabilized *sativa* x *afghanica* hybrid variety of medium height and yield developed by Cultivator's Choice. The medium-green medium broadleaf plants produce copious resin even on the surface of the small leaflets. Some individuals have a pronounced citrus aroma and flavor. California Orange is very potent with a fairly clear high. It requires 8-10 weeks to mature under a 12-hour photoperiod.

BIG BUD

Big Bud is a relatively unstabilized *sativa* x *afghanica* hybrid variety. Big Bud was originally developed in the Portland, Oregon area as a clone for indoor sinsemilla production and was multiplied and distributed through Dutch seed companies.

It is best known for its high yield, especially when it is grown closely packed under high-intensity lights. The medium to dark-green floral clusters are large and dense with a high resin content. Yield, length of maturation and potency are variable because Big Bud has never been stabilized through inbreeding. Approximately 25% of the females will be very high-yielding but late-maturing, and approximately 25% of these will be potent. Since half of the seeds produce male plants, this means that 32 seeds are required simply to assure an even chance of getting one high-yielding and potent plant. If further combinations of traits such as flavor and aroma are desired, then many offspring should be grown and tested. This type of selection of future parental material from rough polyhybrid varieties often proves unfeasible within the confines of a small grow room. It is more economical in terms of population size and grow-room capacity to rely on inbred-line varieties such as Original Skunk #1 for parental material for breeding experiments.

expressing favorable traits. Once individual male plants have been selected, clones of each should be preserved until the SCA and GCA of each has been determined through crosses with several female clones. Male plants are difficult to judge based on their visible traits alone, since they do not produce flowers that elaborate THC-containing resins. Once a male plant with high specific combining ability is selected, it becomes a very valuable addition to the breeder's available gene pool.

Seeding female plants hastens their maturity by one or two weeks, but the seeds must be given time to fully mature. In the end it takes almost as much time to produce good seed as good sinsemilla.

Large late-maturing plants that are growing in the spring on a natural light-cycle can be cloned as soon as they are old enough to have slightly woody stems and long before they flower naturally. If the rooted cuttings are transferred to a grow room set at an inductive photoperiod of 12 hours of darkness, then they will flower and reveal their sex long before the mother plant from which they were taken. If they are females, they will continue to flower, and when the small clone matures, it will give a hint of what the large plant will be like when it matures properly.

It is a fairly simple proposition to select two parents from varieties with favorable characteristics, cross them and select a few offspring that exhibit most of the favorable characteristics from each parental variety. If these unique combinations are cloned, then the improved hybrid clones are preserved for future cultivation with a minimum of work. However, it is much more difficult and involved to undertake the breeding of a stable inbred-line from an F_1 hybrid cross. This takes years of careful selection and grow outs of large number of offspring for evaluation.

A simple analogy can be made with colored flowers. If a pink flower is the goal of a flower breeding program then a red variety might be crossed with a white variety. Almost all of the F_1 offspring will be pink, but how pink are they? Upon careful observation the most pink F_1 individuals can be selected and cloned. However, when the select F_1 hybrid pink offspring are crossed to each other, their F_2 offspring will show great diversity. Some will be varying shades of pink, but many of the offspring will be more red or white than pink. Here is where a breeder's work really begins in an effort to produce a true-breeding pink inbred-line variety rather than simply selecting and cloning the best pink individuals. Parents must be selected that have a high level of pinkness and pass their pinkness on to future generations. These individuals are said to have a high General Combining Ability or GCA.

Selection from huge populations is a luxury rarely afforded to drug cannabis breeders. Original Skunk #1 is one of the only drug cannabis varieties that has been repeatedly selected for many years from large grow-outs due to its widespread use as a commercial variety.

FAVORABLE CHARACTERISTICS FOR INDOOR VARIETIES

GENERAL VIGOR

Parental plants for the production of seed should be strong and vigorous. Weak plants may harbor genetic deficiencies that interfere with their proper growth. Strong, vigorous plants are less likely to conceal genetic weaknesses that may later cause problems. Rapid growth and rich green foliage are signs of vigor.

POTENCY

The potency of a drug cannabis variety is its single most important attribute. If a variety is not potent enough then the smoker will have to consume too much plant material in an effort to get high and will not be satisfied. Potent cannabis is high in the psychoactive cannabinoid compound tetrahydrocannabinol (THC). THC content is controlled by simple inheritance. When a high-THC variety is crossed with a low-THC variety, the F_1 hybrid offspring are relatively uniform in THC content, and the percentage of THC is approximately intermediate between the two parental varieties.

The simplest way an indoor grower can create different hybrids is to cross two diverse gene pools and select only a few of the best offspring. These select plants are cloned by making cuttings and then the clones are multiplied and grown out for production use. The first breeding step of creating F_1 hybrids has been taken. The improvement process need not stop here. At the very least, the best F_1 plants should be inter0-crossed with one another and the best plants from the second inbred or F_2 generation cloned for production use. This allows one more generation of selection and allows the genes from the two parental lines to recombine into additional different combinations that may prove acceptable as clonal material. To ensure success, thousands of F_2 offspring should be grown for selection. However, many advances have been made selecting from F_2 populations of only a few dozen plants. There are no substitutes for close scrutiny and harsh selection. When a very good plant is found, whether it is male or female, a cutting should be made, grown on under a vegetative photoperiod, and serially cloned so its gene pool is preserved for later breeding experiments. The decision to continue improving an already acceptable variety through continuing selective breeding, or to cease selection and preserve the unique products of genetic recombination through cloning, is up to the individual breeder.

Back-cross techniques are effective in creating more potent varieties and in improving or rejuvenating depressed inbred lines. Increases in THC content can be made by crossing an existing low-potency but otherwise favorable parental or P_1 variety with a more potent P_1 variety that may not have other favorable characteristics, such as early maturation or short stature, but is high in THC. Individual female F_1 offspring are back-crossed to select males of the original favorable P_1 variety to produce the first back-cross or BC_1 generation. The best female plants in the BC_1 population are selected for gross phenotype and potency and are back-crossed to males of the original favorable P_1 variety producing the second back-cross or BC_2 generation. The females of the BC_2 generation are selected and back-crossed to the P_1 males as in the BC_1 generation to make the third back-cross or BC_3 generation. This back-cross scheme is repeated until the offspring closely resemble the original P_1 variety, but with significantly higher THC percentage and more potency.

Another way to increase THC content is by constant inbreeding selection within the same variety to create a more potent inbred line. An inbred-line is created by continually selecting brother and sister plants from the same initial parental cross and using them as parents for the next generation. Potency is increased by selecting the most potent offspring of the F_1 generation and crossing them amongst themselves to give the F_2 generation. The F_2 plants are once again selected for potency, and the most potent plants are used as parents for the F_3 generation. However, constant inbreeding often results in a situation known as inbreeding depression that causes a loss of health and vigor in the offspring. The inbred offspring could be very high in THC but so weak

DUTCH SEED STRAINS

ORIGINAL HAZE

Original Haze is a pure-breeding stabilized inbred-line developed from a pure *sativa* polyhybrid created from predominately Mexican and Colombian varieties along with some South Indian and Thai varieties. Original Haze started as a magical mix of the most exotic *sativa* varieties available in California in the early 1970s. Some of the early types were lost but through diligent selection and inbreeding Cultivator's Choice preserved the essence of the variety in their Original Haze. Original Haze produces tall, sparse, light-green plants with narrow leaflets and numerous thin flowers. When grown from seed it is not suitable for indoor production, but small clones can be flowered and the resultant mature plants will be of manageable size. The flowers are oily with a spicy sweet and sour aroma. Original Haze plants can be very potent and almost always have a clear, awake, energetic high. 'Original Haze' takes 12-16 weeks to mature under a 12 hour photoperiod. 'Original Haze' has been inbred for 20 years. Approximately 75% of the plants are female and 10-20% of these plants are very special. The remainder are only so-so. Although 'Original Haze' is troublesome to grow indoors under lights it makes excellent breeding material and is well worth the extra trouble.

HINDU-KUSH

Hindu-Kush is a true-breeding *afghanica* inbred-line variety commonly used for indoor cultivation and as parental material for hybrid crosses. Hindu-Kush plants are short  with dense, leafy flowers, and produce resin over much of their leaf surface. The flowers are rather coarse, with an often strongly acrid earthy aroma and flavor that reminds one of primo Afghani hashish. It usually requires 8-10 weeks of a 12-hour photoperiod to mature.

DUTCH SEED STRAINS

EARLY GIRL

Early Girl is another *C. sativa* x *C. afghanica* hybrid variety developed for over 10 years by Cultivator's Choice. In this case the variety tends 90% towards the *C. afghanica* side and the *C. sativa* contribution is almost entirely masked. Although this hybrid has been stabilized through persistent inbreeding, the offspring continue to show considerable diversity. The dark-green, small to medium height broadleaf plants produce a moderate yield of acrid hashish-tasting flowers of fairly high potency and physical high. The great advantage of Early Girl is that it requires only 7-9 weeks of a 12-hour photoperiod to mature completely. Early Girl also tends to grow in a tall, slender column and is well adapted to close spacing in indoor grow rooms.

EARLY PEARL

Early Pearl is a stabilized early-maturing hybrid variety originally developed for outdoor cultivation in the American Midwest that also performs very well under lights. Early Pearl originates from a hybrid cross between Early Girl and the stabilized *C. sativa* variety Polly from the Sierra foothills of California. Further inbreeding has led to a relatively stable variety. Early Pearl is an early-maturing *C. sativa*-dominated *C. sativa* x *C. afghanica* hybrid variety that produces very resiny, sweet and potent flowers. Early Pearl usually requires only 6-8 weeks of a 12-hour photoperiod to completely mature.

that they could not survive long enough to mature properly.

Many currently popular cannabis varieties were selected from polyhybrid gene pools resulting from broad crosses between drug cannabis land races of various origins. From these diverse F_1 hybrid gene pools relatively true-breeding inbred-line varieties were established and used for further breeding. Some inbred-line varieties such as Skunk #1 have been constantly improved through intense selection and inbreeding for over 10 years without many signs of inbreeding depression. This has been possible because these inbred-line varieties were initially based on and selected from an extremely broad hybrid gene pool and inbreeding depression has had less influence. It is very difficult to prevent inbreeding depression without using a wide range of parental plants in each generation. This often proves difficult within the confines of a home grow room.

Back-crossing and inbreeding are techniques that can be used for fixing many favorable traits and should be considered in the breeding of cannabis varieties for any purpose.

RESIN CONTENT

One of the most important determinants of potency is the amount of resin on the surface of the female flowers. The majority of THC is synthesized and accumulated in the resin glands. Hashish is made from the resin glands of cannabis. Plants that elaborate many resin glands are usually more potent than those with only a few resin glands. Parents are selected from lines that produce large amounts of resin glands on both the bracts and the associated leaves.

FLOWER-TO-LEAF RATIO

The bract surrounding each individual cannabis flower contains the majority of the THC-containing resin glands. Bracts contain far more resin glands than even small leaves. Therefore the most potent floral clusters are those with the highest number of flowers and the fewest number of leaves, or a high flower to leaf ratio. Pure *C. sativa* inbred-line varieties and *C. sativa* x *C. afghanica* hybrid varieties usually have higher flower-to-leaf ratios than pure-breeding *C. afghanica* inbred-line varieties. Some inbred-line pure *C. sativa* varieties such as Original Haze produce sparse stretchy floral clusters but they also have a high flower-to-leaf ratio.

LARGE FLORAL CLUSTERS

Large floral clusters are important because the larger the floral clusters, the more individual female flowers they contain, the more surface they have for the elaboration of resin glands and the more stash the grower gets to smoke. The size of the flowers is largely determined by the number of flowers that are produced within each floral cluster along the stem. It is not enough for a plant to merely produce many floral clusters. Each floral cluster must contain many individual resin-covered flowers.

QUALITY OF HIGH

The quality of the marijuana high varies considerably between different varieties of Cannabis. Some are characterized as sedative, while others are considered mentally stimulating. Afghani #1 and Hindu Kush are both considered sleep-inducing. Original Haze is one of the most mentally stimulating varieties. All three can be extremely potent if they are grown to maturity but they always differ in the quality of the high. Conscious drug cannabis breeders will choose the particular types of highs they prefer and make selections accordingly.

THERAPEUTIC EFFECTS

Variations in the quality of the high may result from variations in the cannabinoid profile of each variety. Although THC is the primary psychoactive cannabinoid, it is not the only cannabinoid. Several other cannabinoids are psychologically or physiologically active and could modify the effects of THC. As cannabis becomes accepted as a therapeutic agent for the relief of symptoms associated with cancer and AIDS chemotherapy and the treatment of assorted other medical conditions, it is likely that certain varieties will prove to be more efficacious for the relief of specific medical conditions than others. This is an important consideration and deserves the attention of cannabis breeders.

TASTE AND AROMA

One of the greatest pleasures of smoking cannabis comes from the variety in flavor and aroma of the flowers and their smoke. The aroma of fresh plants is very consistent between varieties and even beginning growers have little trouble discerning a Skunk #1 from an Afghani #1 or an Original Haze. Each has a very distinctive aroma and the aromas tend to blend when the distinct varieties are crossed. A rich earthy hash-like Afghani #1 crossed with a minty sweet Thai variety often produces offspring that are rich and sweet, expressing flavor characteristics of both parents. The flavors of some varieties are so distinct that they can be detected at first sniff, even when they make up one-quarter or less of the hybrid offspring's genetics.

At the same time breeding cannabis for flavor and aroma can be illusive and frustrating. Over 100 different aromatic *terpenoid* flavoring ingredients have been isolated from cannabis. If we assume that at least 30 different aromatic *terpenoids* are found in any one plant, that there is likely at least one gene controlling the synthesis of each of the *terpenoid* compounds, and the amount of each produced; then there are obviously myriad gene combinations that can influence the flavor and aroma of cannabis. Although some flavor combinations of individual varieties persist in crosses, it is often very difficult to reproduce the flavor of a variety exactly, due to the large number of potential combinations involved in any single cross. Inbreeding has proved to be the most effective way to preserve a desirable varietal flavor and taste, but inbreeding can lead to a loss of potency and vigor.

SHORT STATURE

Short stature is vital in indoor varieties grown from seed that must be short enough when mature to be within the penetration of the grow lights. The use of clones allows very short pieces of female branches to be flowered, and the resultant mature plants are very short. The height of the plant is largely determined by the distance along the stem between flowers, and the length of time the clone continues to grow vegetatively after an inductive photoperiod is started before it begins to form flowers. The farther apart the flowers are, the taller and more stretched the plants will be. The longer a clone remains vegetative, the taller it will grow. Shorter plants are plants that begin to form flowers at close spacing along the stem immediately following a change to a flowering 12-hour photoperiod. Plants should be selected for dense flowers and an immediate response to flowering photoperiod.

EARLY MATURATION

DUTCH SEED STRAINS

NORTHERN LIGHTS

Northern Lights is a stabilized *C. sativa* x *C. afghanica* hybrid variety that was developed in the late 1970s near Seattle, Washington. The Northwest of America was the center of indoor sinsemilla production and indoor cannabis breeding. Due to the poor weather associated with this region, sinsemilla cultivators have long resorted to growing cannabis inside under lights long before growers in other more temperate regions of America. Northern Lights has been highly regarded for many years throughout the Northwest and was multiplied and distributed by Dutch seed companies. The variety was inbred and selected for short early-maturing plants with large floral clusters and resembles its *C. afghanica* parentage most closely. Northern Lights has been preserved much as it originally was through inbreeding without any marked improvements other than hybridization with other established varieties. Northern Lights is a dark-green fairly short variety with leafy but very resiny floral clusters and requires 8-10 weeks of a 12-hour photoperiod to mature completely. Northern Lights has won many awards at the HIGH TIMES magazine harvest festivals in Amsterdam.

GROW ROOM GUIDE · SMUGGLER'S JOURNAL

HIGH TIMES

FIRST ANNUAL CANNABIS CUP AWARDS

MAY 1988 $3.95

THE WINNER: SKUNK #1

Early maturation is of value because the faster a plant matures, the earlier it can be harvested and the sooner the grow room can be used for the next crop. Varieties that mature quickly allow less time for attack by mold, mites and other pests. Early maturation should not be confused with early flowering.

MOLD AND MITE RESISTANCE

The two most devastating pests of indoor cannabis crops are gray molds and spider mites. Mold and spider mites can cause epidemic destruction of indoor cannabis crops, especially when the crop is grown from only one clone. Environmental controls for gray molds and environmental as well as biological controls for spider mites have proved to be the most effective preventive controls of these pests. Of course the most effective preventive control would be to breed resistant varieties for use along with proper environmental controls as crops in indoor grow rooms. Varieties with inherited resistance to these pests are sorely needed.

ORIGINAL SKUNK #1

Original Skunk #1 is a relatively true-breeding *C. sativa x C. afghanica* inbred-line polyhybrid with a heavy tendency towards its *C. sativa* parentage. Original Skunk #1 was originally developed by Cultivator's Choice in the late 1970s for outdoor and glass house cultivation. It has also proved to produce excellent sinsemilla indoors under lights. Original Skunk #1 is a medium-green and medium broadleaf variety of medium height that produces large long floral clusters with very few leaves. The yield per square foot of Original Skunk #1 grown densely packed and strongly lighted can approach 40 grams of dry flowers. The flowers have a strong sweet-and-sour aroma and the taste is full-bodied and satisfying. The high is powerful and fairly stimulating. Original Skunk #1 requires 8-11 weeks of a 12-hour photoperiod to mature completely.

The true-breeding nature of Original Skunk #1 has helped spread the reputation it has earned at harvest festivals in both America and Holland. Original Skunk #1 makes an excellent choice for male breeding material. It was selected from 50 different *C. sativa* x *C. afghanica* F_1 hybrid crosses primarily for its consistent true-breeding qualities in a broad range of crosses. Original Skunk #1 is an inbred-line that came from a naturally combining hybrid selected for its crossability and true-breeding qualities, rather than a forced hybrid made in an attempt to blend two previously selected individual varieties with specific desirable characteristics. In other words, Original Skunk #1 has been selected for its naturally high GCA. Simply crossing a select Original Skunk #1 with almost any other drug variety will improve it. If a grower has a variety that has certain desirable characteristics but lacks potency or yield, it is possible to cross it with an Original Skunk #1, and then select offspring combining the sought after characteristics of the original variety with the many additional attributes of Original Skunk #1. For example, a hybrid cross between the inbred Original Haze and Skunk #1 will restore the potency of the Original Haze and make it a more compact and manageable size while preserving its unique varietal flavor and high. An Original Skunk #1 x Original Haze F_1 hybrid developed by Cultivator's Choice and grown by Dutch Passion seed company recently won first prize at the 1992 *HIGH TIMES* magazine Harvest Festival in Amsterdam. Original Skunk #1 has certainly earned its reputation as the benchmark standard of the sinsemilla industry.

Many of these highly bred cannabis varieties occasionally produce male flowers at the tips of female branches near the end of maturation due to

SKUNK #1

Many dealers consider it the finest marijuana in the world. It is a *sativa-indica* hybrid that was first grown in California. It was then developed by Cultivators' Choice and went on to win several California harvest festivals.

But look again. This is no ordinary Skunk #1. This plant is less than two feet tall and contains the central bud of a much larger plant. It is, in fact, little more than a popsicle stick coated with resinous flowers. And it was grown indoors—in Holland.

Ten years of Dutch growing experiments were necessary to produce plants like this one, techniques that once remained a closely guarded secret.

#145, September 1987

environmental stress during flowering. These male flowers rarely produce viable pollen, and even when they do there are rarely any viable stigmas remaining to be pollinated on the neighboring female plants.

These unique recombinations of genes have lived on as relatively true-breeding varieties and are suitable for hybridization. New varieties are developed each year in an effort to create better sinsemilla. Improved varieties of cannabis can be created by using the varieties readily available from Dutch seed companies for the past few years. Seeds of improved drug cannabis varieties are only sold legally within Holland by Dutch seed companies. True-breeding varieties such as Original Skunk #1 are most valuable as breeding material. Many polyhybrid varieties are also available from a variety of parental lines. They may be fine plants and good for cloning for sinsemilla production, but because they do not breed true, they are not as useful in breeding programs as the inbred true-breeding varieties listed above. It is advisable to create unique hybrids from the available inbred-line varieties rather than relying on other breeders for these simple dihybrid crosses. Individual hybrids are only easily and reliably reproduced by cloning. True-breeding hybrid varieties that grow reliably from seed can only be created through diligent selective breeding. This is a long and challenging project.

Recently cannabis has begun to receive the attention it deserves as a valuable medicinal plant, as well as a valuable fiber and seed crop, rather than merely as a social and law-enforcement problem. The potency and other desirable qualities of drug cannabis varieties were improved by selective breeding throughout the 1980s despite the restrictions imposed by worldwide laws prohibiting cannabis cultivation. We should expect this trend to continue throughout the end of the 20th century and beyond. Whatever the individual goals of the cannabis breeder, and whichever cannabis varieties are available, cannabis breeding will prove to be a truly rewarding experience for many advanced home growers. There are few experiences so satisfying as helping to improve such a valuable plant as cannabis. Good Luck!

TAKING THE GUESSWORK OUT OF HARVESTING

by Mel Frank

Ever have trouble determining the right time to harvest? Ever lose THC by pulling up a plant too early, or by letting a bud go past its prime? As author/photographer Mel Frank explains, knowing the right time to harvest means knowing when a plant's THC-rich resin glands are at their height of potency. All you need to get started is a magnifying glass.

Harvest nears and you're full of anticipation. But you need patience now, not haste. This is the time you must use to examine and then carefully evaluate each plant. If you harvest too soon, your plants may not

HARVEST SECRETS

BY KAYO

Sinsemilla cultivators employ one of two techniques in harvesting their plants. The selection of technique is determined by—among other things—the cultivator's emotional state, security status of the garden and weather.

When environmental conditions are favorable and everything else well controlled, cultivators selectively harvest individual flower clusters as they ripen and mature. The rate at which flowers reach their peak of growth is determined by their position on the plant. Flowers on the top branch-ends mature first. By harvesting these mature clusters, cultivators enable the less mature interior flowers to develop body and character.

When conditions get out of control, or adverse weather is imminent, cultivators find themselves in the position of having to harvest and run. Under these circumstances, the prime consideration is expediency—whatever works in the least amount of time is best. Cultivators might cut the plant at the base of the stem or just pull the plant up by the roots, then run.

#123, November 1985

FUNKY HARVEST

Skunk #1 and Skunk #1 x Northern Lights, grown and hand-watered in a perlite-vermiculite mix under a 1,000-watt MH lamp. I start with 20-20-20, then switch to a 10-30-20 when the plants are forced under a 12-12 light regime. I finish the flowering using a 5-50-17.

Funky Monk
Nashville, TN

#207, November 1992

GETTIN' BETTER

This baby grew under a 1,000-watt MH with CO_2 and all the fixings. Things have gotten better every harvest.

Brother Bilbo
San Bernadino, CA

#181, September 1990

reach full size and potency. If you wait too long, the plants will develop past their prime and progressively lose potency. The goal is to harvest each plant at its peak. Besides, why leave your crop growing longer than necessary, only to worry about having it discovered?

RESIN GLANDS & THC

Resin glands contain 80-90% of the THC produced in a marijuana plant. The bulk of the THC collects in large, stalked resin glands that form on flower bracts and tiny leaves interspersing female flower buds. Intact, healthy resin glands protect and preserve THC. However, during senescence (the growth phase between full maturity and death), plants growing outdoors are especially susceptible to losing potency. Mature resin glands can rupture from fullness; and wind, rain or swings in temperature can break or dislodge resin glands from plants. When resin glands are ruptured, THC is exposed to light and air, which degrades it into nonpsychoactive or much less psychoactive compounds such as cannabinol (CBN). This must be avoided.

Resin glands are barely visible to the naked eye, so use a magnifying lens. Examine the glands that coat the female flowers on your most mature plant. If those glands haven't developed long stalks, then potency is still increasing. If many glands are brown or missing, then the peak has passed and potency is decreasing.

STIGMA INDICATORS

The condition of stigmas (fuzzy white hairs) may also be a helpful indicator of peak potency. At least half of the stigmas in each bud will be brown and withered by the earliest stage of ripeness. Fresh, white stigmas will be at the top of the bud, but resin glands should be intact. When stigmas have fallen from the flowers, the peak potency window has lapsed.

HARVEST WINDOW

You have a window of about one to two weeks during which you can harvest at peak potency. Use these photos of buds and resin glands as your guide. If weather stays mild, then harvest later in this window. With windy or rainy weather, harvest earlier. The photographs of bud and resin glands past their prime warn of potency lost by harvesting too late.

To get the most from your crop, treat each plant as an individual. Even from the same variety, you'll find that some plants mature more quickly than others. So take your time. If you let each plant be the best it can be, you won't be disappointed with the results.

STASH ALERT! HOW TO PRESERVE POT POTENCY

by The Bush Doctor

Growers taking time to harvest a healthy cornucopia of cannabis must also carefully watch over their cut crops. In addition to two-legged thieves, myriad bacteria, molds and insects have been known to rip off your stash while curing, drying or in the fridge. Avoiding these ubiquitous threats is nearly impossible, but there is a way to lessen their impact. The key is being able to manipulate storage conditions.

A variety of bacteria grow on damp marijuana. Many are deadly. Researchers have found klebsiella *pneumoniae*, enterobacter *cloacae* and streptococcus (group D) growing in government-supplied reefer. Salmonella *muenchen* was found in marijuana growing across the Midwest. (Let someone else roll the joints. I don't lick rolling papers anymore!) Under anaerobic conditions (i.e., damp marijuana stored in airtight containers), clostridium species will rot pot; these are the famous botulism bacteria.

In addition, a number of bacteria-like actinomycetes have been identified in confiscated ganja, including thermoactinomyces *candidus*, T. *vulgaris* and micropolyspora *faeni*. These bugs cause allergic reactions (sometimes severe), as well as "farmer's lung" disease.

Insects in pot are less intense. Grow-room critters, such as aphids and spider mites, rarely damage marijuana after harvest. Smith & Olson identified five beetle species from confiscated Mexican weed in San Francisco. They completed this study at the request of DEA agents, whose offices were overrun by the pests. The predominant species, Tribolium *confusum* (confused flour beetle), attacks only seeds, not marijuana proper. Two other beetles cited in the study, Adistermia *watsoni* and Microgramme *arga*, are fungus feeders (the marijuana was moldy). Thankfully, the researchers found no cannabis equivalent to Lasioderma *serricorne*, the tobacco-cigarette beetle. Otherwise some whacked government lab would be growing the bugs en masse to spread across the continent.

Fungi destroy more bud than bacteria and insects combined. Bacteria in marijuana may be more dangerous to humans, but they are rare. Molds are common, and can be nasty: Ramirez reports four policemen developing pulmonary histoplasmosis after pulling up a 5,000-square-meter plot of marijuana in Puerto Rico. Some fungi won't rot pot, but they will put you in the hospital.

Many fungi causing disease in plants die off after their host is harvested. Exceptions include botrytis *cinerea* (the cause of gray mold) and alternaria *alternata* (brown blight). After harvest, your competition becomes aspergillus, penicillium, rhizopus and mucor, the baddest actors on the planet. Each genus causes disease under different conditions:

Ubiquitous aspergillus grows on anything from rocket fuel to astronauts. The genus is millions of years old; while Homo *sapiens* may come and go, aspergillus will remain. Westendorp first found an aspergillus species attacking cannabis in 1854. More recently, Margolis & Clorfene describe a mold that increases potency in marijuana. Their "black weblike fungus" sounds like an aspergillus species. What species, I'd like to know.

Schwartz scraped aspergillus *niger* from the skull of a marijuana smoker experiencing sinus headaches. I frequently encounter A. *niger* growing in ganja stored at room temperature. It does not increase potency. Kagen also reports A. *niger* growing in moldy marijuana, along with two even nastier Aspergilli: A. *fumigatus* and A. *flavus*.

Chusid et al. blame A. *fumigatus* for causing a near-fatal pneumonitis in a 17-year-old. They note the patient buried his

NORTHERN LIGHTS/ HAZE HYBRIDS

I started these Northern Lights/Haze hybrids under 1,000-watt lights. I budded and regenerated them twice in one-gallon pots, then set them out the second week in May at 3,000'-plus elevation in the Sierras. In October, the plants were over nine feet high and produced just under a pound of cured buds. These 17 colas came from one plant.

Sierra Gardener
Portola, CA

#215, July 1993

SPRING HARVESTS
BY CHARLIE FRINK

When short-season plants are placed outdoors or in a natural light greenhouse until about March 21, when the number of hours of light and darkness are equal, they begin to flower. Some plants revert to vegetative growth as the number of hours of light increases. However, some short-season varieties, which show flowering response with 14 hours of light, will come in unaided. If the plants start to revert, they can be covered with opaque black plastic each evening after sunset, and then removed in the morning, limiting the number of hours of light which the plants receive.

Some areas of the country are too cold to grow outdoors in March or April without some sort of protection. Just covering the ground with black plastic so it warms up and retains heat may be sufficient. One grower painted coffee cans black and filled them with water, then covered them with their plastic tops. He used the cans in a circle around each plant. The water heated up during the day and radiated heat at night.

Another inexpensive way to keep plants warm is by using heat mats or heat cables. These electrical devices use very little current to heat the root area. If the roots are kept warm, the ambient air temperature can go lower than usual without affecting the plants adversely.

#114, February 1985

BASIC HYDROPONIC SYSTEMS

WICK SYSTEMS

Special nylon wicks draw nutrients up to roots, vermiculite-perlite (50-50) growing medium—porous, absorbent. Good for leaf crops, starting plants, experiments.

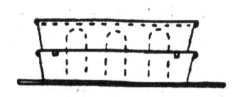

DRIP SYSTEMS

Small feeder tubes supply constant moisture and nutrients to plants. Vermiculite, sand, perlite, peat moss, sawdust (alder).

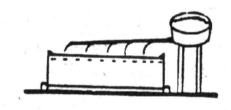

SUBAERATED SYSTEMS AQUARIUM CONVERSION

Air pump delivers air through gravel to roots, through air-wand or air stones. Flush and drain with siphon tube.

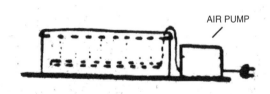

AIR PUMP

AIR-PUMP POWERED SYSTEMS SIPHON TUBE

Air pump used to pump nutrients by venturi action, placement of air entrance 1" below nutrient level in tube; timer controlled

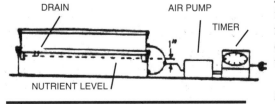

DRAIN

AIR PUMP

TIMER

NUTRIENT LEVEL

marijuana underground for "aging." No doubt the patient was looking for Margolis & Clorfene's fungus, but A. *fumigatus* found him instead. A. *flavus*, on the other hand, kills slowly. It oozes carcinogenic metabolites called aflatoxins. Llewellyn & O' Rear found aflatoxins contaminating Virginian marijuana.

Aspergillus species grow better in warmer climates; penicillium, in cooler climates. Refrigerator storage encourages penicillium infestation. Kagen et al. and Kurup et al. isolated penicillium from marijuana cigarettes. Babu et al. identified P. *chrysogenum* attacking marijuana. (P. *chrysogenum* occurs abundantly in nature, and was Alexander Fleming's source of penicillin.) I isolated P. *italicum* from marijuana stored with an orange peel at 0°C. Adding peels to pot imparts a "pleasant bouquet" (Frank & Rosenthal). In my case, the peel imparted a nidus of infection. P. *italicum*, the "blue citrus mold," is notorious for its ability to spread by contact (i.e., "one bad apple spoils the whole bunch").

Five mucor species have been described on cannabis. Members of this genus grow fast and die young. One of them, M. *hiemalis*, regrettably bioconcentrates (and cannot metabolize) the herbicide paraquat from tainted substrates (Domsch et al.). Mucor's first cousin, rhizopus, occurs in soil, ripe foodstuffs and occasionally on people (especially diabetics). Grebeniuk isolated R. *stolonifer* from hemp stems. In an inoculation experiment, I quickly rotted some damp marijuana with a colony of R. *stolonifer* found growing on bread.

DIAGNOSIS

Rotting marijuana produces a spectrum of odors, from stale to musty to moldy. P. *italicum* perfumes a lavender bouquet, while A. *flavus* smells like a locker room. Clostridium bacteria stink like carrion.

Infested marijuana often darkens in color and becomes crumbly. Anaerobic bacteria turn marijuana into brown slime. Marijuana undergoing rapid decay may feel warm to touch. (At this stage, your stash is ready for the compost heap.) Tufts of fungi are often visible in moldy material. In marijuana stored in darkness, strands look white to light gray. Exposed to light, storage molds spawn millions of colored spores in velvet clumps. A slight tap sends these spores into great billowing clouds. Generally, rhizopus and mucor species produce gray-black spores, penicillium species are light blue-green and aspergillus species are dark green-black.

To check for aflatoxins, inspect your stash under a black light (in medicalese, a "Wood's Lamp"). Material contaminated with aflatoxin-producing A. *flavus* will fluoresce to a green hue under ultraviolet light.

To screen for insects, simply shake samples in a No. 10 steel sieve. Of course, not all bugs found in marijuana cause storage damage. Some are simply "innocent bystanders" caught during harvesting and die right away. Live (and chewing) insects are more suspicious. A hand lens is helpful for I.D.

CONTROL

Avoid damaging plants before they completely dry (even while they are in the ground and growing). Wounded tissues release exudates on which fungi feed and establish a foothold. Lucas says diseased and nutrient-deficient leaves (as well as old yellow leaves) produce more exudates than healthy leaves. Expect more mold problems in poorly grown plants.

The secret to stopping bacteria and mildew is moisture control. Even gray mold dies if plants are carefully and quickly dried. Oven-cured pot rots less than air or sweat-cured crops. Sweat-cured cannabis (remember '70s Colombian?) maintains a "tradition" of aspergillus contamination.

The oven-drying method inevitably leads to a harsh product. So most people air-dry by suspending plants upside down with enough space between them for circulation. Drying rooms should be cool and dry, preferably in uninterrupted darkness. (Most storage fungi require light to sporulate and spread.)

Living cannabis plants are about 80% water. Perfectly dried marijuana contains about 10%-15% water or moisture content (MC). Material below 10% MC becomes too brittle and disintegrates. Fungi cannot grow below 15% MC. Unfortunately, many growers market their crop above 15% MC. Cannabis, like cornflakes, is sold by weight, not volume. Tobacco farmers also allow their product to gain weight by reabsorbing moisture before sale. They term this risky business "coming into order." Recently purchased products should be redried. Freezer storage will not protect damp pot. Placing lemon or orange peels in stored marijuana is discouraged, as they raise the MC above 15%. Dipping penicillium-infested plants in a solution of baking powder will inhibit these acid-loving fungi, but the product must be rapidly redried

Maintaining stored marijuana at 10-15% MC also discourages insects. Insecticides have no application in stored marijuana. Their residues pose a danger to consumers. Also, water-based sprays will kill bugs, but trigger a fungus infection by raising the MC. Fumigants (gas, not sprays or aerosols) contain no liquid, thus they do not trigger mold infestations. But they leave residues in air pockets of fumigated material. Big buds are full of air pockets. Poisons are very useful for disinfecting drying rooms, but only after the crop has been cleared out.

Low temperatures will "freeze" an insect infestation. However, with rewarming, many bugs continue their destruction. Another drawback to freezing above-15%-MC marijuana involves the aforementioned exacerbation of penicillium. Heating marijuana in a 66-93°C oven for 10 minutes will kill most pests. This also dries out the product—again, the cornerstone of control. Marijuana should not be heated longer than 10 minutes or above 93°C to prevent THC oxidation.

CONSUMER CAVEATS

Immunosuppressed individuals and asthmatics should never be exposed to molds, especially aspergillus. People using medical marijuana should take extra precautions:

Ungerlerder, et al. sterilized marijuana with ethylene oxide, reporting no loss of THC from fumigation. These researchers also irradiated their dope with high-dose Cobalt-60 (15,000 to 20,000 Gray Units!) with no loss of THC. This method is not recommended for novices.

Moody et al. evaluated waterpipes for smoking aspergillus-contaminated marijuana. Unfortunately, they found only a 15% reduction in transmission of fungal spores.

In Chicago, goofy dudes spray their marijuana with formaldehyde. This kills insects and fungi, but at a price. The treated weed, known as AMP, causes anoxia and psychomotor retardation when smoked (Spector). According to *Newsweek* (Jan. 20, 1986), a few ill-intentioned dealers dipped marijuana in rat poison or insecticides like Black Flag. They called this product "WAC." Indeed. Have a nice day.

PRESSURE-TANK SYSTEM
Air pump pressurizes lower chamber, forces nutrients up into gravel in growing section—timer controlled.

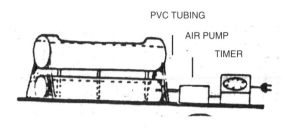

GRAVITY-FLOW SYSTEMS
MANUAL
Bucket containing nutrients raised to flood gravel growing medium; lowered to drain.

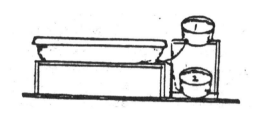

GRAVITY-FLOW SYSTEMS
AUTO (Timer Control)
Timer turns pump on 2-3 times per day, floods gravel. Growing tray drains after pump shuts off by gravity and siphon action.

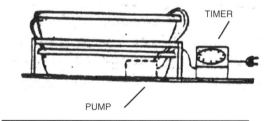

NUTRIENT-FLOW SYSTEMS
Pump supplies constant flow of nutrients across absorbent layer or material; 1" in 4' slope angle assures drainage.

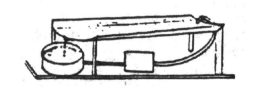

SINSEMILLA TIPS

THE MAN WHO WOULD BE KING OF CANNABIS

THE SEED BANK
1986/1987 CATALOGUE

Nevil, an Australian of Dutch heritage, founded The Seed Bank with a small classified ad in HIGH TIMES in July 1984. His company became a runaway success story.

Two years later, Nevil paid taxes on $500,000 worth of seeds sold to more than 15,000 different growers in the United States alone. His ad in HT jumped to a 1/6 page display ad in October 1985. In 1987, then-Executive Editor Steven Hager traveled to Holland, researched Nevil's biography and dubbed his house "Cannabis Castle." Two months after the article was published, Nevil's HT ad jumped to a full page in color.

Designed to pay homage to the growing cannabis scene in Holland, the 1st Annual Cannabis Cup was held the following year. In 1988, Skunk #1 from Cultivator's Choice took top prize, but the following year, Nevil's Seed Bank swept all five awards. Unfortunately, two weeks before the 1990 Cup, Nevil was arrested while visiting his family in Australia.

Some felt then-Drug Czar William Bennett, who was angered by attacks in HT concerning his alcohol and tobacco addictions, was hoping to shut down HIGH TIMES through Operation Green Merchant and Nevil's arrest. Editor-in-Chief and Cannabis Cup founder Steven Hager was subpoenaed for Nevil's trial. Fortunately, however, Nevil escaped and disappeared. Although his mysterious whereabouts remain unknown, the strains he mailed around the world live on, still being developed at Cannabis Castle. Nevil's life story rivals that of HIGH TIMES founder Tom Forcade, and Hager's biography of him can be found in *HIGH TIMES Greatest Hits: 20 Years of Smoke in Your Face*, published by St. Martin's Press.

#237, May 1995

GROW DUTCH
by The Seed Bank

I decided to set up a garden to produce seeds after growing gardens both indoors and outdoors.

I bought a house and three acres of land so that I could grow all year round. The house has a large cellar which I improved and divided into rooms. The main room is the flowering room, but I want to have a crop every month, so I need to start a crop every month. I have two small rooms for seedlings and a room two-thirds the size of my flowering room. I sex the plants in the preflowering rooms. I sex the plants in these rooms and the females go into the flowering room. I'm planning to build a setup for the males so that they can be properly cared for and milked for pollen well away from the females. At present, pollination takes place in small cubicles. I also have a four-square-meter (43 sq. ft.) room devoted to cuttings of my best stock. They are kept small and in vegetative growth.

Before I flower a plant, I make a cutting of it so that its exact genetic makeup is easily preserved.

To start, I designed the flowering room. The floor has a slight inclination to the center paths (about four centimeters per meter, two and one-half inches per yard) which flow to a sump pump outside the room. The sump is turned on by an automatic float valve and drains the excess water to sewage.

The floor plan was designed so that each plant is within arm's length of the central paths.

The floor was originally brick, but I laid cement so the floor would drain well. Humidity and mold are a big problem in Holland, especially indoors. The drains from the other three grow rooms also lead to the sump. I plan to cover the floor with plastic mats with tubing which are used to heat the roots. Hot water runs through the tubing and keeps the root level warm.

I use rockwool slabs and cut them into slabs 25 x 20 x 10-cm. (8 1/2 x 7 x 3 1/2 inches). This makes the plants easy to move. Since the garden contains many varieties of plants rather than a uniform homogeneous one, it is important to be able to move the plants around so that tall ones don't shade the short ones. It also makes breeding a lot easier. If I was growing a uniform crop, I would use the meter mats, which are pieces of rockwool 100 x 25 x 10-cm., and I would put four plants in each meter mat.

All the bags are covered in white plastic with holes at the bottom for drainage. This helps prevent infections by bacteria or fungus. A 10 x 10 x 7-cm. starting block is placed on the larger block. That's all there is to transplanting The small blocks will keep a plant up to 35 cm. (14 inches).

Each plant is fed with its own dipper, which delivers two liters per hour. The plants are watered three times daily, at the beginning, middle and end of the growing cycle. I use a professionally recommended hydroponic nutrient solution designed for rockwool. The nutrient solution is a lot weaker than standard solutions, because it is given to the plants so often.

Each time the plants are watered, the new water washes away some of the old water and nutrient solution. However, there is some buildup of nutrient salts in the medium. Water here in Holland has a high pH, about 7.8, so we use formulas to lower it to about 5.5. If that doesn't do it, acid is used. When the medium is measured, it ranges below 6.5, which I consider acceptable. The pH is kept purposefully low to make sure the plants can utilize all the nutrients. They are not soluble, and at higher pH levels the nutrients are not always available to the plants. The rockwool itself does not hold the nutrients. It just holds a large amount of water, 10-14 times the equivalent amount of soil, and air is available to the roots throughout the medium.

Water is pumped to the plants from a 1,000-liter tank. The pump has valves and meters to regulate the pressure, and a PVC tube with holes in it to regulate the backflow and at the same time aerate the nutrient solution. The nutrients are stored in two containers in concentrated form. The two solutions are mixed only as they mix with the water in the 1,000-liter tank, or they will have a chemical reaction which will lead to crystallization. There are two final formulas, one for flowering and one for vegetative growth..

A high-efficiency kerosene heater is used to keep the room warm during the cool times. It produces 20 percent by weight of the kerosene CO_2 (8.7 cubic feet per pound). Once the construction is finished, the rooms will be supplied with CO_2-using tanks, and a CO_2 meter and regulator to measure and inject the amount of CO_2.

Right now, the walls are just painted white, but the quality of the white leaves much to be desired. I plan instead to cover them with a thin layer of styrofoam, which is usually used for insulating damp walls and protecting wallpaper. Styrofoam has a reflective efficiency of over 100 percent, according to a horticultural light manufacturer. This is because the light is diffused in a more efficient manner, reaching parts of the plant that would otherwise be shaded. Styrofoam also has the advantage of being easy to hose down. In combination with floor drainage; this assures a clean growing room. It's also easy to install.

The temperature and humidity are controlled by an exhaust fan. The temperature is kept at 25 degrees Centigrade and the humidity at 40-55%. If the humidity or temperature rises above these levels, the fan starts. When they fall below, the fan stops.

The main garden, the flowering room, is illuminated with 400-watt HPS and MH lamps, 2/3 sodium, 1/3 halides. The other rooms are lit solely with HPS lamps. I haven't noticed a difference since adding the halides. The lamps are permanently mounted on the ceiling, on rails. The units are specifically manufactured for horticultural lighting. They have effective and even distribution of light. The bulbs are mounted horizontally so that more light reaches the plants. By increasing the number of fixed points of light, the light is distributed more evenly. Two 1,000-watt lamps provide only two points of light, and with the horizontal mounting and reflectors, the lamps actually throw more light on the plants than 1,000-watt halides. One important reflector innovation is side reflectors on the outer side round lights in the garden. This gets even more light onto the plants rather than the walls. The more fixed points have the same advantage as with light movers, and mounting overhead makes working in the grow room easier.

POPULAR STRAINS AT CANNABIS CASTLE

SKUNK #1
First sold by Sacred Seed Company and later by Cultivator's Choice, this Thai/Afghani/Mexican cross is widely considered the Dom Perignon of domestic marijuana. "Early on, the bud has the aroma of fine perfume, wrote DC in 1988. "Pick it late and it smells like skunk. "
(Skunk #1 won the 1st Annual Cannabis Cup in 1988, while its hybrids won the 2nd, 5th, and 7th Cannabis Cups.)

EARLY PEARL
Originally a hybrid cross of Early Girl and Pollyana, this true-breeding strain only requires 6-8 weeks of 12-hour lighting to mature. "The F1 hybrid is without a doubt some of the finest marijuana ever to have crossed this Connoisseur's lips." wrote DC. "I wish I had pounds of it around all the time.
(Early Pearl has since been blended with many hybrids at Cannabis Castle, including Silver Pearl. Its hybrids won the 2nd and 7th Cannabis Cups.)

NORTHERN LIGHTS
Developed in the late '70s near Seattle, this has become the state-of-the-art indoor *indica*. "It is the result of many years of indoor breeding—three to four crops per year for a total of perhaps 30 to 40 generations in the last 10 years," wrote DC. "The picture in Nevil's catalog is a cutting of my personal favorite, CI #5 F1. Unfortunately, no seeds are available of the strain, only cuttings. If anyone can come up with anything more resinous than this, I'd like to see it. Does not have much taste. The breeder had a very specific goal in mind: high resin content. He certainly succeeded. The grass is a mellow *indica* that gets you pleasantly stoned.
(Nevil experimented with at least eight different strains of Northern Lights. It has become one of the most heavily bred strains in the world. A hybrid won the 2nd, 6th and 7th Cannabis Cups, while the pure #5 strain won the 3rd Cannabis Cup.)

HAZE
A pure sativa polyhybrid first sold by Sacred Seeds, and later preserved by Cultivator's Choice, this legendary strain combines mostly Mexican and Colombian heritage with traces of South India and Thai. Very hard to grow indoors but blends well with other strains.
(Haze hybrids won the 2nd, 5th, 6th and 7th Cannabis Cups.)
#237, May 1995

THE SSSC SYSTEM

FLOWERING CAPS

EBB AND FLOW TABLE

RESERVOIR TANK

THE SSSC CATALOG

Super Sativa Seed Club

THE MARIJUANA SEED CATALOG

The plants are pruned to four main branches while they are in the vegetative growth stage. They are about a foot tall. The lights are cut back to 12 hours. The plants tend to grow a bit more before actually flowering, and finish off 3-5 feet tall. The light level is maintained at 26,000 lux per square meter. This is about 25 percent of the light of a sunny day in Holland.

SUPER SATIVA:
INDOOR GROWING BY THE PLANTLET METHOD
by The Super Sativa Seed Club

We first started growing eight years ago in 10-liter (3-gallon) containers using Colombian and Thai seeds. The plants were allowed to grow under metal-halide lamps for five months and then were flowered for two. After the first crop we harvested, we decided to automate the watering system. In horticulture magazines we saw hydroponic setups; we visited suppliers and straight greenhouse growers, who were happy to show us how they cultivate. (We always look to straight horticulture here in Holland—no need to reinvent the wheel.) We also realized that 90 percent of the plant's potency is genetically determined, so we took a trip to the United States in a quest for good seed. In California we found a *sativa-indica* creeper variety with an excellent Colombian high.

We grew our second crop in rockwool, letting the plants grow for three and one-half months, then flower for two. We ended up with plants 2 to 2-1/2 meters (6 to 8 feet) tall. The harvest was good. In 10 square meters (a little more than 100 square feet) we had 16 plants. The plants averaged 150 grams; the biggest yielded 225 grams. We thought that was a lot. Also, the grass was well received at that time because sinsemilla was still a novelty in the Netherlands. However, we had not yet realized the most important thing about growing in rockwool: it needs good drainage. Also, about 30 percent of the water from the nutrient solution irrigating the material must run off to prevent a salt buildup, which can lower yield and is toxic at high levels. We measured high EC (electrical conductivity) levels. The instrument measured a level up to about EC10, when it should have read about EC2. This indicated that salt residues were building up in the medium.

By the third crop, we had decided to shorten the vegetative cycle, so that the plants were kept shorter and more manageable. We had always thought that plants could not flower until they were several months old, but we experimented and found that cuttings we had placed under a flowering light cycle responded just like their clone mothers. We also found that seedlings placed under the same light-cycle would respond with flowers in about four weeks, the males indicating first. This information caused us to change our growing techniques radically. We continued experimenting, and have now developed a system that produces an incredible yield.

Starting with 10-cm. (about 3-1/2-inch) clones in 6-1/2-cm. (about 2-

1/2-inch) rockwool cubes—or 10 to 15 plants per meter—we let the plants take root. This takes about two to three weeks, depending on the seed variety and weather conditions. We have had our best success taking cuttings from the part of the branch just above where it becomes woody; they root the fastest. With these we have a success rate of about 95 percent. After the cuttings start to grow rapidly, we let them go for another two weeks; each plantlet grows to an approximate height of 30 cm. (about 12 inches) before they are transplanted and placed in a separate flowering room. (By using two rooms there is no downtime; the next crop of clones goes into the flowering room as soon as the previous crop is done.) There are four plants per rock-wool slab, which measures 100 x 20 x 8 cm. (39 x 8 x 3 inches).

The plants are allowed between 10-1/2 and 12 hours of darkness each night. The *indicas* require fewer hours of darkness, the *sativas* more. We try each variety at 10-1/2 hours first, then lengthen the period of darkness if the plants don't respond. We think the more hours of light during the flowering cycles, the larger the buds.

The plant continues to flower for six to eight weeks, and will reach a height of 60 to 70 centimeters (24 to 28 inches), depending on variety. They are harvested when roughly about 50 percent of the pistils turn brown. This is earlier than most Americans harvest, but we prefer the high the younger buds provide, and we can then use the space for the new crop. (To get the American-style ripened bud with the false seed pod forming around desiccated pistils, another week or two of flowering is required.) By transplanting the plants into the rockwool after they root, then placing them in the big grow room, we get five harvests per year from the room. The yield per square meter per year is so large that we hesitate to mention it. But here it is: 1750 grams (about 12 ounces).

We are now working on a shelf growing system so that space can be utilized even more efficiently. For instance, if we have a space 3 meters square and use 2 meters for shelves stacked three high, in effect we have 18 square meters of growing space in a 9-square-meter area.

CYBER-HYDROPONICS

by Bucky Dave and Garbled Uplink

It's every grower's nightmare: puttering around in your isolated grow room on a picture-perfect Saturday morning, adjusting pH levels, CO2 levels and measuring out the nutrients for your state-of-the-art hydroponic growing system. Suddenly the doors come crashing down and a swarm of heavily armored Imperial Storm Troopers laden with weapons and testosterone start barking and screaming at you like pit bulls on crack. Busted! Go to jail, go directly to jail, do not pass Go, do not make the Harvest Festival. But imagine this: The Forces of Darkness creep up on tippy-toe, sweating under the weight of their Kevlar and guns. Their adrenalin peaks as

SEA OF GREEN PRIMER

BY KYLE ROQ

The Sea of Green concept is simple: six mature, one-foot cuttings (clones, plantlets) will give the same yield as one six-foot plant—outdoors. Indoors, because metal-halide/high-pressure sodium light output decreases with distance from the bulb, six one-foot plants will give a greater yield than one six-foot plant—and you won't get stuck endlessly bending branches.

The Super Sativa Seed Club of Holland, who developed the technique (they call it the Plantlet Method) recommends flowering at 10-inch height for greater space utilization and harvest. You'll have myriad smaller plants that won't have time to develop wasteful branches, just large top buds!

And here's the best part: All the plants will give you a guaranteed 100% sinsemilla harvest, the most potent of all buds. There's no wasted space and effort growing males, or searching and breaking crowded branches looking for a change male pollen sac. There's no chance of a premature ejaculator spoiling your crop.

Because the budding plants are cuttings from your favorite female mother(s), they will be identical to her. They're put into a 12-hour flowering period to bud out, while new cuttings are being rooted and vegetated from the same mother. This can be repeated up to two years from one plant.

#145, September 1987

EBB-AND-FLOW TABLE

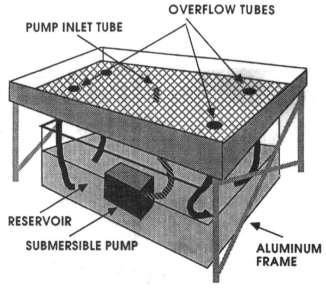

PUMP INLET TUBE

OVERFLOW TUBES

RESERVOIR

SUBMERSIBLE PUMP

ALUMINUM FRAME

SMOKIN' IN THE FREE WORLD

BY STEVE BLOOM

The climactic Awards Dinner, held at Garden Cafe on Wteringschains 75, right across from the Rijksmuseum, brought together the competition, the judges, HIGH TIMES and assorted welcome characters for one final gala event. Huge cone-shaped spliffs passed from table to table and a special platter of space cake and skunk-filled bonbons nearly sent the entire party off into an uncharted stratosphere.

Somehow I collected myself, asked for the audience's attention and, after introducing all the participants, began announcing the winners. Three *indicas* provided by the Bluebird placed second (Northern Lights), fourth (Northern Lights) and fifth (Master Kush). Third place went to Vijaya Seeds' Super Skunk. The grand prize for the best Dutch weed of 1992 and the recipient of the 5th Annual Cannabis Cup Award, I happily told the anxious crowd, was Homegrown Fantasy's Haze/Skunk #1, with a score of 152.5 points. Corrie and Henk graciously accepted the Cup as the crowd applauded.

#212, April 1993

they approach the cabin. These guys have skills, they are as silent as kittycats, but they haven't made the jump into cyberspace yet. They surround the cabin. Their leader gives them the order, and the door is battered down. They rush into the lush, climate-controlled atmosphere with their guns drawn, ready to terrorize yet another hapless farmer. Only this time, there's nobody there. No grower, no prints, no connection to be made between this room and any human entity. An IBM-compatible 486 sits in a corner, connected to various interfaces, controlling the environment and the flow of nutrients. The cops are baffled, stupefied by the very clear sense of ABSENCE surrounding them. Their leader approaches the computer. There is no monitor present, but if there were it would indicate that the system is crashing, erasing its own hard drive, eliminating all data, including the telephone number it just called to let you know that you are not going back to that site. They notice the interface device on the broken door. Even if they knew what the computer was doing, they couldn't stop it. You'd be using the latest in stealth viruses attached to a garden-variety batch file. In their frustration and rage they will dust for prints, and sift through the place looking for evidence, but you have been very thorough, and they will find no connection. From your hotel room in some remote island paradise, margarita and big spliff in hand, you check your remailer and discover that your grow room is history. You close out the mail drop and answering service issued to the alias you used to rent the place, maybe shed a wistful tear or two over the loss of your investment, and enjoy another shitty day in Paradise, as free as the birdies in the bright blue sky.

Sound like science fiction? Sound too expensive? Wrong on both counts. The necessary components of this system are here now, and you can upgrade the intelligence of your grow room for under $4,000. "Aboveground" gardeners and horticulturalists are doing it already.

Consider the present-day "dumb" automated growing system: Most of you who have gotten into hydroponic gardening are well aware of this option, which consists of a series of programmable event timers with fans, lights, a CO_2-control valve, etc. plugged into the timers. You simply program the on/off events, and hope all goes well. But Hope is a pretty shaky construct, and Murphy's Law always wins in the end. What can you do?

THE INTERNET SOLUTION

Since Fate does have a mind of her own, you can never be sure all your events will be timely. What if the humidity shoots sky-high due to some intense storm front, and eventually infiltrates your grow room? What if one of your fans blows? What if a fluorescent burns out? The low-tech timers would be rendered helpless. You'd be soaking up the rays, thinking about the next vacation after harvest, only to find upon your return that there is no harvest.

Ron Edwards, reporting in *The Growing EDGE* recently, gave some high-tech solutions to such problems in his article "Computer Control Systems": "...the X-10 controller...uses your house wiring to send and receive signals. This means that no additional wiring is needed to control a light, fan or just about any electrical device remotely.... X-10 systems have been around for quite a few years. The systems started out as basic controllers for lights and appliances...but the real breakthrough came with the introduction of the CP290 computer interface. This opened the door to control up to 256 devices with 128 events. The CP290 will send an on or off command to the appropriate module such as 'A1 on' or 'A2 off'.... A1 could be a light, a fan or a CO2-control valve. The CP290 is limited to a cycle of one minute. You can control your indoor grow room, green house, clone area or your whole house easily.... But it is still a 'send only' system, capable of sending an on or off signal to the appropriate receiver/module. The next step up in computer control is the 'smart' interface.... (There are several smart interfaces now on the market. They range in price from $60, if you don't mind writing your own software, to $400.)"

You need a system capable of if/then programming, as in: *If* the temperature is 85°, *then* turn on vent fan two. A smart system, built around Homebase software (a sophisticated send/receive package for controlling and monitoring events and equipment) can control light, temperature, nutrient flow and pH levels, according to need. Sensors, transmitting X-10 and ASCII code, feed into Homebase, providing full monitoring of significant environmental ambiance. With your equipment plugged into an X-10 interface, you can control all on/off events. Still, you have to be able to monitor the room.

So your sensors are feeding the PC, but you need to monitor the conditions, occasionally adjust timed events and make sure the Feds haven't crashed down the door. Using a common business application like PC/Anywhere, you can call in from wherever you are via your ultra-tech subnotebook (covered with decals from that Star Trek model you never assembled because the last harvest was so good) and take over the PC in the corner of your grow room. It's just like being there, but you're not. These business software packages are common, easy to install and can be had for less than a hundred bucks.

Homebase, a system designed to control all electronic events in the home, can do a decent job of monitoring your perimeter and inform you of any breach of security. If the cops break in, Homebase would then send a code, let's call it "OHSHIT," to a batch file containing any one of thousands of garden-variety computer viruses, which would quickly and irretrievably take out every piece of information (including log-in records) on the host PC in your grow room. Virus-infected files are easily obtained from hacker BBS systems. Just make sure you select a virus such as Deicide or Viper which completely overwrites the hard drive, file allocation table and boot sector. These viruses render your PC useless as evidence.

Suppose the feds were able to infiltrate your perimeter without tripping "OHSHIT." To protect your location, you could send your monitored environmental data through an anonymous remailer on the Internet to an e-mail address that would be completely untraceable. Anonymous remailers are essentially electronic mailboxes run by computer hackers for the express purpose of removing any possibility of tracing the source of a transmitted message. Many of these remail systems offer data encryption, which garbles the data for all but those with the appropriate translation software. This decoding software can be downloaded from most sources that offer encrypted remailing. It is also possible to send your transmission consecutively through more than one remailer, giving you an added measure of security. Using a remailer, the Feds could never intercept the source of your daily monitoring data. And even if they had fingered your location and were sitting in front of your host PC, they would only be able to pinpoint an anonymous mailer thousands of miles away, not your location. The front-line Feds are far behind in this ultra-tech realm. Of course, we recommend you leave no monitor on your host PC in the grow room, as an added measure of security. Its very unlikely they would be packing a monitor or a laptop. They're just not that sophisticated yet.

Using the anonymous remailers, the only risk of having your location fingered would be when you need to log into your host PC to adjust events.

CYBER-SECURITY TIPS

When done using computer files to store data concerning any questionable matters, simply erasing these files using "DEL" or "ERASE" may give a false sense of security. The file is NOT erased! It is simply removed from the directory. Any authority could use "UNDELETE" to regain the files. A surer way to get rid of files is to use a program by Norton Utilities called WIPE. This utility will go over the file as many times as requested by the user, with one character. The government uses this technique. Unfortunately, it too is not certain. Computer disk-head alignment can be off a little with each write operation, and I have heard of cases where this misalignment left recoverable magnetic traces of WIPED files. This is very rare, though.

Today's typewriters are a storehouse of disaster. Unlike the older models, which worked with an ink ribbon, newer typewriters use a plastic strip. This makes for better type quality, but also leaves a copy of the typed letters on the strip. It would be no problem for any authority to unroll the strip and gather a copy of the text.

Today's phone systems can have a built-in feature that transmits the caller's number to the called party. It the authorities are at a residence and you call and that party has a Caller ID device, your number is now with the authorities! A way around this is to call the phone company and ask them to have your number blocked. I did, and my friends tell me it comes up as "PRIVATE" on the Caller ID system.

Sherlock Bones
Lynn, MA

#238, June 1995

COMPUTER GROW RESOURCES

The Growing EDGE, New Moon Publishing, Inc. 215 SW 2nd Street, Suite #201, Corvallis, OR 97333. For subscription phone (503) 757-0027. Great, cutting edge-grow info.

Home Control Concepts, 9520 Padgett Street #108, San Diego, CA 92126. Phone (619) 693-8887. Reseller of hydroponic equipment and software.

Home Automation Laboratories, 550 Highlands Parkway #450, Smyrna, GA 30082-5141. Phone (404) 319-6000. Carrier of Homebase software and X-10 transmitting sensors.

Custom Home Control. Phone (619) 696-8128. Custom grow room planning and installation with full computer implementation.
See alt.gathering.rainbow@igc.apc.org for details on Clipper Chip technology (from Wired 2.04/Electrosphere).
#230, October 1994

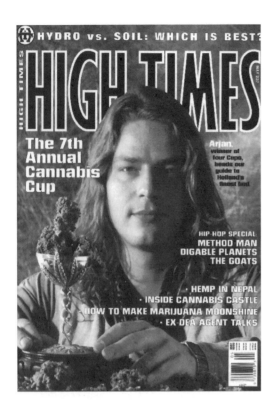

7TH ANNUAL CANNABIS CUP

BY PETER GORMAN

The judges sat in a circle around an open space in the center of the hall. In the center was the council's sacred staff and ceremonial water pipe. Jah Levi opened the council with a silent prayer, and the pipe was lit and passed.

Council rules were simple: Anyone who wished to talk was free to do so, as long as they brought an offering for the council pipe. Eagle Bill volunteered free cannabis for anyone who wished to speak but had no offering. The idea was for the judges to talk about the best varieties of grass and hash they'd found—informal Cup nominations—while sharing it with as many others as possible. With the competition for Cups open to all coffeeshops and all forms of cannabis, the councils were intended to get as much information out to the judges as possible.

Alan Dronkers from the Sensi Seed Bank entered the room with a silver platter heaped with cannabis and took the staff. He thanked everyone for coming, then spoke about the significance of Jack Herer's work and explained that it was in admiration of Herer that they had developed their new Jack Herer bud, a *sativa/indica* mix, which he wanted us to taste. Eagle Bill filled a pipe with a bud of the new strain and passed it to Herer himself for a ceremonial first taste of his namesake. Herer took a huge mouthful, coughed most of it up, grinned and passed it on. Alan Dronkers broke up the colas and passed them out to the crowd for sampling.

#237, May 1995

If you are comfortable with Homebase, it would take you only a few minutes to log in and adjust the necessary events. This risk indeed pales in comparison to returning to your actual grow room every few days to check and adjust conditions.

This is just one of many applications the information superhighway offers. It is an exciting technology that has raced far ahead of ethics, law enforcement, and government or corporate control. The US military, which built the Internet, could not have foreseen this application and is most likely shaking its ugly head in disbelief. Use it, and actively oppose all attempts at controlling this technology. A word of warning: Resist the government push for the Clipper Chip, and under no circumstances employ any equipment with it installed, unless you can find a specialist to subvert its function.

THE GREAT HYDRO vs. BIO DEBATE
Two Dutch Growers Face Off
with Arjan and Wernard

On Saturday, Nov. 26, the Cannabis Cup Hydro vs. Bio debate took place in the packed first-floor auditorium of the Pax Party House in Amsterdam. Nearly 200 people came to hear two of Holland's premier cannabis cultivators, Arjan—a former grower—and Wernard, and one former US grower, Kyle Kushman, discuss the merits of growing hydroponically versus biologically—water versus dirt. Afterwards, the three fielded questions from the audience. Below are the key points made through the thick haze of pungent smoke that filled the room.

ARJAN—*A former cannabis grower, Arjan is the founder and owner of the Green House, a coffeeshop that picked up four Cannabis Cups this year—including both the Hydro and Bio Cups, for Master Kush and Cytral Skunk, respectively. Arjan also won the Best Coffeehouse in Amsterdam Cup and the Imported Cannabis Cup for his Charas Malana.*

I don't believe there is really much difference between growing cannabis hydroponically or biologically. There are four really important things necessary for both systems: water, heat, nutrients and the movement of the air.

In Holland, 90 percent of the growers use rockwool slabs if they grow hydro, and most bio growers start their clones in [rockwool], too. A few people are using aeroponic systems and other new techniques, but they are very new and still quite experimental.

One of the advantages of working with rockwool is that there's much more air circulating around the roots, and because of that, the nutrients get to the plants more quickly, so the plants grow a bit faster. Both hydro and bio require the same nutrients, but the soil is more compact in bio systems, so it takes longer for the plant to receive its nutrients, and therefore longer to grow. Another system that's popular here is the use of grow rocks, which provide even more air to the roots because the water comes down from the top of the system in a sort of circle, pulling the air with it.

The thing you have to watch with hydro growing is the plant nutrients. If you mess up with a hydro system, you will be punished within 24 to 48 hours. On the other hand, if you fix the problem, you'll see improvement in 24 hours. With soil, you can get away with many more mistakes than you can with hydro growing. Generally, you'll have five to seven days before something happens to the plants, and you will still be able to save them.

When you see photographs in magazines, you often see yellow leaves. Most growers don't want to admit that if they have this problem, it's their own fault, because the nutrients that are being sold all over the world are pretty good. If your plants do turn yellow, it's almost always a pH problem. If you grow hydro, you need to be much more accurate than you do with soil growing. Otherwise, you will lose control of the garden. With rockwool, for instance, the pH will change much faster than with soil, so you have to adjust it nearly every day. You also have to make sure that within the rockwool, the pH and EC [electrolyte] levels are good.

The nutrients we use have a pH between 5.5 and 5.8. The rockwool is neutral—it has a pH of 7.0—so for the plant to get its nutrients, you have to make sure that the pH in your rockwool slabs is between 6 and 6.5. This is also true for aeroponic systems. We keep the EC between 1.5 and 1.8. There are certain cannabis strains for which you can go higher than that, but they are the exception.

With the strains we grow here hydroponically, we also have to be very careful with humidity. These plants yield in the last 10 days to two weeks, and the potential for mold—which can spread to the whole garden very quickly—is highest during that time, so we make sure our humidity is very well controlled. In Holland, the best time to grow is in winter, because it's cold outside and most houses have central heating, which takes the humidity out of the air. For hydro growing, we usually keep the humidity level at 50 percent, though at night you can go up to 60 percent without any problems.

About five years ago we also began using CO_2 systems. I used them for three years, but after that we took them all out. Why? Because with both aeroponics and hydroponics, we had such a great amount of air exchange and so many lights in our little rooms—they were about 300 to 400 square feet—that all the CO_2 we put in the rooms was blasted away by the exhaust fan. And the exchange of air is much more important than the CO_2.

WERNARD—*The founder and owner of Positronics Sinsemilla Salon and the chairman of the Sinsemilla Fan Club, Wernard has been an innovator in Holland's cannabis-cultivation industry since 1981. An ardent believer in bioponically grown marijuana, Wernard's Positronics won two Cannabis Cups this year—for Best Booth at the Hemp Expo and a Bonus Judges' Cup—as well as taking both second and third place in the Bio-Cup category for his Orange Bud and Northern Lights, respectively.*

To me there's no doubt about whether I should be involved in bio or hydro because I found out that marijuana works best when the quality is the best, and I found out the quality is best when it is biologically grown. So a long time ago, I made the bio choice, and I'll stick to it.

HEALTHY TOKING

Something I look forward to with relegalization of the righteous herb is certified organic weed. But even organic herb can have negative effects on the body. In my recent studies of Ayurvedic medicine, I came across an interesting bit of advice for mitigating the toxic effects of marijuana, and, in fact, all psychedelics.

Ayurveda is a holistic system of medicine indigenous to India for more than 5,000 years. And remember, our Indian brothers and sisters are no strangers to the herb, with documented use going back 3,000 years.

According to Ayurvedic practice, smoking a pinch of powdered calamus root along with the herb neutralizes what are considered to be marijuana's toxic effects on the liver and brain cells.

After finding calamus at an herbalist, I've been grinding it into powder in my coffee grinder. I find the taste slight and pleasant. Sprinkled on top of a bowl, it gets a good, glowing burn going, which means a better smoke because you don't fry the herb directly. Calamus is believed to bring clarity and expansion to consciousness, and is also supposed to be good taken like snuff to relieve clogged sinuses or sinus headaches. It is also used as an anticonvulsive to prevent epileptic seizures, and as a bronchial dilator and memory enhancer.

Steve
Long Beach, CA

#234, February 1995

PRESERVING POT POTENCY

I have been receiving HIGH TIMES since the beginning. During this time, I have read of many ways to store buds. So far, the method that I have found to be the best is the "canning" method. I have used this technique for 10 years and have never failed with it. The buds are preserved, forever, in the same condition as when they were put in the jar, no matter how many years in there!

1. Heat to over 150 degrees.

2. Place product into jars with twist-top lids (which have rubber rings sealed inside lid). Pack tightly and leave a 1/2" space on top.

3. Place jars and lids (lids not on jars) in oven, on rack or pan, in upright position.

4. Leave in over 10 minutes. This may overdry the top layer, but not to worry.

5. Remove from oven, place lids on jars and twist to seal tightly. The jars should be hot to the touch so use a towel.

6. Leave jars covered with towel until they cool.

7. The jars can be stored indefinitely and can be buried.

R.D.
Washington

#144, August 1987

MAX YIELD'S GUIDE TO CLOSET HYDRO

CLOSET HYDROPONICS

BY MAX YIELD

The debate rages on between those who grow organically and those who grow hydroponically. Those who prefer organics claim a certain "earthiness" to the flavor and aroma of their weed that they say is lost with hydroponics. Hydroponics fans (myself included) maintain that as long as you aren't overloading the plants with fertilizer, hydrobuds are just as tasty as others.

Moreover, in my experience, hydroponic systems are cleaner, easier to use and require less monitoring and maintenance. Growing organically requires that the soil mixture be balanced with the right amount of nutrients in the right proportions. If a problem develops, it will take time for it to show, and it will be difficult and time consuming to correct.

In hydroponic systems, you can alter the balance of the nutrients and their availability at will, so it's easier to discover any problems and correct them quickly. This allows the plant to express it full genetic potential so as to maximize potency.

Most commercial gardens employ one of the three most common hydroponic techniques: drip irrigation, flood irrigation or the ebb-and-flow system. The small-scale closet gardener has a space no bigger than 4' x 4'. That's when wick hydroponics becomes the best option.

#240, August 1995

Whenever there were difficulties in growing we always tried to find biological solutions to them, whether we were growing indoors or outdoors. This is one of the differences between bio and hydro growers. Hydro growers are a little more into technique. I know the feeling, because it's nice to work with water and nutrients and pumps and valves and everything. It's interesting. But it is actually much more interesting to find the simplest solution with the most simple toys and fertilizers that you can.

In 1984, I started to collect clones. There were people everywhere in Holland who had various strains, and I thought it might be a good idea to collect clones from them in some sort of library. In the beginning, I barely knew what to do, since cloning was pretty new in those days. I used to fill cups with a little bit of soil and a little bit of water and then put the clone in there. For some reason, 10 to 15 percent made it. And I had some huge lights in my garden which were on day and night that must have looked funny to my neighbors, so I had to move everything inside. Which is how I learned to make clones.

Cloning these days is done on basically the same principle that we discovered. That is, the best thing to do is to grow the mothers in peat-moss cups and keep the clones underneath. We use just one 400-watt bulb for lighting, because at 400 watts you have tiny little plants, and tiny plants are better for cuttings. When you use more lights, the plants grow too fast. We take cuttings the second week, which is when the good flowers are at the size we want.

We keep about 10 mothers in one drum, and we can take about 200 clones per square meter per week. The mothers are kept in biologically fertilized soil and can be used for about four to five months before they are done.

When we first started growing indoors in the early '80s, our greenhouses were really just tents covered in plastic, because it was inexpensive. But we now know that the THC level is higher when you grow under plastic than when you grow under glass, so that was good. But then growers in those days thought that big was beautiful, so people tended to grow big plants and 100 grams per meter was considered good, and that was bad. So not everything we thought then was right.